The Secret Thoughts
of Successful Women

The Secret Thoughts of Successful Women

WHY CAPABLE PEOPLE SUFFER FROM THE IMPOSTOR SYNDROME AND HOW TO THRIVE IN SPITE OF IT

VALERIE YOUNG, Ed.D.

CROWN
BUSINESS
NEW YORK

Published in the United States by Crown Business, an imprint of the Crown
Publishing Group, a division of Random House, Inc., New York.

www.crownpublishing.com

CROWN BUSINESS is a trademark and CROWN and the Rising Sun colophon
are registered trademarks of Random House, Inc.

Crown Business books are available at special discounts for bulk purchases for
sales promotions or corporate use. Special editions, including personalized covers,
excerpts of existing books, or books with corporate logos, can be created in large
quantities for special needs. For more information, contact Premium Sales at
(212) 572-2232 or e-mail specialmarkets@randomhouse.com.

Library of Congress Cataloging-in-Publication Data
Young, Valerie, Ed.D.
The secret thoughts of successful women: why capable people suffer from the
impostor syndrome and how to thrive in spite of it / Valerie Young.—1st ed.
        p. cm.
1. Women—Psychology 2. Success. I. Title.
HQ1206.Y68 2011
155.3'33—dc23   2011016330

ISBN 978-0-307-45271-9
eISBN 978-0-307-45273-3

Printed in the United States of America

Book design by Maria Elias
Jacket design by David Tran

10 9 8

First Edition

This book is dedicated to the codiscoverers of the impostor phenomenon, Dr. Pauline Clance and Dr. Suzanne Imes. By putting a name to the feelings, they have helped free countless people—including myself—from needless self-doubt.

[CONTENTS]

The Secret Thoughts
of Successful Women

Introduction

Women don't give themselves enough
credit for what they can do. You see it in the
twenty-one-year-old senior just coming out
of school, you see it in the Ph.D. candidate
just coming out of graduate school, and
you see it in the professional who's been
working for ten or fifteen or twenty years.

> —Director of minority-student affairs at a
> prestigious women's college

Countless books promise to reveal the "secrets" of success. This is not one of them. You're already successful. You just don't own it. And that's what this book is about—helping people just like you who have already achieved some measure of academic or professional success to *feel* successful. This book exposes the kinds of hidden fears and insecurities well known to millions of accomplished women—and men—and explores the myriad of reasons why they secretly feel undeserving of their hard-won success.

For the record, you don't have to feel especially "successful" to relate to the dichotomy of the public face of confidence and competence on the one hand and the private voices of self-doubt on the other. You could have won the Nobel Prize in physics, an Oscar, and the respect of peers and competitors alike, and still you would wonder, *"What if they find out I'm not as smart as they think I am?" "Can I really pull this off?" "Who do I think I am?"*

Fortunately, this book shows you how to, in the words of the famous Apple ad, "think different." Not only about things like competence, luck, faking it, failure, and success, but about yourself. Will you become more successful as a result? Undoubtedly. Once you have the tools to transform your thinking, you'll find yourself reaching new heights. In fact, this book will help you positively thrive.

Frankly, this is the book I wish I'd had in 1982. I was four years into a graduate program in education and procrastinating terribly on writing my dissertation. One day while I was sitting in class, another student began reading aloud from an article by a couple of psychologists from Georgia State University, Dr. Pauline Rose Clance and Dr. Suzanne Imes, titled, "The Impostor Phenomenon in High Achieving Women." Among the 162 high-achieving women they sampled, Clance and Imes uncovered a pervasive pattern of dismissing accomplishments and believing that their success would disappear once others discovered the awful secret that they were, in fact, "impostors."

My head was nodding like a bobble-head doll's. *"Oh my God,"* I thought, *"she's talking about* me*!"* When I looked around the room, everyone else—including the professor—was nodding too. I couldn't believe my eyes. I knew these women. I'd been in class with them, I'd taught alongside them, I'd read their work. To me, they were intelligent, articulate, and supremely competent individuals. To learn that even *they* felt like they were fooling others rocked my world.

A group of us began to meet as a kind of informal impostor-support group, where we did what women commonly do under stress—we bared our souls. We talked about how intimidated we felt when we discussed our research with our respective faculty advisors, about how more often than not we left these sessions feeling confused and inept. How we'd clearly put one over on the admissions office, and how anyone who looked too closely would realize we weren't scholar material after all. A few of us were convinced that certain professors had overlooked our obvious intellectual shortcomings simply because they liked us. We all agreed that these feelings of fraudulence were keeping us from finishing our dissertations in a timely fashion—or, in my case, from even starting.

The nineteenth-century English literary critic John Churton Collins was right when he said, "If we knew each other's secrets, what comforts we should find." Just being in the company of like-minded women was tremendously reassuring. Everything was going pretty well until about the third meeting. That's when I began to have this nagging sense that even though they were *saying* they felt like impostors . . . I *knew* I was the only *real* impostor!

Turning Pain into Gain

A few months later I came across a column in the *New York Times* by then ABC news correspondent and author Betty Rollin, with the headline: "Chronic self-doubt: Why does it afflict so many women?"[1] Despite an impressive track record, Rollin admitted to being plagued throughout her professional career by a constant fear of "screwing up." She wondered why more men weren't reduced to tears, as she often was, by the "I'm-in-over-my-head-and-this-time-they're-going-to-catch-me" feeling that accompanied each new assignment.

So one day Rollin decided to put the question to a young male producer she worked with at ABC, someone who, she was quick to point out, "is as competent as he thinks he is." Here's how Rollin described the exchange:

"When you're on a story," I asked him, "do you ever think it's not going to work out?" "Sure," he said merrily. "All the time."

"Do you worry about it?" "Sometimes," he said, not sounding sure.

"When it doesn't work out, do you usually figure it's your fault?"

"No," he said, sounding sure.

"Suppose it is your fault. Does it make you feel terrible?"

"Nah," he said.

"Why not?"

He looked at me. "Aren't I entitled to make a mistake once in a while?"

It's been decades since I first read those words, but I still recall how this simple rhetorical question stopped me cold. Entitled to make a mistake? This was new information to me—and, as I came to learn, to an awful lot of other women too. I was beginning to see that even if the myriad of occupational obstacles facing women at that time vanished altogether, our own inner barriers might well prevent us from taking full advantage of opportunity.

I realized then that I had a choice, I could let my own secret fears continue to stand between me and my goals, or I could channel my energy into trying to understand them. I chose the latter. The impostor phenomenon or the impostor syndrome, as it is more commonly referred to in the popular media, became the impetus for my doctoral research, in which I explored the broader question of why so many clearly intelligent, capable women feel anything but.

My search for answers entailed in-depth interviews with a racially diverse group of fifteen women: executives, clinicians, social service providers, and academic advisors. I wanted to hear from them about the kinds of internal barriers to success they'd observed in the women they managed, counseled, or advised. What I learned became the basis for a daylong workshop called "Overcoming the Imposter Syndrome: Issues of Competence and Confidence for Women," which I co-led with fellow grad student Lee Anne Bell.

Lee and I booked a small meeting room at a local hotel, put up some flyers, and hoped that at least a few people would come. When forty women showed up, we knew we'd hit a nerve. We facilitated several more packed workshops before Lee relocated to pursue a career in higher education. I continued to speak on the impostor syndrome and in 2001 renamed the program "How to Feel as Bright and Capable as Everyone Seems to *Think* You Are: Why Smart Women (and Men) Suffer from the Impostor Syndrome and What to Do About It."

Taking impostor feelings out of the realm of therapy and into an educational arena has proved tremendously successful. To date, more than fifty thousand people have attended this workshop. Simply giving people an alternative way of thinking about themselves and their competence has yielded some amazing results. Women reported asking for—and getting—raises. Corporate execs who had participated in a workshop as students told of being so transformed that years later they asked me to address their employees. Writers who had played small for years became prolific. People who had lacked the confidence to start or grow a business suddenly found the courage to go for it.

The core of what you'll learn stems from my original research. Now and then I draw from the professional and management experience gained in my own seven years in a Fortune 200 company and sixteen as an entrepreneur and pioneer in Profiting from Your Passions® career coaching.

However, most of what you will discover here comes from the collective experience and wisdom of my workshop participants over a quarter of a century.

During that time I've led workshops for tens of thousands of students, faculty, and staff at more than sixty colleges and universities including Harvard, Stanford, Smith, MIT, and Cal Tech. Unfortunately, the impostor syndrome does not end with a diploma. Some of what you'll learn comes from working directly with employees in such diverse organizations as Intel, Chrysler, Ernst & Young, UBS, Procter & Gamble, EMC, Bristol-Myers Squibb, IBM, the Society of Women Engineers, and American Women in Radio and Television, and with numerous groups of Canadian women entrepreneurs.

In addition, I've run seminars for groups of nurses, psychologists, optometrists, administrative assistants, jewelers, cancer researchers, social workers, and attorneys—all of which has been incorporated in this book. Despite their various situations and occupations, the women and men I've worked with have one important thing in common: They are not impostors. And, as you will soon discover, neither are you.

The Impostor Syndrome Then and Now

Clearly a lot has changed for women since 1982. I wish I could report the same with regards to women and the impostor syndrome. In fact, of the four overarching themes in this book, the three that emerged from my initial research are no less apt today:

1. *How you define and experience competence, success, and failure has everything to do with how confident and competent you feel.* Not only is adjusting how you think about competence, failure, and success the fastest

path to overcoming the impostor syndrome, bar none, but it won't happen unless you do. Period.

2. *Women's self-limiting attitudes and behavior barriers must be viewed in the context of certain sociocultural expectations and realities.* If you have difficulty always seeing yourself as competent and qualified, it may be because at times society has a hard time seeing you that way too. In spite of all the progress, the fact remains that being "too" *anything* that's considered unfeminine can cause people of both genders to perceive you to be less competent and a less desirable hire.

3. *It is impossible to separate women's achievement experience—including "fear of success"—from the feminine drive to affiliate with others.* Relocating for school or a new job, receiving a major promotion, or training to work in a predominantly male field are just a few of the situations where you may feel uncertain of yourself. It could be the impostor syndrome talking. In some cases, though, what you assume is fear of success may in fact be a heightened sensitivity to the potential ramifications of success on your relationships with others.

There is one aspect of the confidence conversation that was not present in the 1980s that you'll learn about here. Then women were striving to break down the cultural, educational, and legal barriers to higher-paying occupations that had been historically male-only. Now that the structural barriers have largely fallen, the quest for work/life integration, satisfaction, and meaning has for many women superseded the singular pursuit of money, status, and power. Overall the change is good. However, it's also complicated things, making it harder at times to tell if you're holding back because of self-doubt or a shift in priorities.

Can Men Feel Like Impostors?

When psychologists first began to study the impostor phenomenon, they suspected it was something experienced primarily by women. That has proven not to be the case. In fact, it is one of the few psychological issues initially thought to affect primarily women that has later been determined to relate to both genders.[2] Men are attending my seminars in increasing numbers, and among graduate students the male-female ratio is roughly fifty-fifty.

This of course begs the question, if men identify with the impostor syndrome too, why is this book aimed primarily at women? It's a legitimate question and frankly one I struggled with. I've heard from or worked with countless men who suffer terribly from their fraud fears, including a member of the Canadian mounted police, an attorney who argued before the Supreme Court, a corporate CEO, and an entire team of aerospace engineers, one of whom spoke of the "sheer terror" he feels when handed a major assignment. In the end, though, I decided there were more reasons than not to focus on women.

Articles about the impostor syndrome invariably cite the fact that numerous studies have found no difference between men and women. Some articles do mention the multiple studies where women scored significantly higher on impostor scales.[3] Nearly all point to the single study in which men outscored women.[4] However, few mention that these subjects were college professors. Given that academia is a breeding ground for impostor feelings, I think you'd be hard-pressed to replicate this finding in other settings.

Perhaps the real question is, if men experience the impostor syndrome equally, why aren't more clamoring for a solution? Of the sixty-six dissertations on the impostor phenomenon, 90 percent are by women. Speaking from my own experience, I can tell you that every seminar I've conducted for undergraduate students, members of professional associations, or corporate audiences has *always* been at the invitation of a program or committee whose mission it is to attract, develop, retain, and advance female students, members, or employees. All of which would seem to confirm impostor-syndrome researcher Dr. Joan Harvey's explanation that "men take it for granted and just live it, while women want to do something about it."[5]

More important, this book is aimed at women because the impostor syndrome holds them back more. Betty Rollin says it best when she writes: "I know the theory that says men are as scared as we are and they just repress it. Well, ok, then maybe repression works. Because when I look around the workplace I see an awful lot of men who are less competent than they think they are and as many women for whom the opposite is true: Women who are far more competent than they know and, if they keep it up, more than anyone else will ever know."

The next obvious question is, can men who experience the impostor syndrome benefit from this book? In a word—absolutely! All the more so if you are a man of color, have working-class roots, or identify with any of the other "at-risk" groups I talk about in this book. Similarly, if you know, teach, manage, mentor, parent, or coach a male or groups of males who are susceptible to the impostor syndrome, you will gain greatly from this book as well.

Although the book is geared toward women, I've tried to make it as helpful to male impostors as possible. For one, you'll find I've included a number of male voices here. Also know that when I refer to men or to broader gender differences relative to the impostor syndrome, unless otherwise noted, I'm not referring to distinctions between male and female impostors. In other words, when I talk about impostors in general, I'm talking about men too. If you are a man who identifies with the impostor syndrome, *I have a favor to ask*. After reading this book, I invite you to take a moment to send any feelings, thoughts, or experiences that you consider unique to male impostors to me at maleimpostors@impostor syndrome.com. I'd love to have your voice more fully represented in future editions.

SINCE WE'RE ON THE TOPIC OF GENDER: I've been doing this work long enough to know that anytime you talk about social difference you open yourself up not just to debate but to potential misunderstanding. Some argue that addressing differences reinforces stereotypes. Others prefer not to mention gender differences at all, seeing *difference* as synonymous with *conflict*. Still others may misconstrue points raised here to mean that I believe men to be a bunch of overly confident blowhards. Or the opposite—that men have it all together and women are insecure shrinking violets. Neither, of course, is true.

You and I both know that *all* women are not one way or *all* men another. Still, when speaking about gender differences, it is impossible to avoid making certain "genderalizations," and this book is no exception. With that, I ask your permission to use *men* and *women* here as shorthand, recognizing that discussions of differences of any sort can only be statements about averages.

How to Get the Most from This Book

As trite as it sounds, the more you put into this book, the more you'll get out of it. That may seem obvious, but I've met plenty of people who tell me they've read all the advice books out there but "nothing worked." My question to them is always the same: "Did you apply the advice?" The answer is always no. It's always easier to keep reading than it is to stop and do the exercises, and trying on new behaviors does require you to stretch in sometimes uncomfortable ways. Yet it's only by actively engaging in the process that we learn.

I know the impostor syndrome can cause great anguish, which is precisely why I've tried to bring a bit of levity to a subject that can carry such an emotional punch. It may seem impossible now, but I guarantee that by the end of this book you'll laugh at the absurdity of fully capable people—yourself included—feeling like impostors, fakes, and frauds. As the great Bugs Bunny once said, "Don't take life too seriously. You'll never get out alive."

Finally, the fact that you're reading this book tells me you're ready to "think different." That you've decided once and for all that the time has come to see yourself as others do. I want everyone to know just how bright and capable you really are. But the person I most want to acknowledge your brilliance is *you*.

Feel Like an Impostor?
Join the Club

The whole problem with the world is that
fools and fanatics are always so certain
of themselves, and wiser people so full
of doubts.

— Bertrand Russell

You don't have to look far to find intelligent, competent, talented women who feel anything but. Reflecting on her early days as a rising star at Revlon and later Avon, Joyce Roché, the former president and CEO of Girls Inc., remembers thinking, "Somewhere, deep inside, you don't believe what they say. You think it's a matter of time before you stumble and 'they' discover the truth. You're not supposed to be here. We knew you couldn't do it. We should have never taken a chance on you."[1]

When entrepreneur Liz Ryan, founder and CEO of WorldWIT, a women's online discussion community, won the Stevie, the business equivalent of an Oscar, she didn't feel like a winner. As she took the stage in New York to receive her award from Bill Rancic of *The Apprentice*, all Ryan could think was, *Who the hell am I? I'm just a mom with an overflowing laundry room and a two-year-old with applesauce in his hair.*[2]

Countless other women feel the same way. After graduating near the top of her class, a bright engineering major named LaTonya* was accepted into a highly competitive doctoral program. Instead of feeling proud, she was worried, telling me, "I was certain they'd made a mistake. I keep waiting for the other shoe to drop." Dawn, desperate to get off the fast track, invested thousands of dollars and considerable amounts of time training to become an executive coach. Two years and a hundred coaching hours later, she had yet to hang out her shingle, explaining, "I can't shake the feeling that I faked my way through the program."

What you've just seen is the impostor syndrome in action. What about you?

Take the Quiz
- Do you chalk your success up to luck, timing, or computer error?
- Do you believe "If I can do it, anybody can"?
- Do you agonize over the smallest flaws in your work?
- Are you crushed by even constructive criticism, seeing it as evidence of your ineptness?

*Unless otherwise noted, all names have been changed.

- When you do succeed, do you secretly feel like you fooled them again?
- Do you worry that it's a matter of time before you're "found out"?

If you answered yes to any of these questions, then you of all people know it doesn't really matter how much acclaim you've received, how many degrees you've earned, or how high you've risen. True, there are a lot of people who regard you as intelligent or talented, perhaps even brilliant. But you're not one of them. In fact, you have profound doubts about your abilities. No matter what you've accomplished or what people think, deep down you're convinced that you are an impostor, a fake, and a fraud.

Welcome to the Club

Despite the fact that we've never met, I suspect I already know a lot about you. For starters, you probably seem remarkably able and accomplished to the outside world. But secretly you believe you are merely passing for competent. When you do manage to nail the presentation, ace the exam, or get the job—*which you almost always do*—you see yourself as lucky or industrious, never intrinsically good at what you do. People who know or work with you have no idea that you lie awake at night wondering when they will finally discover what an incompetent sham you *really* are.

I also happen to know that you are intelligent, even though you don't always feel that way. Part of you knows this too. It's just that it's tough for you to maintain a consistent image of yourself as smart. And while we're on the subject, I don't necessarily mean you're book-smart. Although there's a pretty good chance you have at least one degree—perhaps even two or three.

You're also an achiever who by most standards is considered

successful—although here too you may struggle to see yourself that way. I'm not talking just about achieving wealth, fame, or status (although you very well may have). You don't have to have graduated first in your class or made it to the top of any ladder. But you do have to have achieved something to feel fraudulent about. Usually it's something you didn't expect of yourself, or have not yet mastered, at least not to your ridiculously high standards. Am I close? I thought so.

The Impostor Club has untold millions of members around the world. It's made up of women and men of all races, religions, and socioeconomic classes. They come from a wide range of educational backgrounds from high school dropouts to multiple Ph.D.'s, from such diverse fields as law enforcement, music, and medicine, and from entry level to CEO.

Finally, a Name for the Feelings

You may not even have known that these vague yet overwhelming feelings of self-doubt and angst actually have a name. I didn't either, not until my first year in graduate school when I was introduced to a 1978 paper titled "The Impostor Phenomenon in High Achieving Women" by Pauline Clance and Suzanne Imes. At the time both psychologists were at Georgia State University, where they observed that many of their students who excelled academically admitted during counseling that they felt their success was undeserved.

At its heart, the impostor syndrome, as it's more commonly known, refers to people who have a persistent belief in their lack of intelligence, skills, or competence. They are convinced that other people's praise and recognition of their accomplishments is undeserved, chalking up their achievements to chance, charm, connections, and other external factors. Unable to internalize or feel deserving of their success, they continually doubt their ability to repeat past successes. When they do succeed they feel relief rather than joy.

You may find that these feelings fade over time as you get more knowledge and experience under your belt. Or like many, you may experience impostor feelings consistently over the entire course of your career. For some people, the feelings of faking it extend into other roles, such as parenting and relationships. For instance, mothers who work outside of the home who try to pass off store-bought pies as homemade so as not to feel judged by the stay-at-home moms at the school fund-raiser. Or feigning interest on a date when you feel anything but.

The fraudulent feelings we're talking about here have to do with insecurities related to your knowledge or skills and as such occur primarily in academic and professional arenas. Not surprisingly, impostor feelings crop up most during times of transition or when faced with a new challenge, such as tackling an unfamiliar or high-profile assignment.

No one knows for sure how long the impostor syndrome has been in existence. For all we know, the first cave artist brushed off admiring grunts with "Oh, this old painting? Any Neanderthal could have done it." What is known is that the phenomenon is remarkably common. How common? In a study of successful people conducted by psychologist Gail Matthews, a whopping 70 percent reported experiencing impostor feelings at some point in their life.[3]

For the record, the impostor syndrome has nothing to do with you literally pretending to be someone you're not. Nor do you behave like real frauds, who actually do cheat their way to the top. In fact, people who identify with the impostor syndrome have proven to be less likely than non-impostors to engage in academic dishonesty such as plagiarism or cheating.[4]

It's also easy to misconstrue the impostor syndrome as just a fancy name for low self-esteem. It's not. Some studies have been able to link the two. But the fact that others have failed to find a strong connection tells us it's possible to feel insecure without feeling like a fraud. That's not to say you don't sometimes struggle with self-esteem (who doesn't?). However, that you identify with this syndrome at all suggests that your self-esteem is at least solid enough for you to set and achieve your goals. And achieve you have.

"Sure I'm Successful—but I Can Explain All That"

There's plenty of evidence to prove your success—good grades, promotions, raises, status, recognition, perhaps even awards and other accolades. But in your mind none of that matters. Like all impostors you are a master at coming up with ways to explain away your successes. See if you recognize yourself in any of these statements.

I got lucky. A perennial favorite is to chalk accomplishments up to chance. You think, "I may have lucked out this time, but next time I may not be so fortunate."

I was just in the right place at the right time or *The stars were right.* A candidate selected for a plum executive post believes it's because the selection committee drank a bit too much wine at dinner and the alcohol clouded their judgment.

It's because they like me. Being likable offers another handy hat on which to hang your success. You could be class valedictorian and still tell yourself, "It's only because the teachers liked me."

If I can do it, anyone can. You're convinced that your success has to do with the supposed simplicity of the task. A postdoctoral student in astrophysics from the California Institute of Technology told me, "I figure if I can get a Ph.D. in astrophysics from Cal Tech, anyone can." (I had to break it to her that most people, me included, can't even balance their checkbooks.)

They must let anybody in. You secretly believe that your success is a result of others' low standards. When a college administrator got word that she'd been accepted to a graduate program at Smith College, she told me she had second thoughts about attending. "I thought, what kind of standards do they have there?" It's the impostor version of the Groucho Marx joke: "I don't care to belong to any club that will have me as a member."

Someone must have made a terrible mistake. Maria Rodriguez and Linda Brown went to different colleges in different decades. Despite having never met, they said exactly the same thing: "I have a pretty common name. Deep down, I think that the admissions office mixed up my application with someone else who had the same name and they let the wrong person in."

I had a lot of help. There is certainly nothing wrong with sharing credit. But to you, any form of support, collaboration, or cooperation automatically cancels out your own contribution.

I had connections. Instead of seeing connections as giving you a leg up, you're convinced that knowing someone is the only reason you got into school, landed the job, or got the contract.

They're just being nice. The belief that people who speak highly of your work are just being polite is so thoroughly ingrained that whenever I get to this place in my presentation, I need only utter the first few words: *They're just being*—and the entire female audience finishes the sentence with *nice.*

They felt sorry for me. Impostors who return to college in midlife have been known to wonder out loud if perhaps the professors aren't just taking pity on them. Knowing they're trying to juggle kids, a job, and school, they suspect that their professors are intentionally going easy on them.

Excuses, Excuses

- A postdoctoral student with an impressive curriculum vitae insists, "I just look good on paper."
- A graduate student who gets into a research program that is so competitive only one new student is admitted per year decides she was chosen because the school was looking for diversity . . . and she was from the Midwest.
- A student majoring in microbiology engineering quickly sets the record straight to those who are impressed by her field of study by explaining that it just "sounds impressive because it has a long name."

Fooled 'Em Again

On one hand, you have to admit that it takes an exceptional mind to think up so many creative excuses for success. So take a moment to pat yourself on the back right now. But don't congratulate yourself too long because you also have a problem, don't you? After all, if you are unable to claim your accomplishments on a gut, visceral level, then when you are confronted with actual evidence of your abilities, it's unclear to you how you got there. Even though your achievements clearly emanate from you, you feel oddly disconnected from them. And without this connection between yourself and your accomplishments, the only possible explanation you're left with is that you've fooled them.

Rationally you would think success would alleviate feelings of fraudulence. The more successful you are, the more evident it is that you really do know what you're doing. But for you just the opposite happens. Instead of reducing the pressure, success only makes it worse because now you have a reputation to defend. Instead of being cause for celebration, things like praise, financial rewards, and status can feel oppressive. You think, *Now they'll expect me to be that good every time—and I have no idea how I pulled it off the first time.*

Rather than spurring you on, success may lead you to drop out altogether. This is especially true if you are perceived to be an "overnight" success. A rapid ascent to the top of the hill suddenly lands you in unfamiliar territory. You wonder, *How did this happen? Did I pay enough dues? Do I deserve to be here?* Whether success came early or late in your career, the prevailing sense among impostors is, *They'll expect me to be competent down the road, and I'm not at all sure I will be.* That's because in your mind, one success is unrelated to the next. Rather than being cumulative, each accomplishment is its own sum game. This makes success a very tenuous thing. You think, *Sure, I've done well up until now . . .*

But Wait Until Next Time

You know your good fortune can't last forever. So instead of basking in your achievement, you live in fear that your ineptness will finally be discovered and that you will be humiliated—or worse. Because you're convinced that each new endeavor will be your undoing, your run-up to each test, presentation, or challenge brings tremendous anxiety and self-doubt. You think, *One false move and I'm out.* This apprehension is typically followed by success, and finally by skeptical relief. It is a pattern that endlessly repeats itself.

Of course, in your mind "next time" is when you'll finally be unmasked. Like Deb, a law-firm partner, who despite a solid track record approached each new case with a growing dread. To her own surprise, one day she found herself absentmindedly perusing the want ads for waitressing jobs. As she struggled to understand her own behavior, she realized that back when she was a waitress during college at least she knew what she was doing.

There may be days when the notion of being unmasked actually brings a tinge of relief. As humiliating as being exposed as an impostor would be, you can't help but imagine how much easier your life could be if you could just drop this charade of trying to act like a respected, capable professional. Besides, you know you could always learn how to say, *Would you like fries with that, sir?* or do something else you believe to be *"more on my level."*

Even if you don't harbor such fantasies, you're well aware of what it's like to be perpetually waiting for the other shoe to drop. For Jodie Foster it first happened when she put her acting career on hold to pursue an undergraduate degree and then again after she won the best actress Oscar for *The Accused*. "I thought it was a fluke," Foster explained in a *60 Minutes* interview. "The same way when I walked on the campus at Yale. I thought everybody would find out, and then they'd take the Oscar back. They'd come to my house, knocking on the door, 'Excuse me, we meant to give that to someone else. That was going to Meryl Streep.'"[5]

For some people the fear and anxiety caused by the impostor syndrome can be debilitating. One first-time manager was so consumed with the idea that she'd bluffed her way into the job that she experienced chest pains. Fearing the worst, her assistant called an ambulance. Fortunately it turned out to be an anxiety attack. Your fear of exposure is unlikely to land you in the hospital, but the stress does have consequences.

Sadly, every day exceptional students drop out of school. People take jobs far below their abilities or aspirations or otherwise fail to rise to more mentally challenging and financially rewarding opportunities. Still others abandon long-cherished dreams of writing a book, becoming a photographer, or starting their own business, all in an attempt to avoid detection.

These are, of course, the extreme cases. Fortunately, the vast majority of people with impostor syndrome don't give up. Instead, like you, they press on in spite of the nagging self-doubt. They get the degree, advance in their field, take on the challenge, and succeed—sometimes spectacularly so. Still, the anxiety remains. Fortunately, though, you won't have to suffer much longer.

From "Impostorism" to Confidence

As you embark on this journey to feel as bright and capable as you truly are, there are a few things you need to know. First and foremost is that you are neither broken nor sick. True, something is not quite right about your impostor *feelings*, but there is nothing wrong with *you*. I'm not going to try to talk you out of those feelings, at least not yet. I know you well enough to know that you wouldn't believe me anyway. More important, you're going to do that yourself soon enough. All the tools, insight, and information you need to overcome the impostor syndrome await you here.

Up until now your shame, along with the mistaken belief that you're the only one who feels like a fraud, has kept you from speaking up. However, in picking up this book you've acknowledged something you may have kept hidden for years, and by breaking the silence you have taken what is an essential step in beating the impostor syndrome.

Throughout this book I'll be encouraging you to both get support from and give support to fellow members of the Impostor Club. I mention this now because you may have learned the hard way that sharing with people who don't get what you're going through is often not helpful. Your family, friends, or close colleagues either pooh-pooh your self-doubt, insisting that you're "worrying over nothing," or have grown impatient when their reassurances of your brilliance are constantly brushed aside. It's not that they don't want to be supportive—they do. But if you perpetually agonize over striking out only to consistently hit the ball out of the park, after a while even your most ardent supporters will find it hard to sympathize

The good news is that you're not alone anymore. Even better news: It really *is* possible to unlearn the self-limiting thinking that feeds your impostor feelings. How can I be so certain? Simple. The reason I know you so well is that *I am you.* Allow me to also officially introduce myself by letting you in on my not-so-secret secret. Namely, I am a recovering impostor. See, I told you you were in good company!

The Bottom Line

You've become adept at explaining away or minimizing evidence of your success and hence never really owning your accomplishments. Because you believe you've fooled others into thinking you are brighter and more capable than you "know" you are, you live in fear of being unmasked as an impostor.

Now that you have a name for the feelings and the knowledge that you are not the only one who feels this way, you can finally begin to turn this impostor business around and see yourself as the competent person you really are.

What You Can Do

- The impostor syndrome packs too much of an emotional punch to try to reason it away. Overcoming it requires self-reflection as well. Keep a notebook handy to capture "ahas" as they occur as well as to write your answers to exercises you'll find throughout this book. With everything in one place, you'll be able to more easily trace your entire journey from impostorism to the more confident you who you'll meet at the end of this book.

- For a more engaged experience, consider reading this book as part of a book club or with a friend.
- If this is the first time you're learning about the impostor syndrome, take a moment now to identify your biggest take-aways so far. What did you learn here that surprised you or you found most helpful? What thoughts, feelings, and/or behaviors did you recognize in yourself? What questions do you have? Write them down now.

What's Ahead

The question is, Why do intelligent, accomplished women—and men—from Indiana to India fall victim to this faulty thinking? To unlearn the impostor syndrome, you need to know where it comes from. So let's begin there.

[2]

Consider the Source

The more one analyzes people, the more all reasons for analysis disappear. Sooner or later one comes to that dreadful universal thing called human nature.

—Oscar Wilde

You did not come by your impostor feelings all by yourself. These irrational feelings of inadequacy can get sparked by a host of things. When you have an "impostor moment," it's tremendously helpful to understand the possible reasons behind it. That's because when you shift away from the personal it allows you to put your responses into perspective more quickly. It's the difference between thinking *Yikes, what an incompetent fraud I am!* and knowing *It makes perfect sense that I'd feel like a fraud. Under the circumstances, who wouldn't?*

Not only do you no longer need to feel the shame that comes from the mistaken assumption that you're the only one who feels this way, but as you are about to discover, feeling like an impostor is not only normal, but in certain situations it's to be expected. This alone can go a long way toward lowering your anxiety and raising your confidence.

Seven Perfectly Good Reasons Why You May Feel Like an Impostor—and What to Do About Them

You are about to discover seven perfectly good reasons why fully capable people like you wind up feeling like impostors. Even if you can't relate personally to every reason, knowing about them will help you see the larger picture. None of the seven are unique to women, and most are situational. As such you may identify with one or some more than with others. However, there's one source that everyone can relate to. Raise your hand if . . .

1. You Were Raised by Humans

Since it looks like almost all of you have your hands up, we'll spend a bit more time on what is for some the start of their impostor story. Your family—with help from teachers, coaches, and other significant adults in your life—had a profound impact on shaping your early self-expectations and, therefore, how confident, competent, and even successful you feel today. Discouraging messages especially can linger for years. In his memoir, crooner Andy Williams speaks of never having been able to get out of his head what his father had told him when he was a child: "You're not as good as them, so you have to work harder." They were words that prompted a "crisis of confidence" that haunted Williams throughout his long and exceptionally successful career.[1]

Impostor feelings can be spawned by far more subtle messages as well. If you were the kid who came home with all As and one B and your parents' only response was "What's that B doing there?" there's a good chance you grew up to be a perfectionist. If your parents were preoccupied with grades to the exclusion of anything else, you may have come to believe that being loved depended on being smart.

Or you may have grown up in a family where your talents and accomplishments went unnoticed. You made honors or took home the trophy and all you heard was "That's nice," or worse, they said nothing. For kids, approval is like oxygen. The absence of praise during childhood can make it difficult as an adult to own your accomplishments and feel deserving of your success. If that resonates, you should know that there are any numbers of reasons why a parent would withhold praise—none of which involve a lack of love.

Your parents may have been afraid that praise would give you a big head or that you'd come to depend on it. If you always brought home the gold, your parents may have simply come to expect it. If you had siblings who struggled academically, your parents may not have wanted to single you out for your achievements. Depending on your parents' own education level, it's possible they simply didn't value schooling. Or they were raised to believe that modesty and not calling attention to oneself are virtues.

On the other hand, you may have been lavished with praise no matter how well you did. As enviable as this may sound to the approval-deprived, unearned applause has its drawbacks. After all, if everything you did was considered remarkable, you may never have learned to differentiate between good and great, or between taking a shot and giving it your all. You may have grown so dependent on constant validation that if your professors or employers fail to continually stroke you, then you immediately start questioning your performace. Or you don't value the judge, believing, "They love everything I do because I'm their kid."

It's possible too that you grew up in an atmosphere where the norm was to emphasize effort over outcome and everyone got a trophy or gold star. Certainly this approach kept many kids who are not natural athletes or students literally and figuratively in the game. However, you may be among those who grew up to experience confusion at the lack of correlation between results and praise. Jack, a bright graduate student at Carnegie Mellon University, believes his parents' inclination to praise *only* his approach is what led to his own tendency to rationalize away his accomplishments and to feel guilty when the process doesn't match the outcome. For example, if Jack aces a class without extraordinary effort, he feels undeserving of the grade. He wonders too if the impostor syndrome actually fuels some high-achieving people, explaining, "I have long felt driven to do something that will completely surprise and impress my parents, instead of eliciting the same stock praise for all occasions."

As you can see, early messages about achievement, success, and failure run deep. At eighty-one, Andy Williams says he's "finally beginning to believe that maybe I am as good as the others after all." It might take a lifetime to fully uncover and recover from the childhood roots of your impostor feelings. But that's not to say you can't get a jump on things here.

For example, it may help to think back to an early success, preferably something you were proud of. It could be something you excelled at, that came easily to you, that you won or achieved. What was your response at the time? Were you excited, embarrassed, surprised, or proud? Did you celebrate, or did you beat yourself up for not doing even better? Did you tell your friends or keep a low profile? How did your family and/or other significant adults respond to this success? Did they reward, praise, encourage, or ignore you? Were they excited, disappointed, ambivalent, or proud? How do you think this experience has impacted how you respond to success today?

Of course, there's the other side of the achievement coin—failure, challenge, and mistakes. Here you'll want to think back on a memorable "failure" or challenge you experienced as a child or young adult. Was there something you found especially difficult—for example, reading, math, art, learning a language, or athletics? Perhaps something you performed poorly at or blew, like the big game, a test, or a class presentation. Did you consider things like not making honors or winning a prize at the science fair to be a failure?

How did you respond to this early difficulty? Were you embarrassed, disappointed, or upset? Did you beat yourself up or shrug it off as no big deal? Did you try harder, or did you feel discouraged and give up? Did you share your feelings with others? What was your family's response? Were you punished, comforted, encouraged, protected, ignored, or rescued? If relevant, how did teachers, coaches, or other significant adults in your life respond? Finally, what impact do you think this experience had on how you respond to failure, difficulty, and risk taking today?

Children who grow up to feel like impostors can also be affected by what psychologist Joan Harvey refers to as "family myths and labels." In families with multiple children or close cousins it's common for children to get labeled according to their perceived traits or talents. There may be "the funny one," "the athletic one," "the sensitive one," "the responsible one," "the bad one," and so on. If another sibling was dubbed "the smart one," you may have been torn between believing the family myth and desperately wanting to prove your parents wrong. If, however, you did get to be the chosen one, you may have felt tremendous pressure to live up to the label. Either way it's no picnic.

Even if you had the most supportive family in the world, you no doubt learned to measure your adult achievements through your family's eyes. Of course different families can have very different definitions of what constitutes success for their children. For the Korean American teenager Patti in Paula Yoo's novel *Good Enough,* the expectation was crystal clear. Under the heading "How to Make Your Korean Parents Happy," Yoo placed three things:

1. Get a perfect score on the SATs.
2. Get into Harvard Yale Princeton.
3. Don't talk to boys.*
    *Boys will distract you from your studies.

Your own messages may have been far less explicit, but still you somehow knew what success looked like. In some families it meant that you graduate high school or train to enter a trade. In others, success was getting a four-year college degree. In some that wasn't good enough—you had to earn an advanced degree. In still others it was about the "right" college or even earning the "right" degree—often in things like law, medicine, or engineering. Then there are families for whom education was not the focus at all. Instead children were expected to go into the family business, join the military, marry and have children, enter the clergy, or grow up to be a contributing member of one's racial, religious, or cultural group—something some African, Latino, Native, and Asian Americans refer to as "collective success."

What about you? How was success defined in your family? If success centered on education, what did your parents expect of you academically? What would a typical report-card conversation sound like? What did your family assume you would grow up to do or be? In the eyes of your family, would you say you've met, exceeded, or fallen short of their expectations? What, if anything, does your family have to say about your current level of achievement? If your family doesn't speak of such things, what do you *imagine* they're thinking or feeling? Once again, what impact has all this had on how you feel about your success today?

We all want to feel like our family is proud of us. If you've achieved at the level of success established by your family—and you're good with that—then everybody's happy. But when you succeed on different terms than what was anticipated, you may wonder, *Am I really successful?* Go far beyond what your family had envisioned, and you might feel guilty for outdoing your parents or siblings. Fail to live up to parental expectations, and you may experience shame. Either scenario can send you running to the nearest therapist.

No matter how old you are, you never fully outgrow the need for your family's acknowledgment and approval. But needing it and getting it are two different things. If your parents designated another sibling as the family genius, as much as you may like to, you can't unring the bell. On the other hand, if you did happen to be crowned "the smart one," accept that you're not always going to be able to live up to the title. Once you make the decision to stop wasting your time and emotional energy try-ing to maintain your family's approval, you'll free up a lot of time in your schedule. You can't change the past. The future, though, is yours for the making. Mary Ann Evans, better known by her pen name, George Eliot, said, "It's never too late to be what you might have been." It's also never too late to be the confident, self-affirming person you were meant to be.

Finally, don't lose sight of the fact that your parents were raised by humans too. If you were underpraised, it's possible that your parents never received praise themselves. Or maybe the reason they demanded academic perfection from you was that their parents demanded it of them—or they wish their parents had. When you can finally understand and forgive your parents, you'll be able to do the same for yourself.

2. You Are a Student

Since 1985 more than sixty colleges and universities have invited me to their campuses to speak. Occasionally it's to address faculty and deans. Primarily, though, it's to talk to a group that's especially vulnerable to the impostor syndrome—students. It makes perfect sense really. What other group do you know who have their knowledge and skills literally tested and graded practically on a daily basis?

If you graduated from high school near the head of your class or were otherwise recognized for your academic excellence, you probably got used to being seen as the best and the brightest. But then you went off to college, where suddenly you were just one of many. Now who are you? On the other hand, if you were an average student in high school and then went on to do well in college or beyond, you might question how you managed to pull it off.

It's possible that you began your academic life quite confident, only to have your confidence squashed by an insensitive educator. It's a story I've heard far too often. One distraught engineering student was told by her professor, "You are certainly not brilliant, but you may be able to muddle through." Another master's student who worked under a cruel and condescending advisor told me that the most encouraging comment he heard in four years was "Nothing in your thesis is too egregious." Translation: "Your work doesn't suck too bad." With feedback like that, how could anyone's self-confidence not suffer?

The higher the achievement stakes, the more likely you'll wind up feeling like a fraud. If you were considered academically gifted or enrolled in honors classes, you may feel more pressure to be brilliant. Or you may have skated through your undergraduate years relatively confident, but once you decided to get an advanced degree you began to wonder whether you really had what it takes to go from student to scholar. In any of these scenarios you wonder, *Do I know enough? Can I really do this? Am I good enough?*

If you're a student, there are a few things you want to keep in mind. One is that every field, from law to psychology to art, has its own specialized and often unnecessary convoluted language. In order to be deemed sufficiently knowledgeable or scholarly, you're required to "elevate" things that could just as easily be described in everyday language. At times the language can be so dense that even when you're relatively well versed in an area, you may still have to read the same sentence over and over again to comprehend what's being said. Whether you eventually decipher it or not, the fact that you had to struggle in the first place can set off your impostor alarm. Truth be told, if more experts communicated with the goal of making their work accessible to a larger population, everyone, including you, would feel a lot smarter—and be more informed.

When you're surrounded by well-educated people it's easy to assume that everyone else is somehow "smarter" than you. Some are. Some aren't. Either way, as Thomas Armstrong points out in *7 Kinds of Smart: Identifying and Developing Your Multiple Intelligences,* there are different ways of being smart—and "book-smart" is just one of them.

When intellectual insecurity does strike, try to remind yourself that not only did you sign up to have your knowledge and ability tested on a regular basis, but you *paid* for the privilege. After all, getting an education costs good money. So approach being a student as you would being any paying consumer and take advantage of every possible resource available to you, including tutoring and academic advising. Recognize too that some subjects are going to come more easily to you and others you're going to have to really work at. If you're struggling to do the work, stop being embarrassed or judging yourself as inadequate and seek assistance instead.

Most of all, you need to recognize that the impostor syndrome is part of the student experience, and all the more so if you're in graduate school or belong to any of the other groups covered in this chapter. Just knowing this can go a long way in helping you see your lack of confidence less in personal terms and more as part of the collective student experience. So repeat after me in your most confident voice: I'm a STUDENT. I'm here to LEARN. I'm SUPPOSED to feel stupid!

3. You Work in an Organizational Culture That Feeds Self-Doubt

It is entirely possible, of course, to work in an environment that fosters cooperation and mutual support and *still* feel inept. However, if you happen to be trying to make it in a culture known for eating its own, there's a greater risk for the impostor syndrome to take hold.

Adversarial organizational cultures are hardly new. Nearly a century ago the distinguished physicist and chemist Marie Curie observed that within her field "there are sadistic scientists who hurry to hunt down errors instead of establishing the truth."

Take academia. Scholarly debate and rigorous investigation are what motivates many people to pursue a career in higher education in the first place. But what you might not have bargained for, especially if you're in a highly competitive research setting, is a culture where spirited debate and inquiry can quickly turn hostile and derisive. It can be so intense that physicists at one university refer to these exchanges as "combat physics."

In fact, Diane Zorn at York University in Canada insists that the less desirable elements of academic culture, such as aggressive competitiveness, scholarly isolation, nationalism among and between disciplines, and lack of mentoring, are *the* reason the impostor syndrome is so rampant on college campuses and not just among students.[2] In the only study in which men actually identified *more* strongly with the impostor syndrome than women, the men were university professors.[3]

Things are somewhat different in the business world. Here success is measured not by the ability to punch holes in other people's theories but by your skill at beating the competition and getting promoted. Still, there is no shortage of egos, one-upping, and infighting. Having spent a decade in the corporate world, I've seen firsthand how overbearing executives can belittle subordinates, how despite the party line, everyone knows there really is such a thing as a "dumb question," and how risk taking is acceptable—as long as you always get it right. If the place where you spend most of your waking hours makes you feel stupid or inept, your self-confidence is bound to suffer.

If you feel intimidated or out of your league in your job, stop assuming it's because you're not smart enough or sophisticated enough and recognize the ways in which your organizational culture may be contributing to your impostor feelings. Is asking for help—or even information—considered a sign of weakness or a legitimate request? Is admitting a gap in knowledge seen as normal and necessary for learning or as a sign of incompetence? Is perfectionism the unspoken rule?

Only you can decide whether your workplace nourishes your intellect or feeds your insecurities. If you're in an especially hostile setting, reach out to like-minded colleagues within or across disciplines or fields. Collaborating or even just talking with people who understand and who can validate your work is an effective counterbalance to being in a less-than-supportive environment. If nothing works, take Oxygen Media CEO Gerry Laybourne's advice: "If they make you feel stupid . . . move on." While you obviously can't change jobs overnight, you would be wise to keep your eyes open and your résumé up-to-date.[4]

4. You Work Alone

You can work all by yourself and still feel like a giant fake. In fact, in some ways working alone can cause you to question your competence even more. After all, being your own boss means you have no real job description, no management feedback, and no outside performance standards to guide you. So instead you come up with your own, which makes for tough going when you work for a demanding and unforgiving boss like yourself.

Working alone also puts you more at risk for professional isolation. Not having anyone to bounce ideas or decisions off of makes it easier to second-guess yourself. With no one to point out your blind spots or pat you on the back, you can get discouraged more readily and become mired in self-doubt.

Because it's so easy to lose perspective when you work alone, one of the best things you can do is connect with another solo worker for regular check-ins. It's less important that the other person be in your business or field than it is to have someone to help hold you accountable for follow-through and deadlines, to troubleshoot problems, brainstorm ideas, and offer that much-needed feedback that you really do know what you're doing.

5. You Work in a Creative Field

After his novel *Everything Is Illuminated* made the *New York Times* best-seller list, Jonathan Safran Foer told a reporter, "I can be very hard on myself. I convince myself that I'm fooling people."[5] Award-winning author Maya Angelou also worries that her success is a big ruse, once saying, "I have written eleven books, but each time I think, 'Uh-oh, they're going to find out now. I've run a game on everybody, and they're going to find me out."

It's not just writers. The Internet is full of impostor confessions from people in the entertainment industry who despite receiving much acclaim still worry about being unmasked. She may be a bona fide star, but as the stakes got higher, Kate Winslet says, there were times when "I would wake up in the morning before going off to a shoot, and think, I can't do this. I'm a fraud."[6] And Don Cheadle says that when he looks at his work, "All I can see is everything I'm doing wrong that is a sham and a fraud." It doesn't matter which side of the camera you're on.[7] When he's on the set, Michael Uslan, the producer of the Batman movies, says, "I still have this background feeling that one of the security guards might come and throw me out."[8]

And why wouldn't they—or you—have these feelings? The very nature of creative work makes those who do it vulnerable to feeling inadequate, especially if you are not formally trained. For one, your work is highly public. Plus you are defined not only by your work but by artistic and literary standards that are completely subjective. How many other occupations do you know where a person's work is judged by people whose job title is "professional critic"? It's a challenge to maintain confidence when you know you are only as good as your last painting, your last movie, your last book, when even the brightest stars fade quickly, and where success requires that you prove yourself over and over again in ways few others must.

But what if you really have achieved a certain degree of notoriety? You might expect to feel more confident. Instead it can cause you to question yourself even more because the reactions of those around you can be so skewed. "When you're a celebrity," says writer A. J. Jacobs, "anything that emerges from your mouth that vaguely resembles a joke is cause for gut-busting laughter from everyone within earshot."[9] With all that adoration it's only natural to question whether you really deserve the attention.

Given the nearly universal nature of impostor feelings among your fellow creative types, what if you were to stop fighting it and instead get with the program? The reason I've included so many impostor confessions from well-known actors throughout this book is that evidence of their talent is commonly recognized. Even Meryl Streep, the most Academy Award–nominated actor in history, gets cold feet at the beginning of every new project, telling a reporter, "You think, 'Why would anyone want to see me again in a movie?' And I don't know how to act anyway, so why am I doing this?"[10] *Meryl Streep*, for crying out loud! If that doesn't tell you something about how normal *and* absurd the impostor syndrome is, nothing will.

As esteemed choreographer Martha Graham once said, "No artist is pleased. [There is] no satisfaction whatever at any time. There is only queer divine dissatisfaction, a blessed unrest that keeps us marching and makes us more alive than the others." When so many of the most acclaimed people on the planet feel like impostors, why wouldn't you? Instead of berating yourself, do a little happy dance at the blessed unrest that allows you to share the human insecurity with some of the most talented people of all time.

6. You Are a Stranger in a Strange Land

A sense of belonging can go a long way in fostering self-confidence. Conversely, when you feel like an outsider you are in a sense wearing a mask, a situation that can easily open the door for impostor feelings to slip in. There are a few different ways you may feel like a fish out of water, including operating outside of your culture or socioeconomic class or being in a work environment that feels highly foreign.

If you do work or study in another country, for instance, then you know what a constant struggle it is to fit in. In addition to all the normal expectations and pressures facing anyone doing demanding work, you've got to do it while navigating a different culture and perhaps language as well. Little wonder a whopping 85.7 percent of foreign-trained medical residents in Canada tested high for impostor feelings."[11]

A sense of belonging can also be a function of your socioeconomic class. British students who attended private schools prior to college, for example, ranked low for impostor feelings.[12] If, on the other hand, you sprang from blue-collar roots, you may feel like a poser. When she stepped onto the Princeton University campus from the Bronx, the future Supreme Court justice Sonia Sotomayor says, she felt like "a visitor landing in an alien country." For the entire first year, she was "too embarrassed and too intimidated to ask questions."[13]

As a first-generation professional who has "made it," you may find yourself in the precarious position of not fully fitting in. You may have an underlying sense that *"I don't really belong here. I don't really deserve this."* While hobnobbing in your new world, you may half expect to be tapped on the shoulder and asked to leave. "I have spent my years since Princeton, while at law school and in my various professional jobs, not feeling completely a part of the worlds I inhabit," Sotomayor says. "I am always looking over my shoulder wondering if I measure up."

Regardless of geography or class, if you are a woman working in a corporate environment, whether you know it or not you are also operating in an alien culture. That's why you'll find scores of books seeking to educate women about how to navigate the unwritten rules of organizational politics but none specifically aimed at teaching men how to make it in a world that is culturally speaking neither strange nor new.

This is no small matter when you consider that in the private realms of relationships, home, and family, women are far less likely to struggle with impostor feelings. You don't feel like a fraud when you're sorting laundry or think it's a fluke that your pet adores you. True, there may be times, when, for instance, you feel like you're winging it as a parent. But that's different from questioning your intellectual capacity or chalking your parenting success up to luck or charm.

If the impostor syndrome were merely a matter of confidence or upbringing, says Wellesley Centers for Women senior researcher Dr. Peggy McIntosh, you would feel fraudulent in all aspects of your life. Instead, the places where women are most apt to feel incompetent and illegitimate are in the public spheres of power and authority. This is true for men too, of course. But here again the difference is that up until a few short decades ago these arenas were the near exclusive domain of men.

Since women do not have a long history of belonging in these spheres—especially at the highest levels—the feats of the great and powerful wizards of industry, finance, science, politics, and even art can, for some, seem downright mysterious. You may see important people doing important things and think surely that what they're doing is beyond your abilities or comprehension. If you don't understand the game for what it is, you may be so intimidated that you never even try.

If you fall into any of these categories, the first thing you need to do is give yourself a break. When you are outside your cultural comfort zone, for example, you're bound to have more insecurity about your competence than a native does. If you are a first-generation professional, the fact that you got where you are without the benefits that accompany social class makes you both commendable *and* exceptional. When impostor feelings hit, give yourself extra points for performing as well as you do.

Next, look for ways to address the isolation that goes along with feeling like a stranger in a strange land. If you're a student, tap into campus programs that serve international students. If you are a professional working abroad and there are no resources that offer contact with others from your culture, look for online venues that can connect you with others either elsewhere in the country where you currently reside or back home. Once you do, look for opportunities to raise the impostor syndrome not as a confession, but as an interesting topic of discussion. Given the universal nature of these feelings, I guarantee that once you name the feelings, you'll find people who will identify.

Remember too that regardless of the reason, whenever you feel like a stranger, a certain amount of fakery is required just to fit in. The important thing is not to take the discomfort of feeling out of your element to mean you are somehow less intelligent, capable, or worthy than others. You are where you are because you deserve to be. Period.

7. *You Represent Your Entire Social Group*

Clare Boothe Luce once remarked, "Because I am a woman, I must make unusual efforts to succeed. If I fail, no one will say, 'She doesn't have what it takes.' They will say, 'Women don't have what it takes.'" The playwright, magazine editor, ambassador, and congresswoman launched her career in 1935. And yet some eight decades later the pressure to carry the competence torch for one's entire gender, race, sexual orientation, and so on is still on.

Some years ago a young woman who was blind attended one of my workshops. The recent college grad struggled with the same impostor feelings as everyone else in the room. But she also expressed tremendous anxiety about being the first sight-impaired person at her new workplace. "If I'm not 'Super Disabled Person,'" she explained, "I worry the next time someone with a disability applies for a job, they'll think, 'Uh-oh, we tried one of *those people,* and it didn't work out." It's a situation highly familiar to people of color as well.

You don't have to be blind to see the pressure that comes from feeling like you have to represent not just yourself but your entire social group, pressure that makes you more vulnerable to the impostor syndrome. Upon her retirement, Supreme Court justice Sandra Day O'Connor reflected on her pioneer status. "My concern was whether I could do the job of a justice well enough to convince the nation that my appointment was the right move. If I stumbled badly in doing the job, I think it would have made life more difficult for women."[14]

Merely *thinking* about being in the minority relative to men has been shown to lead to palpable anxiety in women (something we'll explore in more detail in a future chapter). At best, you feel self-conscious; at worst, intimidated. Add to that any assumptions that you got where you are solely as a result of affirmative action (which in the minds of some translates into the belief that you are automatically less capable) or that you cruised on the basis of good looks. Either scenario can undermine your confidence and up the pressure to prove yourself.

If you don't think numbers impact performance, think again. As researchers at Massachusetts Institute for Technology discovered, once the percentage of female students in a department rose above about 15, women's academic performance improved. Girls who attend single-sex schools have higher career aspirations than both boys and girls at coed schools.[15] Studies repeatedly show that if you attended a women's college, you are likely to have higher self-esteem and more intellectual self-confidence than your counterparts at coed institutions. The same is true for African Americans who attend historically black colleges.

So what can you do? First, know that it's not you. There really are well-documented and important differences between how men and women in the workplace tend to communicate, assert authority, negotiate, use humor, and navigate organization politics. Understanding these differences can help you recognize when a perceived slight may be more a matter of style than of sexism. In these situations a sense of humor can go a long way.

If you are a person of color working in a predominantly white environment, you may have had to figure out how to navigate within the dominant culture. At the same time, embracing your own culture can actually serve as a powerful buffer against self-doubt, with one study finding that high-achieving women of color who drew collective self-esteem from being a member of their racial or ethnic group felt less like impostors.[16]

Other things you can do are actively build relationships with people of any ilk who support your academic or professional goals. Join or form a professional network within your workplace or community. If you do not live or work in a racially or ethnically diverse setting, make the effort to attend conferences and other networking events outside your area.

Last, don't confuse the discomfort caused by feeling outnumbered with the idea that you're not smart enough or are in some way not worthy of being there. You are where you are because you deserve to be. Being one of a token few can be stressful. Which makes it all the more important that when impostor feelings do strike, you give yourself extra points for performing as well as you do. You may be expected to represent your entire social group, but you need not accept that responsibility. You have as much right to fall as flat on your face as the next person; assert it.

The Bottom Line

There are seven perfectly good reasons you might feel like a fraud: family expectations and messages; being a student; working in an organizational culture that feeds self-doubt; working alone; working in a creative field; being or just feeling like a stranger in a strange land; and having to represent your entire social group. Once you recognize that many people in similar scenarios experience these same self-doubts, you can put your own impostor feelings in less personal and more situational terms.

What You Can Do

- Step back and examine how family messages and expectations may contribute to your impostor feelings.
- Note which situation(s) discussed here you identify with. For each one complete this sentence: *How I feel is perfectly normal given the fact that* _____.
- Make a note of any aha moments you had when reading about your situation.
- If you still believe you are the only one who feels like a fraud, seek out opportunities—in person or online—to connect with others in your situation and raise the topic of the impostor syndrome. I guarantee that you will not feel alone for long.

What's Ahead

There is an undeniable connection between how you are perceived from the outside and how you feel on the inside. For women the impostor syndrome is as much a shared experience as it is an individual one. As you are about to learn, another critical piece of the impostor puzzle is societal assumptions about female competence—assumptions that go a long way in explaining why impostor feelings are more prevalent in women.

[3]

It's Not All in Your Head

Women are considered just a little less competent. Their problems are just that much less urgent. Their experience is not quite as valid.

—Dee Dee Myers, former White House press secretary

An executive at an international investment bank invited me to deliver a talk on the impostor syndrome at her company. Sandra had talked with a number of female managers who she knew would benefit, but her motive was not completely unselfish. Despite her impressive title and even more impressive salary, with every new promotion she thought, *Don't these people realize I'm just winging it here?* It had to be reassuring, then, when within twenty-four hours more than two hundred people signed up to attend.

Among the responses Sandra received was an email from another executive. His reply read simply: "I don't need this. I really am smarter than people think I am." My client marveled at the mirror-opposite responses between her and her colleague. "Where does he get that kind of confidence?" she asked. Not long afterward I received an email containing a strikingly similar story from a highly regarded research scientist who'd attended an impostor workshop the previous day.

> My husband is a nice guy who is successful and pretty far up the executive ladder. Last night at dinner, I was telling him about the impostor syndrome. He said to me completely sincerely and non-arrogantly that he could not relate at all because he feels like he is genuinely smarter than anyone gives him credit for. LOL!!:-) I just have to laugh at our differences. It is funny.

You know, it really is *funny* how so many presumably intelligent, capable men exude this level of confidence while as many equally bright, competent women struggle to do the same. How women find it so hard to recognize their own competence while men feel unacknowledged for their brilliance by others. How research consistently finds that in fields ranging from finance to teaching to athletics, males regard themselves to be more knowledgeable, secure, or capable than women rate themselves. The question, of course, is why.

In the last chapter you learned seven perfectly good reasons why you—or anyone—might come to feel like a fraud. Some, like being a student, working in a creative field, being one of the few people who look like you in your workplace, working alone, or studying or working in a different country, are highly situational, which means that it's conceivable that you could avoid the impostor syndrome altogether if you steered clear of these triggering scenarios. Others—how you were raised or being a first-generation professional—you really can't get around.

There is one more all-permeating situation that you can't avoid: your gender. That's why we're going to shift our view from situational factors to how society can make you feel less competent than you really are. Factors that also help explain why impostor feelings are more commonly expressed by women. As we explore the ways in which certain social realities compound female self-doubt, keep in mind that not all women have the same experience. If you happen to have been on the early front lines breaking down barriers that kept women from being full and equal members of the workforce, or if you work in a job that is atypical for women, then you probably have more "war stories" than if you were the beneficiary of these forerunners or work in a more female-friendly environment.

Even different women who work for the same organization can have dramatically varied experiences depending on the level or department they work in and whether they work in the home office or out in the field. The type of work you do matters too. If you're in a female-dominated field such as social services or education, you may not face many obvious double standards. But if, for instance, you make your living in front of a camera, then you know full well that if you balloon up to a size 4, your career can tank, while leading men such as Denzel Washington, John Travolta, and Russell Crowe can go from hunk to chunk with no dip in box-office appeal or earnings.

Some of what you learn in this chapter may be depressing or discouraging. However, knowing what's going on will help you to contextualize your impostor feelings more and personalize them less. As you step away from your experience you'll see that there's a lot more to your impostor story than meets the eye. From there you can explore how external realities might have affected what's going on inside you.

Understanding that there are forces that can work against you can also help you learn how to deal with them. At the same time, this is not about casting yourself or women as a whole in the role of victim. True, there are ways society can have an enormous impact on how competent you feel. But you have a role as well, which is why you'll be invited here to take stock of ways you yourself might unwittingly collude in undermining your own success.

Judging Women

It's often said that we are our own worst critic. However, what you may not realize is the extent to which your competence is being critiqued by other people—people who despite knowing nothing about you have nonetheless made determinations about you based solely on your gender. You already know, for instance, that you chalk up your accomplishments to chance. Well, as it turns out, you're not alone. Research has found that people are more likely to attribute a man's success to ability and yours to luck. In other words, when he achieves a positive outcome it's because he has "the right stuff," but when you pull it off it's because you just got lucky.[1]

Then there's the old joke about how a woman has to work twice as hard as a man to be considered half as good. Somewhere along the line women added the punch line "Fortunately that's not difficult." Well, guess what? As it turns out, it really *is*. As Swedish immunologists Christine Wenneras and Agnes Wold discovered, for women scientists it can literally be *two and a half* times more difficult.

Wenneras and Wold wanted to determine why, despite the increasing numbers of doctoral degrees for women in science worldwide, men still dominated the highest levels of academic research. So they investigated how research grants were awarded. They had their work cut out for them. The Swedish Medical Council's unshakable belief in its system of meritocracy made gaining access to the private peer-review system so difficult that it took two years and even a court order for them to succeed.[2]

Once the curtain was finally pulled back, what they found stunned the overwhelmingly male scientific community. Women scientists had to produce 2.5 times more research and/or published work to receive the same competence scores as male applicants.[3] Put another way, the men were able to go further by doing significantly less, confirmation that despite objections that affirmative action would "lower standards," mediocrity has never been an impediment to male success.

> I am working for the time when unqualified
> blacks, browns, and women join the
> unqualified men in running our government.
> —Sissy Farenthold, Texas state representative

Being female means that you're held to a higher standard in professions where you might expect evaluation to be purely objective.

- When orchestras use a screen to conceal the identity of the auditioning musician, female musicians are twice as likely to advance from the preliminary rounds and their chances of being selected in the final round increase severalfold.[4]
- Female high school science teachers received lower evaluations than male teachers from recently graduated students even

though both proved equally effective at preparing their students for college.[5]

- Both male and female psychology professors evaluating the credentials of fictitious candidates for an assistant professorship showed a two-to-one preference for "Brian" over "Karen," rating "his" credentials as superior, even though the credentials were identical.

Not only is the bar set higher for women, but the burden of proof is on you to prove your competence in ways rarely required of men. For instance, even when fictitious male and female tenure candidates were deemed equally likely to be promoted on the basis of a superb curriculum vitae, reviewers were four times more likely to ask the female candidate for supporting evidence, such as proof that she had won her grants on her own or a demonstration of her teaching.[6] I've heard similar "prove it" stories from countless female students and students of color accused of plagiarism by professors who thought their paper was "too good."

> Our struggle today is not to have a female Einstein get appointed as assistant professor. It is for a woman schlemiel to get as quickly promoted as a male schlemiel.
> —Bella Abzug

Even so, if these kinds of double standards are ticking you off, you may want to curb your anger. That is, *if* you want to be seen as competent. Men such as Donald Trump and John McEnroe are famous for blowing off steam and letting the chips fall where they may. Certainly one reason they get away with it is because they don't care what people think about them. However, the fact that they're male means they also *don't have* to care. In experiments involving mock job interviews, observers concluded that the angry male candidates not only deserved more status and a higher salary but could be expected to do better at the job than angry women. In other words, irritability in men is regarded as a sign of status. But when women lose their temper they're seen as *less competent.*[7]

Not everyone needs research to prove how costly negative assumptions about female competence can be. In a post titled "Why James Chartrand Wears Women's Underpants," the widely read founder of the Web design and copy business Men with Pens James Chartrand revealed that "he" is actually a "she" presenting herself as a man. The reason? Not only was it significantly easier to get freelance work as a man, but Chartrand reports that the implied credibility and respect meant less negotiating over fees and even having the same bid submitted as a man win out over the one submitted as herself. Writing under a male pseudonym, says the thirty-something Canadian, "opened up a new world. It helped me earn double and triple the income of my true name, with the same work and service. No hassles. Higher acceptance . . . Business opportunities fell into my lap. People asked for my advice, and they thanked me for it, too."[8]

Connecting the Dots to Your Life

You already know you hold yourself to a higher standard, expecting of yourself perfection with ease. Do you think other people's unrealistic expectations might compound the problem? When you already question your competence it's bound to make it harder to determine whether, for example, the reason you didn't get the promotion is that you really were lacking in some way or because you're being judged by a different standard.

That's why you need to step back and explore what role gender or other bias based on race, age, or disability may play in your feeling less competent than you really are. For example:

- When you do well, do other people make comments about how "lucky" you were?
- Have you ever felt you had to overdeliver or otherwise been held to either a higher or a lower standard because you are a woman?
- Are there times when you feel like you have to prove your qualifications in ways men don't?

If you answered yes to any of these questions, take time to reflect on how these experiences have affected how confident and competent you feel today. From now on, don't automatically assume that the reason you were passed over or asked to provide additional proof of abilities or credentials is because you're somehow lacking. At the same time, be aware that there really are reasons unrelated to gender or racial bias why decisions go a certain way or careers stall. We all have blind spots. So before you cry foul, ask yourself a few questions:

- Do I need to gain more experience or a track record before I can reasonably expect to be moved ahead?
- Are there ways I can improve my skills at presenting ideas, negotiating, or interviewing?
- Who can I look to for objective feedback about things I could be doing better or differently to get where I want to go?

The Importance of Being Lesser

Being female means you and your work automatically stand a greater chance of being ignored, discounted, trivialized, devalued, or otherwise taken less seriously than a man's. Take something as basic as art. Despite being equally creative and painstaking, ceramics, embroidery, weaving, and other mediums associated with women are relegated by historians and curators alike to the inferior status of "crafts." Similarly, the scholarly, scientific, or literary work of women has generally not been considered as "important" or "brilliant" as that of men. Books and films produced by women or that appeal to them are frequently derided as "chick lit" or "chick flicks." But you rarely hear a similarly rhyming term used to describe the often violent action films popular among male audiences.

It's unlikely that the stray demeaning remark or indignity will undermine your self-confidence in any lasting way, especially if it comes from a stranger. It's the cumulative effect of often subtle put-downs that can take a toll. For example, of the hundreds of highly successful male executives and entrepreneurs I've worked with, I've never heard a single one protest that his work was being trivialized. But it's something women complain about a lot.

Little is one of those words men don't take kindly to—at least not when it's used in reference to them. But it's a word that's freely tossed around to refer to your work. Like when a young professor I know announced excitedly that her grant had come through, only to feel totally deflated when the dean responded, "Oh, you mean the little one?" Even when made innocently, belittling comments like "Why don't you share your little idea with the group?" "I hear you're starting a little consulting business." "When is your little show happening?" send the message that what you have to offer is not really serious.

If researchers looking at children are right, males may have simply grown up learning to take females less seriously. In play pairs, even among children as young as two and a half, boys pay attention to protests from other boys. But when girls tell boys to stop doing something, the boys ignore them.[9] Fast-forward a few years and even on what researchers had set up as a collaborative science project, the experience of being the only boy differed dramatically from that of the lone girl. When teams consisted of three girls and one boy, the girls deferred to the boy, who spoke twice as much as all the girls combined. But when the situation was reversed, the boys ignored and insulted the lone girl.[10] Jump ahead to adulthood and this pattern continues. Midlevel women in high-tech describe their largely male work environment to be so "competitive and unfriendly" that it requires "a concerted effort to be assertive in order to be heard."[11]

Naturally, everyone wants to feel heard. It's likely, though, that for you feeling heard matters even more. If you've ever sat in a classroom or meeting and felt your contributions were ignored, you won't be surprised to learn that when female students feel their questions are dismissed by professors, their self-confidence declines; conversely, feeling heard boosts women's confidence.[12]

You don't have to convince United States Supreme Court justice Ruth Bader Ginsburg that feeling heard matters. Speaking of her experience as a female attorney in the sixties and seventies, Ginsburg told *USA Today*, "I don't know how many meetings I attended . . . where I would say something, and I thought it was a pretty good idea . . . Then somebody else would say exactly what I said. Then people would become alert to it, respond to it." Three decades later Ginsburg admits that there are times when the lack of diversity on the high court can still be wearying. "It can happen even in the conferences in the court. When I will say something . . . it isn't until somebody else says it that everyone will focus on the point," said Ginsburg.[13]

When you feel like an impostor, you're prone to undervalue yourself.

Widen the lens a bit and the question becomes, how could you not? As more women enter a field, the pay scale drops and so does the job's status. And when you live in a society where money and status are revered, having less of both only reinforces the perception that the work you do is not as highly valued—at least not when a woman does it. *Miami Herald* humor columnist Dave Barry raised this point when he suggested, "The obvious and fair solution to the housework problem is to let men do the housework for, say, the next six thousand years, to even things up." Joking that "the trouble is that men, over the years, have developed an inflated notion of the importance of everything they do, so that before long they would turn housework into just as much of a charade as business is now. They would hire secretaries and buy computers and fly off to housework conferences in Bermuda, but they'd never clean anything."[14]

It's easy to smile at the truth in Barry's joke. But it's no laughing matter when your job is the one routinely made smaller. Just ask former Clinton White House staffer Dee Dee Myers. In her book *Why Women Should Rule the World*, Myers offers a revealing look at the subtle and not-so-subtle ways women are rendered less important. She tells of the intense pressure then president-elect Bill Clinton was under to make good on his promise to create a government that "looked like America." Unfortunately, his initial appointments looked like more of the same. That's when insiders hatched a plan to appoint Myers to be the first female White House press secretary—*kind of*. Myers got the news from transition-team members George Stephanopoulos and Ricki Seidman. I'll let Myers take it from here:

"[They told me] I would have the title of White House press secretary. But the job would be a little different. George would be director of communications; he would handle the daily briefings, as he had during the transition, and I would be the backup briefer. He would take the press secretary's office in the West Wing; I'd have a smaller office in the same suite.

He'd carry the highest rank of assistant to the president (as all previous press secretaries had); I'd be a deputy assistant—a lower rank that came with a smaller salary (natch)." Of the offer, Myers says, "Suddenly, I found myself staring down the barrel of a predicament that I knew was all too common among women: responsibility without corresponding authority."

Once in the White House, Myers had the lesson reinforced. It turned out that despite having less responsibility, a deputy in another office was making ten thousand dollars more a year than she was. So Myers went to chief of staff Leon Panetta to straighten out what she presumed to be a simple and easily remedied oversight. Instead Panetta explained that the other guy had taken a pay cut to work for the president, there was no money in the budget for a raise (we're talking eight hundred dollars a week here, folks), and besides, he had a family and she didn't. When Myers tried to press her case, Panetta abruptly ended the meeting with "It's not going to happen."

You don't have to be especially motivated by power or money to recognize the diminishing effect such experiences can have on a woman. Myers writes, "The president and the senior staff made the job less important than it had been. And that made *me* less important."

Connecting the Dots to Your Life

If you've been selling yourself short, it may be because the world you live in does too. To begin to connect the dots, look for instances in your own life when you have felt ignored, trivialized, or otherwise taken less seriously. Instances when you had to work harder for your voice to be heard and/or ways you may have been devalued financially. Do you see possible connections between these external realities and your internal struggle to feel competent and deserving?

Even when you understand the larger social landscape, you can't control what other people think or do. There are, however, things you can do to mitigate certain situations or at least be mindful of. Take showing anger at work. You can still get riled if you want, but at least be aware that doing so puts you at risk of being seen as less competent. Know too that when women explain why they are angry, researchers found people more apt to cut them slack, whereas they are less forgiving of men who do the same because offering reasons for their emotions is considered a sign of weakness.

It really is harder to take yourself seriously when the people around you don't. But that doesn't mean you don't have a role here. Remember how the one boy in the science-project group spoke twice as much as all three girls combined? We've all run into men who hog the stage—but who lets them? If you don't feel heard, pay attention to how you may contribute to this dynamic: Do you use the more traditionally female mode of communication, which is to defer and wait your turn? That's fine to do when the stakes are low. But there are situations where in order to be heard you have to forgo the usual rules, starting with the belief that you always have to follow the rules.

It's not enough, for example, to raise your hand. You have to *keep* it raised, even if it means not doing what you're told—a lesson Facebook COO Sheryl Sandberg says she learned, ironically after delivering a speech to employees on why there are so few female leaders. Shortly after her talk Sandberg was approached by a young woman who said her big take-away was that she needed to keep her hand up. The employee went on to explain that after her talk Sandberg said she would take two more questions. Once she did, the employee put her hand down and noticed that all the other women put their hands down too, only to watch as Sandberg continued to take more questions—all from men who kept their hands up.

If you want to be heard, you're going to have to step out of your comfort zone in other ways too. Impostor syndrome or no impostor syndrome, you're probably not comfortable tooting your own horn. You can have all the confidence in the world and still be reluctant to self-promote out of a steadfast belief that a person's work should speak for itself. It doesn't. Men understand this, which is why they're more comfortable tooting their horn, no matter how small the instrument.

My work has brought me in touch with scores of highly successful female partners in major law firms. On more than one occasion I've watched them collectively roll their eyes over their male colleagues' willingness to submit minor activity updates to the firm's internal newsletter. Said one attorney, "Some of these guys think nothing of publicizing little things like that they went to a Rotary Club breakfast. Unless I was the keynote speaker, I'd be embarrassed to broadcast something so uneventful."

Whether you think it's "right" or "trivial" is irrelevant. What matters is that while you keep your nose to the grindstone banking on others paying attention, these guys are busy keeping their name in front of people in a position to help further their career. If you're not naturally gifted at self-promotion, don't worry; like any skill, it can be acquired. Read a book, take a class, or hire a coach. I know it's hard to talk about how great you are, especially when you're not convinced yourself. But it's a heck of a lot harder to get noticed if you keep your own accomplishments a closely guarded secret. If you're not telling your story, who will?

Similarly, don't make the mistake of simply assuming that doing a good job means you'll automatically be noticed and rewarded. You won't. It's true that Dee Dee Myers did not get the raise she was due. But at least she *asked*—something economist Linda Babcock and her colleagues discovered women often fail to do. After digging deeper into why the starting salaries of male master's degree students were on average almost four thousand dollars more than women's, they found that eight times as many men asked for more money. Put another way, 93 percent of the women accepted the first offer.

Men "always seem to go for the biggest brownie on the plate," says Myers, adding, "What's more, they expect the other guys (and sometimes the gals) to do the same." And if you think four thousand dollars is not that big a deal, think again. As Babcock and Sara Laschever point out in their aptly titled book, *Women Don't Ask,* over the course of a career the financial consequences of even a relatively small initial difference can cause you to eventually forfeit at least one million dollars in income. Say the authors, "This is a massive loss for a one-time negotiation—for avoiding what is usually no more than five minutes of discomfort."

It is true that when your work, your voice, or your job is considered less significant, it complicates your ability to recognize—never mind *appreciate*—what you have to offer. On the other hand, you can't expect other people to value your work if you don't. In a literal sense, valuing yourself means making sure you have the information you need to attach the proper value to your expertise and labor.

- Do you know the going rate for people in your field?
- If not, check with industry-specific associations for salary surveys.
- If you work for yourself, go online to do a fee or price check. I guarantee you'll find people or companies with far less experience or inferior products who command far more than you do.

Once you have the information you need, remember that valuing yourself means raising your hand—and keeping it raised. It's about knowing what you want and deserve and going for it. As you assess your current situation:

- Do you routinely let those in a position to advance your career know about your goals and accomplishments, or do you wait to be noticed?

- Do you tend to accept whatever is offered even if you think it's inadequate?
- Are there ways you're settling for less or otherwise not stepping up to "claim a bigger brownie"?
- If so, what's the worst thing that could happen if you ask for more or otherwise advocate on your own behalf?
- What are the consequences of not keeping your hand up or asking for more?

If you want more money, more staff, a promotion, to work from home, to get your art onto a gallery wall, or for someone to mentor you, then there's only one way to get it: A-S-K. Obviously, just because you ask for something doesn't mean you'll get it. But as opera diva Beverly Sills once said, "You may be disappointed if you fail, but you are doomed if you don't try." Or, as is often required, if you don't *retry*.

Stereotypes Matter

The pioneering congresswoman Shirley Chisholm once said, "The emotional, sexual, and psychological stereotyping of females begins when the doctor says, 'It's a girl.'" Diversity experts Rita Hardiman and Bailey Jackson point out two other truisms about stereotyping. Namely, the group with more power always does the naming, and the naming group either denies the existence of a given trait or behavior in their group or, when they do admit to it, the trait or behavior is renamed in positive terms.[15]

You know the drill: He's commanding; you're bossy. He's assertive; you're a bitch. He's persistent; you're pushy. He's decisive; you're impulsive. He's blowing off steam; you're hysterical. He's carefully weighing his options; you can't make up your mind.

Males are of course pigeonholed by stereotypes too. But careerwise, which side of these stereotypes would you rather be on? In a man's career, being competitive, aggressive, high-achieving, and a workaholic—all hallmarks of a type A personality—are an asset, but these same characteristics are considered a career liability in you. This alone goes a long way in explaining why the impostor syndrome is prevalent among type A females but not type A males.[16]

> Men are taught to apologize for their
> weaknesses, women for their strengths.
> —Lois Wyse, author and columnist

Even the rules for communication are different. Not only do you have to figure out what to say and how to say it, you also must worry about the *way you sound* saying it. If you speak in a decisive manner using a lower pitch and downward inflection, both of which are considered more characteristically masculine, you're perceived as aggressive. But here's the rub. Women who talk in a more conventionally feminine manner, using a higher pitch, softer volume, and upward inflection, are perceived as *less competent.*[17]

Stereotypes matter because they are so easily internalized as the truth, which, as repeated studies have shown, can in turn affect behavior. The phenomenon is known as "stereotype threat," and was first documented by Stanford researchers Claude Steele and Joshua Aronson. Everyone knows females are lousy at math, right? Precisely because we all do "know" this supposed "fact," merely informing female students prior to a math exam that the test is gender-neutral causes them to perform better. Telling female students the opposite, that the test had demonstrated gender differences in the past, they performed substantially worse.[18] Stereotype threat comes into play in more subtle situations as well. The simple inclusion of a check box for gender on a math test causes women to perform worse than men.[19]

There's more. Separate studies found that compared with subjects who were not reminded of a negative stereotype, females who were prompted

- were less likely to attempt math problems on a test[20]
- were less interested in assuming leadership positions[21]
- were more likely to attribute their failure at a computer task to their own inability, whereas men blamed their failure on faulty technical equipment[22]
- switched career preferences away from those involving strong math skills after being exposed to TV commercials depicting women fussing over their appearance or engaged in stereotypically female activities[23]

Similar findings have been found based on race and class. When African American students were told they were being tested on verbal ability, it triggered racial stereotypes about intelligence, causing them to do worse than students who did not receive this information.[24] Likewise, when students in France were reminded of their socioeconomic status, those from low-income groups performed more poorly than those from high-income groups.[25]

Stereotypes impair men's performance as well. Men who were told that a test measured "social sensitivity," on which "men do worse than women," performed more poorly than those who were told the test measured "complex information processing." In this same scenario, women's performance did not differ.[26]

Stereotypes matter because even so-called positive stereotypes limit us by falsely altering behavior. When a golf-putting test was framed as measuring "natural athletic ability," African American students did better than white students. But when the test was positioned as testing "sports intelligence," the opposite was true for both groups.[27] Similarly, when reminded of their ethnic identity, Asian American women performed better on a math test than a control group. But when primed to think about their female identity, they did worse.[28]

Stereotypes matter because generations of women grew up having their self-perceptions shaped by stereotyped notions of men's versus women's work. It was not long ago that paid work options for females were largely confined to teacher, nurse, secretary, social worker, or domestic. If you grew up middle- or even working-class, you learned that a job was something to "fall back on" in case something happened to your future husband. If you were encouraged or even expected to get a degree, college was frequently seen as an end in itself, not necessarily a step toward something else. It was a place for you to become a well-rounded individual in order to attract a mate, who *was* expected to utilize his training.

If you are of this generation, any pride you feel about breaking into traditionally male roles may be complicated by a sense of not really belonging. One senior vice president who grew up assuming she'd go to college, marry, have a bunch of kids, and then settle into being a mother and homemaker told how her plans abruptly changed when her husband died before they'd had children. Suddenly forced to support herself, she took the only job available at the time as a secretary. Over the years she worked her way up to senior vice president. Yet even today the executive admits that there are moments when she looks in the mirror and thinks, *What am I doing here? This isn't what I was supposed to be doing. You don't belong here. You are such a fraud.*

Stereotypes matter because they continue to contribute to how the next generation of girls see themselves. Certainly a lot has changed for girls growing up today. Barbie dumped Ken in 2004, and girls today are as likely to own a pirate, astronaut, or Hispanic presidential candidate Barbie as they are a princess or nurse Barbie. Ask them about their career aspirations, and most girls will tell you the sky's the limit. And for the most part they're right.

Dig deeper, though, and girls tell another story too. While 71 percent aspire to go to college full-time after high school, a survey by Girls Inc. revealed that more than a third believe most people think the most important thing for girls is to get married and have children.[29] Girls today are also keenly aware of the intense pressure they feel, at ever younger ages, to fit a uniquely female model of success. Along with heightened expectations about physical perfection, being thin, and dressing "right," stereotypes about girl's needing to speak softly, not brag, and assume caretaker roles persist. "Society appears to be making some room for girls to transcend traditional expectations about abilities and aspirations, just as long as they also conform to conventional notions of femininity," conclude the researchers.

Finally, stereotypes matter because although you may be playing on the same field as men, in a world that sees and treats powerful, successful women differently than it sees and treats powerful, successful men, the rules of the game are not the same—a double standard that played out on an international stage during the historic 2008 United States presidential primary election as two ambitious women battled for the number one and number two jobs in the country.

In a *New York Times* critique of the media's treatment of Democratic presidential candidate Hillary Clinton, Judith Warner cites ample evidence of what British columnist Andrew Stephen referred to as a time of "gloating, unshackled sexism of the ugliest kind." Something Republican vice presidential candidate Sarah Palin would likewise discover when she entered the race a few months later.

None of this was lost on young people. The election is long over, but the consequences may be felt for some time to come. Pre- and postelection surveys conducted by Girl Scouts of the USA showed that the election had significantly increased both girls' and boys' appreciation for the difficulties women face. Girls of course were the most disheartened. Following the election, a majority of girls now believe it's more difficult for a woman than a man to become a leader and fewer believe they have an equal shot at a leadership position. Can you blame them? "Clearly, in an age when the dangers and indignities of Driving While Black are well-acknowledged, and properly condemned," writes Warner, "'Striving While Female'—if it goes too far and looks too real—is still held to be a crime."[30]

Connecting the Dots to Your Life

The poet Adrienne Rich writes, "The most notable fact that culture imprints on women is the sense of our limits. The most important thing one woman can do for another is to illuminate and expand her sense of actual possibilities."[31] Striving while female may not always be easy, but it is worth it. Despite the higher bar and additional hoops, women have made and continue to make their mark everywhere from the Senate floor to the trading floor, the boardroom to the operating room, the tennis court to the Supreme Court. And so can you.

By far the best defense against the confidence-zapping effects of stereotypes is self-awareness. We were all, men and women alike, raised to see the same behavior differently depending on gender. When you are having an impostor moment, be aware of how stereotypes may affect how you see yourself. Be aware too of ways you may inadvertently reinforce certain stereotypes about yourself or other women. For instance, even when you "know better," do you expect a female manager or physician to be more caring or empathetic? Are there other ways you expect more from women than men or are more critical of women who demonstrate more traditionally male behaviors? When you see a powerful woman on television, is your first thought, *What's up with her hair?*

This is important because as easy as it would be to blame all of this on male bias, the sad reality is that in each of the studies cited here, *women held other women to a higher standard as well.* Be aware too that precisely because sexism and racism are often subtle, you can suck up a lot of energy trying to suss out whether what's happening is a function of bias, office politics, or simply bad manners. Regardless of the source, you're going to have to decide which battles to fight and which to let go. Some battles can and should be fought. But sometimes you may need to walk away and save your energy for another day. When confronted with gender bias, ask yourself:

- How important is it? If the answer is not very, then let it go.
- If it is important, ask, *"Is there anything I can do about it?"* If the answer is no, let it go.
- If the answer is yes, ask, *"Would the likely outcome be worth it?"* If so, go for it. If not, let it go.

The Bottom Line

Remember the wise words of Eleanor Roosevelt: "No one can make you feel inferior without your consent." Despite all the gains women have made, the essential truth remains: If you are male or pale, you are presumed competent until proven otherwise. Much of the bias against female competence—bias held by both men *and* women—is subtle and largely unintentional. But that does not mean it's trivial or inconsequential.

Succeeding in any endeavor or field takes hard work, determination, and patience. Making it as a woman requires this and more. On top of being aware of the ways you hold yourself back, be mindful of the subtle and not-so-subtle ways external realities can whittle away at your self-confidence.

Your impostor experience may feel deeply personal, but there is a larger social context. Knowing this can help you connect the dots between what's happening out there and your own false sense of inadequacy.

What You Can Do

- Stay alert to the ways in which society as a whole views female competence negatively.
- Take questions about female competence seriously but not personally.
- Look for ways you may collude in devaluing or stereotyping yourself and other women.

What's Ahead

There is more to your impostor story than what's going on "out there." It's time to take a more inward look at how the impostor syndrome plays out in your life.

4

Hiding Out

At any time I still expect that the no-talent
police will come and arrest me.

—Mike Myers

I f you believe that up until now you've somehow managed to fool people
into thinking you're smarter or more talented than you "really" are, then
what's your number one fear going to be? Being found out, right? Perpetually waiting to be "outed" as an impostor is stressful and exhausting.
So naturally you have to find ways to manage the stress of being found

guilty of the crime of impersonating a competent person. No surprise there. But have you ever stopped to consider how you go about doing that exactly?

You've managed to escape detection for so long, you're probably not even aware of how automatic or well rehearsed your defensive behaviors truly are. Or that these behaviors have implications that go beyond avoiding detection. That is, until today. Together we are going to shine a spotlight on that person you have cast all these years as an impostor, a fake, and a fraud. The insight you will gain will prove helpful in developing healthier ways of dealing with and ultimately eliminating your fraud fears.

Seven Ways Impostors Try to Stay One Step Ahead of the "No-Talent Police"

You did not choose to feel like an impostor. But whether you know it or not, you have found a way to handle it. In fact, there are at least seven ways people with the impostor syndrome have unconsciously learned to both manage the anxiety of feeling like a fake and to make sure they remain safely undercover. The codiscoverers of the impostor phenomenon, Pauline Clance and Suzanne Imes, along with various collaborators, point to four coping and protecting mechanisms: diligence and hard work, holding back, charm, and procrastination.[1] In my own work I've observed three more: maintaining a low or ever-changing profile, never finishing, and self-sabotage. As you read through the descriptions, pay close attention to the one that speaks most directly to you. This information will come in handy shortly.

Overpreparing and Hard Work

In the mid-eighties, I and several others were invited to appear on a Boston-area television show to talk about the impostor syndrome. One of the guests was a medical student named Karen. Toward the end of the show the host turned to Karen and said, "But, Karen, you're in medical school, so you're obviously intelligent." Without missing a beat, Karen replied, "Not really. I just work harder than everybody else."

If you believe everyone around you is inherently more intelligent or capable, then one way to avoid detection is to rely on extraordinary effort to cover up your supposed ineptness. To be clear: This is different from good old-fashioned hard work. No one gets to where she is without working for it, and that includes you. What we're talking about here is doing things like obsessing about every aspect of a minor presentation or studying and restudying material you have already mastered. Such behavior is driven by the belief that the *only* reason you're successful is because of your Herculean effort. So, every aspect of your work is approached as if it were crucial.

Non-impostors who work hard do so because that's what's required to get the job done. When their diligence pays off, it enhances their confidence. But when your work pays off, you mostly feel relief. Because your efforts are motivated by an underlying sense of phoniness, say Clance and Imes, any good feelings you have following a success are short-lived.

Being a workaholic is a difficult cycle to break. In addition to protecting you, this strategy actually contributes to your success. When you stay later, study harder, or practice longer than the people around you, obviously you have a greater chance of doing well. So in that regard, diligence does "work." However, the anxiety that fuels your behavior remains untouched.

That certainly was Joyce Roché's experience. The former president and CEO of Girls Inc. grew up one of eleven children in a working-class family. After earning her graduate degree from Columbia University, she quickly became a rising star at Avon and Revlon. To go so far so fast in the 1970s was remarkable for any woman. It was even more so for an African American. Looking back on the fourteen-hour days she put in as she ascended to senior management, Roché realized that the reason the glow of success wore off so soon was that "somewhere, deep inside, you don't believe what they say . . . The threat of failure scares you into these long hours. Yet success only intensifies the fear of discovery."[2]

The other thing about hard work is that it can be quantified. We already know that you don't credit yourself for less tangible measures of competence, such as talent or intelligence. But you can count how many hours you're logging. And so can everyone around you. You think, *I may not know what the hell I'm doing, but at least no one can fault me for not giving 150 percent.* Once on the workaholic treadmill, it's terribly hard to get off because you believe it's the sole reason for your success. And the longer you continue to succeed, the less apt people are to find out that you're a fraud.

You may wonder, *Who* doesn't *feel overworked these days?* If you're having trouble telling whether your own pattern of overpreparation and hard work is simply what the situation calls for or if it's doing double duty to cover for your impostorism, apply the gut test. If it's telling you, *"That's me!"* trust that it is.

Holding Back

As a protecting device, holding back can take many forms. For example, if you're not a fan of hard work, then you may try to skirt detection by doing precisely the opposite. Low-effort syndrome, as psychologists refer to it, is commonly seen among bright teenagers who steadfastly refuse to apply themselves. But adults use it too. You know you could achieve more, but you don't. The unconscious thinking here is *If I'm going to fail, better people think it's because I'm lazy than because I'm stupid.* Besides, the less reason you give people to judge your performance, the less chance you'll be judged.

Part of you understands that expending effort to achieve a goal also makes you vulnerable. After all, what if you put in all that time and energy to build a business or study for the boards and you still fail? No, it's far less painful not to try than to expose yourself to others' judgment of your work and risk falling short. Plus, if you never really give it your best shot, you can always claim (if only to yourself) that you could have been a great writer, artist, leader, or lawyer—that is, if you'd really tried.

Of course many impostors do try. Still, you may hold back in other ways, like taking yourself out of the running for promotions, shying away from honors classes, or avoiding anything that makes you too vulnerable. Holding back can also take the form of what Clance and Imes refer to as "intellectual inauthenticity." You remain silent in the face of opposing opinions. Or you attempt to figure out (or suck up to) hiring managers or higher-ups by telling them what they most want to hear.

As a student you may gear your research to complement and endorse your advisor's own work and opinions or otherwise engage in "intellectual flattery" to impress those in a position to judge your competence. Even if you don't skew your research, you may still verbally flatter your advisor, figuring it's harder to be critical of someone they like. The problem is, rather than feeling proud of your success, you wind up feeling like a phony. Secretly you wonder, *Would they think I was so great if I were really myself?*

Maintaining a Low or Ever-Changing Profile

You can be highly successful and still try to shield yourself from scrutiny by finding ways to maintain a low profile. You may have unconsciously chosen a field or a career that allows you to work autonomously or otherwise be relatively inconspicuous. For instance, you may have been drawn to self-employment in part because it allows you to circumvent the kind of supervision and routine evaluation employees must undergo. You think, *Sure I'm successful running my own business, but if I had to get a job, who would hire me?* If your company does require a public face, you may decline interviews and speaking engagements or designate someone else to be the out-in-front person.

If you work in a job or field where it's impossible to remain safely under the radar, you have to find another way to take care of yourself. So you unconsciously adopt an ever-*changing* profile. As an impostor you feel like you have a big target on your back. What better way to dodge those you believe have overestimated your abilities than to make yourself a moving target? As a student you do things like regularly switch majors, advisors, or research topics, or you become a perpetual job hopper or career changer—not as a logical career move but as a defense mechanism. I once read about a hospital president who was in the habit of moving on every three years because that was how long he figured it would take the current board to figure out that he was an impostor.

Use of Charm or Perceptiveness to Win Approval

A part of you feels inadequate. But another part of you believes you're quite remarkable. If only you could find the right person to recognize your brilliance and then help you embrace it too. Once you find someone you admire, you use your social skills to impress him in hopes that he will see you as "intellectually special." The problem, say Clance and Imes, is that if your efforts are successful, then you dismiss his feedback, believing that the *only* reason he thinks you're special is because he likes you. Plus, in your mind, the fact that you even *need* outside validation just reinforces the fact that you are a fraud.

Another way I've seen personality come into play is the calculated use of humor. If you are blessed with a quick wit, you may have come to rely on it as a way of deflecting attention away from those aspects of yourself where you feel most fraudulent, such as your intellect. As one sales representative told me, "I figure if I can just keep 'em laughing, maybe they won't see that I don't have a clue." But when you do manage to impress, you feel like a phony.

Procrastination

Everyone procrastinates from time to time. When you feel like an impostor, though, it can also be a way to put off whatever situation you fear will lead to your eventual undoing. If you're self-employed or in school, there's a good chance that procrastination is your coping mechanism of choice. After all, it's a lot easier to drag your feet when you're accountable primarily to yourself. When I was a graduate student not only did I have the cleanest house in Amherst, Massachusetts, but every room of my rental needed to be painted personally by me.

You tell yourself it's because you "work best under pressure." And maybe you do. But you also know that when you leave important things until the last minute, there's greater chance that quality will suffer. On an unconscious level, Clance says, procrastination is a way to give yourself an out. Take Kate, a bright political science major who desperately wanted to land a coveted internship in Washington. To earn a spot required completing a lengthy application, which included writing a heady essay. Kate had months to work on it. But instead she waited until the very last minute, literally dashing it off the day before the deadline and popping it into overnight mail. She didn't get the internship.

Kate probably wasn't deliberately trying to blow her chance. However, once she did fail, her procrastination provided a built-in excuse because she could tell herself, *I'm disappointed, but hardly surprised. After all, I just whipped it off at the last minute.* But here's the kicker. If she *had* managed to pull it off, she wouldn't have felt deserving because she knew the application did not reflect her best efforts. For the chronic procrastinator, the resulting success just reinforces your belief that you fooled them again.

Never Finishing

Granted, it may be by the skin of your teeth, but ultimately most procrastinators do get the job done. *Most.* There are others who take procrastination to the extreme by starting only to never finish. Like the doctoral candidate who completes all of her course work only to languish in a state of incompletion (sometimes for years) known as being ABD—all but dissertation. Or the artist who works ceaselessly on the same piece of work but never completes anything. Or the aspiring self-bosser who endlessly researches, plans, and tinkers with a business idea but never gets it off the launch pad.

By not finishing, you not only shield yourself from possible detection but you also effectively avoid the shame of being criticized. After all, if someone does question your work, your talent, or your expertise, you can always insist that *it's still in progress* or *I'm just dabbling.*

Self-Sabotage

In some cases, the fear of being exposed can be so anxiety-producing that you subconsciously do things to undermine your very success. This is different from withholding effort because on the surface anyway, you're still striving. Here, however, your actions have the effect of undercutting your prospects for success. You may do things like show up late or unprepared for an important audition or appointment. Perhaps the night before a big performance you stay up too late or drink one too many glasses of wine. If you do poorly, you can blame it on the fatigue or the hangover. If you do well, then you feel undeserving because you know you dodged a bullet.

Or you may unwittingly employ a self-sabotage strategy known as "other-enhancement." This happens in situations where you're competing against or being compared with another person and you do things like point out information or coach her in some way or otherwise provide some advantage that will enhance her chance of doing well. In doing so, you've strategically obscured the link between your performance and its evaluation. Since "technically" you've done nothing to actually interfere with your own performance, you may still do well. However, if you *are* outperformed, then you've preserved the ambiguity about your failure by creating a convenient excuse that you helped the other person. Plus, by helping someone else, you preserve your image as someone who is self-less—something that is especially important to women.

Substance abuse is another way to avoid success and thus escape the emotional burden of impostorism altogether. A distressed mother once wrote me for advice after her twenty-five-year-old daughter was arrested for drunk driving. For the previous year and a half the young woman had been a mere three credits away from completing a degree in graphic art. "After her arrest," wrote the mother, "my daughter confided in me that she feels she doesn't really deserve the degree anyway because she has somehow just fooled her professors into thinking she's good."

At the same time, just because someone risks his career by flirting with disaster does not mean it's because he feels like a fraud. But that hasn't stopped some in the media from blaming the impostor syndrome for all sorts of self-destructive behavior, from the sexual impropriety of Hugh Grant, Bill Clinton, and Eliot Spitzer to the misconduct of disgraced *New*

York Times reporter Jayson Blair.[3] It is possible of course that these men did act out of feelings of inadequacy. However, the impostor syndrome should not be blamed for every stupefying display of self-destruction.

Put a check mark next to the coping and protecting mechanism that resonates most with you:

____   Overpreparing and hard work

____   Holding back

____   Maintaining a low or ever-changing profile

____   Use of charm or perceptiveness to win approval

____   Procrastination

____   Not finishing

____   Self-sabotage

To be clear: None of these coping and protecting behaviors do anything to actually alleviate your impostor feelings. That's not their job. Their job is to keep you safe from harm by avoiding the shame and humiliation of being unmasked as well as to relieve some of the stress that comes from feeling like a fraud. As self-defeating as these behaviors are, we don't engage in them because we are masochists. We engage in them because we are doing the best we can to protect ourselves under particular life circumstances.

In other words, you really *are* trying to take care of yourself. So in that sense you need to appreciate whatever coping and protecting behaviors you've created. Most impostors rely on one strategy more heavily than others. Don't be alarmed, however, if you employ multiple coping mechanisms. It just means you're *really* taking care of yourself!

What Are You Getting Out of This?

Becoming more aware of how you've tried to manage this impostor syndrome of yours is important, but it's just the beginning. To really understand what's going on requires digging a bit deeper. So we're going to borrow from the work of Dr. Gerald Weinstein. Weinstein's book *Education of the Self* [4] has at its core a self-discovery process that consists of a series of questions designed to help you see and modify a self-limiting pattern of behavior—in this case the impostor syndrome.

For example, you already know that your pattern is there to keep you from being unmasked. But that's not all it does. To get at the broader function of any pattern of behavior, you need to ask yourself three questions: What does this behavior help me avoid? What does it protect me from? What does it help me get?

On their face, all these questions seem to ask the same thing. However, when you begin to answer them you'll discover that each comes at the issue from a slightly different angle, which in turn helps you peel back layers you may not have gotten to otherwise. For example:

1. *What does my behavior help me avoid?* If you never push yourself intellectually, you avoid the humiliation of trying and coming up short. If you never finish writing your dissertation or your business plan, you don't have to show your work to others, which keeps you from receiving negative feedback.

2. *What does my behavior help protect me from?* By constantly changing jobs, you protect yourself from finding out whether you could have gone higher. If you maintain a low profile, you protect yourself from scrutiny.

3. *What does my behavior help me get?* This question is often the hardest to answer because it's difficult to imagine how sabotaging your own

success, for example, could get you anything but stress and misery. Go deeper, though, and you'll no doubt see that you're getting more out of your behavior than you think.

For example, when you put in eighty-hour workweeks, there's a good chance you'll be recognized by higher-ups. When you constantly call your friends to anguish over what you are convinced will be an impending failure, you're probably going to get a lot of sympathy and stroking. When you keep a low profile, you automatically get a degree of security and safety. And in a very practical sense, when you procrastinate, you get more time to do things that are more fun—or at least easier than whatever it is you're putting off doing.

Similarly, if you are prone to overpreparing, you probably spend a fair amount of time mentally replaying worst-case scenarios—a phenomenon psychologist Albert Ellis calls "awfulizing." *Not only will I fail the qualifying exam, but I'll become a laughingstock. No one will want to work with me again. I'll be tossed out of my profession. I'll end up living in a cardboard box down by the river.*

As distressing as this mental disaster movie may be, Wellesley College psychology professor Julie Norem argues that this behavior is actually highly adaptive. Overpreparing helps ensure your success in part because of what she calls "defensive pessimism." This is when you have unrealistically low expectations, then devote considerable energy to anticipating everything that could go wrong and planning for all possible scenarios. Mentally running through every conceivable negative outcome, says Norem, helps impostors reduce anxiety by taking concrete steps to minimize potential problems.[5]

Now it's your turn. To uncover additional ways your impostor pattern serves you, ask: What does this behavior help me avoid? What does it help protect me from? What does it help me get?

Uncovering Your "Crusher" and Exposing the Lie

You think you developed your protecting strategy solely to keep people from finding out you are an impostor. However, a *core* function of all self-limiting patterns is to protect us from what Weinstein calls the crusher. The crusher is a core negative belief we hold about ourselves. At its heart, your crusher has to do with a basic feeling of inadequacy and unworthiness. You developed your pattern in part so that you wouldn't have to face this hidden negative belief.

You may assume that everyone who identifies with the impostor syndrome would share a common crusher, namely: *I'm a fraud.* Go below the surface, however, and you'll realize that your own crusher reflects a deeper, more painful belief that is unique to you and your pattern. Let's say, for instance, that the way you attempt to protect yourself from the shame of being found out is to not speak up in meetings or in class. You tell yourself it's because you don't want other people to think you're stupid. But the real reason you hold back is to escape having to face the crushing "truth" of your own core belief, which is, "I really *am* stupid."

It's important to recognize that you didn't develop your crusher overnight—or by yourself. This irrational negative belief has been reinforced through interactions with family, teachers, coworkers, and, as you learned in the last chapter, by the culture at large.

One way to identify your crusher is to imagine the statement you would most dread hearing said aloud about you in your impostor scenario: *You'll never measure up. You have no special gifts. You're not as intelligent as other people. You have no talent. You're not an original thinker.* Or simply, *You're unworthy.* If your crusher is not immediately obvious, then imagine that your best efforts to protect yourself failed and you are publically revealed to be a fraud.

Take a few moments now to quiet yourself and tune into your own crusher. Giving voice to your crusher statement can be an intense emotional experience. At the same time, you can't change what you don't understand. Tough as this step can be, it is essential to expose this false belief to the light of day so it can be seen for the lie that it is. I know your crusher feels true. *But you can't believe everything you think.* The real truth is this:

WITHOUT EXCEPTION,
ALL CRUSHERS ARE LIES.
YOURS INCLUDED.

I don't expect you to fully believe this—at least not right away. Right now all I want you to do is become consciously aware of the lie you've avoided confronting up until now.

What's All This Protection Costing You?

The good news is that your coping and protecting behaviors really do keep you safe from harm. They help you escape the humiliation of being discovered and having to confront the pain of your crusher. At the same time, as the adage goes: You never get something for nothing. Even though your pattern serves a protective function, we always pay a *price* for that protection.

The way to hone in on your pattern cost is to ask these questions: What will happen if I never change this pattern? What price would I pay? What opportunities would I miss? What options or possibilities would be closed to me?

Some of the costs are the same for all impostors—things like living with the anxiety of waiting for the other shoe to drop or allowing your fraud fears to, in the words of one workshop participant, "steal the joy of the ride." Others are highly specific to you and your situation and may include things like *If I don't finish my research, I'll never graduate or get tenure* or *If I keep procrastinating, I'll miss my chance to get the job in France.* See if any of these costs resonate with you:

If I never change this pattern . . .
- I'll only get safe, dead-end jobs that don't fully utilize my gifts and passions.
- My health will suffer.
- I will live with the regret of never knowing how far my talents and effort could have taken me.

The price I would pay is . . .
- Unnecessary psychological stress and fatigue.
- I'll earn less money, which will limit me from doing things I want to do in life.
- I won't get to meet valuable mentors and contacts who can help me achieve my goals.
- I won't have the chance to learn from my mistakes so I can really grow.
- I'll never get recognition for my work.
- I'll never know what it's like to really feel and own my successes and then build on them.

The opportunities I would miss would be . . .

- The satisfaction of taking risks—win or lose, knowing I tried.
- Learning new things about myself and the world.
- Receiving valuable feedback—both positive and critical–that I need to grow and improve.
- I'll never learn what I need to know to advance in my field.
- The excitement, challenge, and growth involved in flexing my mind and enjoying my own progress.

The options and possibilities that would be closed to me would be . . .

- The option of taking my career (or business) to the level I know it can reach.
- Other more challenging and satisfying job possibilities.
- Gaining the experience I need to further my reputation.
- The chance to make a positive difference in the world.

Now it's your turn to decide for yourself: What would happen if you never changed your coping and protecting behavior? What price would you pay? What opportunities would you miss out on? What options and possibilities would be closed to you?

You already knew that the impostor syndrome was a huge drag on your energy and potential. However, if I'd asked you before to outline exactly what your attempts to evade the No-Talent Police were costing you *specifically,* you may have been hard-pressed to do so. But now you know. Being conscious of the price you pay for all that protection means you now have a more personalized incentive to continue taking the steps required to unlearn this unnecessarily self-limiting pattern.

At the same time, letting go of any habitual response, even when you know it's in your best interest to do so, is not easy. The familiar, even if it's not working, is always more comfortable than the unknown. But growth is not meant to make us comfortable. Its purpose is to stretch us so we can perform at our full potential and achieve our highest purpose.

The good news is that all of the information you identified here constitutes your "before" picture. The feelings, thoughts, and behaviors that embody your impostor pattern now do not represent the self-assured person you are going to be. The ultimate payoff for the work you put in here will come at the end of this book when your "after" picture fully emerges.

In the meantime there really are small things you can do to become the self-assured person you are meant to be. For example, if you know that you're procrastinating or that you have yet to finish an important task, then put a stake in the ground right now and set a completion date. Next, build in accountability by publically declaring your deadline. Then get out your calendar and make an appointment with yourself to work on this project. Time blocking, as it's called, helps ensure that you don't schedule other things on the days—or part of a day—you've set aside to work on this task.

On this last point, stop telling yourself that you can't possibly work on something unless you can devote an entire day to it. Anything that involves a lot of steps or time to complete almost always gets done in small focused chunks of time over a period of days, weeks, months, or even years. To get yourself started, set a timer for forty-five minutes to an hour and focus all of your attention on chipping away at that one thing. When the timer goes off, you can stop. However, since the hardest part was getting started, there's a good chance you'll keep going. Either way you'll not only *get* more accomplished but you'll *feel* more accomplished too.

If you've been relying on charm or perceptiveness to win approval, rather than continuing to seek validation from others, make a point of celebrating your next accomplishment. If you've been engaging in intellectual flattery, ask a role model to lunch and practice talking about your own views or work. If you know you've been doing things to sabotage yourself, pay attention to what you're doing and why, then practice what it feels like to show up for yourself. If you've been avoiding applying yourself, pick one goal to tackle this week.

Other things you can do: Ask someone you trust for feedback. Share something with another person that you're proud of, maybe something you wrote or won. Write yourself a letter of recommendation so that you can see your accomplishments and attributes through someone else's eyes. Resolve to accept your next compliment graciously. Rewrite your résumé, adding accomplishments and skills you had previously omitted or downplayed. Speak up without self-judgment in your next meeting or class. Take a public-speaking seminar or join Toastmaster. Role-play a challenging exchange/event. Make a list of the reasons why you deserve a raise or promotion. Join a study group, writing group, or other support group designed to help people stay on track. Spend five minutes a day visualizing yourself being confident in a situation where you typically feel anything but.

The Bottom Line

Marie Curie said, "Nothing in life is to be feared, it is only to be understood. Now is the time to understand more, so that we may fear less." Although impostors everywhere share the fundamental fear of being unmasked, not everyone handles it the same way.

Up until now you probably weren't aware of how you've managed to keep your impostorism under wraps all these years. That's why it's important to untangle the unconscious coping and protecting strategies you use to handle your impostor syndrome. In doing so you gain valuable insight into how your self-limiting pattern serves you—and at what cost. This is your "before" picture. Knowing this information will help you later in this book when you create the picture of the strong, self-confident person you were meant to be.

What You Can Do

- Identify the coping and protecting mechanism you use to manage your impostor anxiety and keep from being found out.
- Untangle your impostor pattern by determining its function, naming your crusher, and assessing the hidden costs.
- Choose one action step to take this week.

What's Ahead

You've spent far too long denying yourself the credit you deserve. An essential step in ditching your impostor pattern is to set the record straight about the *true* reasons behind your success.

5

What Do Luck, Timing, Connections, and Personality **Really** *Have to Do with Success?*

I wasn't lucky. I deserved it.

—Margaret Thatcher

What if you believed in no uncertain terms that the reason you got the degree, the job, the role, the deal, or the corner office was because you deserved to get it? In other words, what if you really and truly *owned* your accomplishments as your own and not some fluke? If that were the case, then there wouldn't be anything for you to feel fraudulent about, would there? Unfortunately, that's not the case.

Instead you've spent years essentially giving away your success. And the way you've done this is by crediting your accomplishments to anybody or anything—except yourself. You tell yourself, *It was dumb luck . . . The stars were aligned . . . My father got me in the door . . .* Or, *Oh, the judges just liked me.* The time has come to reveal the true reasons behind your success.

"All We Want Are the Facts, Ma'am"

Detective Joe Friday of the iconic 1950s television show *Dragnet* had a famous catchphrase. If a witness who was being questioned began to wander off track by offering extraneous information, Friday would redirect them with "All we want are the facts, ma'am." We already know you've deemed yourself guilty of the charge of impersonating a competent person. So you probably won't believe me yet when I tell you that you and everyone else in the Impostor Club are a pretty competent bunch. How do I know? Evidence—hard evidence.

In the last chapter you learned that countless people have felt like they're waiting for, in Mike Myers's words, the No-Talent Police to come and arrest them. I want you to imagine that this competence-enforcement unit actually does exist and that they've just hauled you in for questioning. However, instead of trying to wrench from you a false confession that you've committed success fraud, this squad is out to prove your innocence. But in order to do that they need evidence—and that proof is going to come from you.

Evidence can take many forms, depending on the situation. Academic competence and success are measured by qualifying exam scores; getting into a top school; earning good grades, degrees, academic scholarships, internships, and awards; letters of recommendation from faculty; licensing; and the like. Employee success is typically viewed in terms of job titles, salaries, performance evaluations, promotions, raises, citations, or awards. In other cases it could mean being tapped for an appointment or winning an election.

In creative arenas, competence and success are gauged by things like getting a part, a grant, a contract, recognition, selection for a juried show. It could be winning a writing contest, receiving an award, or indeed being able to make a living as an artist, writer, musician, poet, actor, or craftsperson. Of course, evidence of entrepreneurial competence and success varies widely depending on the business you're in, but essentially it comes down to your ability to make things happen in order to generate profit.

The problem isn't that you deny the existence of such evidence in your own life. The problem is your compulsion to explain your success away with qualifiers. But not this time. This time you're going spill the beans about everything you've ever done, from passing a particularly hard class in school to being asked to chair an important committee—any shred of proof that you are, in fact, an intelligent, talented, resourceful, and otherwise fully capable human being.

And this time you're going to do it without explaining it away. If in the process of creating your achievements history you're tempted to stray from the what, when, and where, remember: "All we want are the facts, ma'am." Either you got good grades or you didn't. You wrote the thesis or you didn't. You got promoted or you didn't. You performed onstage or you didn't. You made the sale or you didn't. No qualifiers, no ifs, ands, or buts.

Take ten minutes to create your list now.

The Verdict Is In

When you leave out all the qualifiers and just stick to the proof at hand, you get a very different picture of who you are and what you've accomplished. Indeed, after thoroughly and dispassionately considering all of the evidence, the only conclusion any rational person could come to is that you are innocent on all counts. So innocent, in fact, that if it were up to our No-Talent Police, why, you'd be tossed out of the Impostor Club this very minute.

Fortunately or unfortunately, you and I both know that ultimately the only one who can free you of the belief that you are a fraud is you. That's why you need *perspective*. And to get perspective it's essential to clear up some fundamental misconceptions you and other impostors have about how success happens. As you are about to learn, rather than diminishing or negating your achievements, factors like luck, timing, connections, and charm actually do play a role—a *legitimate* role—in everyone's success—yours included. Just not in the dismissive ways you've been thinking.

What's Luck Got to Do, Got to Do with It?

To a certain degree your success—and everyone else's—is a result of some kind of luck.

- It was writer Ray Bradbury's chance encounter in a bookstore with the British expatriate writer Christopher Isherwood that gave him the opportunity to share his first book with a respected critic.
- Award-winning correspondent and anchor Christiane Amanpour found her way into journalism because her younger sister had dropped out of a small journalism college in London. When the

headmaster refused to refund the tuition, Christiane replied, "Then I'll take her place."[1]

- In what is perhaps the flightiest example of all, mixed-media artist Hope Sandrow made quite a name for herself in the art world doing poultry portraiture. It all began when she went looking for her cat in the woods near her house and happened to find a lost Paduan rooster, the colorful exotic fowl prized by sixteenth-century European painters.

When you hear these stories, do you think these individuals are any less capable? Do you now perceive them as less deserving of their success? As frauds? Of course not. Then why would you think this when serendipity plays a role in your own success?

Not only is luck an element in individual success, it factors into organizational success as well. So much so that accounting giant Deloitte insists that when it comes to business success, luck is not one factor, it's the *central* factor. In a 2009 company white paper titled "A Random Search for Excellence," Deloitte states that the overwhelming majority of research claiming to study unexpectedly successful companies "may very well be studying merely lucky companies."[2]

Looked at more broadly, if you are lucky enough to have grown up in an industrialized nation, then you had a better chance of not being born into severe poverty and hence a better shot at achieving financial success as an adult. Similarly, if you had the good fortune to attend a decent school, or to catch the attention of a great mentor, or to work in an organization that appreciates the benefits of a diverse workplace or of advancing people from within—then lucky you, because your prospects for success just went up considerably.

Indeed, the major premise of Malcolm Gladwell's *Outliers: The Story of Success* is that many of the world's most successful people rose on a tide of advantages, "some deserved, some not, some earned, some just plain lucky." When Bill Gates was about to enter seventh grade his parents sent him to an elite private school. Luckily for him the Mothers Club used proceeds from a school rummage sale to buy the students a newfangled thing known as a computer terminal. By the time the first PC came along a few years later, Gates was way ahead of the geek pack, with thousands of hours of programming experience under his belt.

Anyone can be lucky. It's what you *do* with luck that makes the difference. Keep in mind that Gates's classmates also had access to this early computer. Notice, however, that Microsoft Corporation was not started by the Lakeside class of 1973. It was co-conceived and built in part by the person who had the wisdom to work with the advantages presented to him, the initiative to take action, and the perseverance to see it through. As the American business tycoon Armand Hammer once said, "When I work fourteen hours a day, seven days a week, I get lucky."

For years I've preached that successful people really are "luckier"— however, not totally due to serendipity. Rather, successful people routinely put themselves in situations where good things are likely to happen. They show up in places where they're apt to meet interesting people. They are lifelong learners who frequently attend classes, symposiums, and conferences. They set goals and follow through with deliberate action.

Successful people are also intensely curious. They talk to strangers seated next to them on airplanes, at their kid's sporting event, standing in line for tickets, or working behind the counter of their local café. And because learning is so important to them, they ask lots of questions. These are all things that less successful people rarely do. But because successful people do them, it effectively positions them to attract good fortune in the way of contacts, advice, assistance, and collaborators. Of her own rise to fame, *Good Morning America* anchor Robin Roberts writes, "I learned how to put myself in a position for good things to happen to me. Even when I felt outnumbered or afraid, I made sure I was ready to grab the ball when it came my way."[3]

On the flip side, there's a danger in viewing success *solely* in terms of luck. You see someone who is living your dream of writing children's books, being a motivational speaker, or hosting her own radio show, and you think, *She's so lucky.* But what you really mean is, *Sure, that happened for her, but it will never happen for me.* And in this case you're probably right. Not because you are inherently unlucky but because when you frame success as totally the luck of the draw, like the lottery, your chances of achieving it are one in millions. As famed success mindset expert Earl Nightingale said, "Success is simply a matter of luck. Ask any failure."

Sometimes Timing Really Is Everything

Timing is the twin sister of luck. People who feel like frauds sometimes believe that they are where they are because they happened to be in the right place at the right time. If you've been dismissing your own achievements in this way, I've got more news for you: Sometimes timing really *is* everything.

In certain situations, Gladwell discovered, success can come down to the year or even the month in which you were born. For instance, in youth sports like Pee-Wee baseball and hockey there's always a cutoff date based on age. The reason there's a preponderance of future sports stars born in the months just after the cutoff date is that as kids they enjoyed a physical advantage over other young players. Yet you're never going to hear these adult athletes discount their accomplishments as merely a matter of being in the right womb at the right time. Instead they know they did what all successful people do—they took advantage of the timing edge life gave them and got up every day and worked their tails off to make it into the major leagues. And that's what you need to do. If timing has worked in your favor, be grateful. Then put in the effort it takes to make sure your great timing pays off.

The key is to learn how to use timing to your advantage. Successful people understand that a timely follow-up with a valuable networking contact or hot sales lead can mean the difference between seizing the moment and blowing it. And when things do pan out, they give themselves full credit because they recognize that having a knack for knowing when to act—and then doing it—is a skill in itself.

About Connections

From legacy admissions to college to nepotism in job hiring, the well connected do have a better chance of getting ahead, especially at high levels. It's perfectly all right to acknowledge your good fortune in being given a leg up. Just as long as you don't dismiss the role ability plays. Maybe your mother did graduate from Spelman or Vassar or an insider did vouch for you with an agent. But no institution, reference, or employer is going to risk its reputation or the bottom line if it doesn't think you're up to the task. Someone may have opened the door, but once inside you were the one who delivered the goods.

Besides, connections are only as good as the people who use them. Flip through a high school yearbook from any affluent community, and I guarantee you will find people who, despite having every advantage including phenomenal connections, failed to rise to their potential. In certain situations being *too* well connected can actually hurt a person's credibility. Being related to the rich or famous means you face a certain amount of skepticism as to whether you could make it on your own merits. That's why Ivanka Trump doesn't take her position in her famous father's company for granted, once telling an audience, "There may be more intel-ligent people, there may be people who are more experienced . . . but I'll work harder."[4]

Personality Rules

The term "winning personality" exists for a reason. Just as luck, tim-ing, and connections play a legitimate role in success, so does likability. Women especially tend to underrate its importance. It's rare to hear a man talk in the same dismissive "Oh, they just like me" way women do. Rather than consider personality to be an excuse for their success, men tend to see it for what it is—a form of competence.

If you've ever been on the hiring side of a job interview, you probably know that all things being equal, the more likable candidate will almost always get the job. It may not be fair, but the reality is that in most situa-tions, a great personality trumps even supposedly nonnegotiable qualifica-tions such as training or experience. When you understand this, you can stop being so consumed with proving how smart you are and put equal effort into demonstrating that you're the kind of person these future co-workers would want to spend forty-plus hours a week with.

Even in fields often thought of as less people-oriented, it's under-stood that personality is a legitimate element of competence. In fact, when electrical engineers at the famous Bell Labs think tank were asked to name the most valued and productive engineers on the teams, they didn't name the people with the best academic credentials or the highest IQs. Instead they chose those with the highest levels of social intelligence.

If you happen to be blessed with a great sense of humor, it's all the more likely that you falsely believe that the *only* reason you got where you are is that "they just like me." The fact is, it's been found that the people who rise to the top of organizations not only possess social intelligence but are also considered funny by others.[5]

Of course some people do initially skate through on charisma alone, but ultimately those around them catch on. Charm and personality are the frosting on the performance cake, but it's your underlying ability to do the job that is the cake itself. Being the kind of person others want on their team is on a par with any other skill. So if you've got it, work it!

Learning to Own Your Success

Now that you see how luck, timing, connections, and personality are part and parcel of the success equation, your old excuses are gone. To prove it, take out the list of accomplishments you created at the start of this chapter and look for instances where any of these factors really did play a role. Next to these write down actions you took that built on your good fortune, timing, connections, or charm that ultimately led to your success. This is where you want to make sure to give yourself well-deserved credit for things like persistence, initiative, going the extra mile, making use of breaks or contacts, or that winning personality.

Hopefully now you see that there really are times when external factors enter into your success equation—and everybody else's. What the impostor in you truly needs to get is that luck, timing, and all the rest may have helped success along, but *you* were the one who made it happen. Once you really understand that outside factors take nothing away from you or your achievements, it will forever change how you frame your past accomplishments as well as your future performance.

For starters, now when you look at the achievement history you created earlier, hopefully you will see it for what it is—unqualified evidence that you are indeed the bright, capable person everyone thinks you are.

Viewed with a fresh eye, all those successes you'd previously given away can now be put back into the *I did it* column, where they rightfully belong.

From here on you'll want to practice doing things to strengthen the mental link between you and your accomplishments. For starters, pay more attention to when and how you minimize your accomplishments. Maybe you don't run around telling everybody you lucked out in getting the big promotion, but you may notice that you wave off compliments more often than you think.

If so, instead of pushing the compliment away, practice responding with something more appropriate, like *Thank you.* Once that becomes second nature, step it up a bit with statements like *I really appreciate you saying that* or *Thank you—it makes me feel good that all my hard work paid off.*" Simply hearing yourself say these words in reference to something you did can help you internalize your accomplishment more fully.

You probably think that you're just being modest. But did you ever consider how constantly pointing out why you don't deserve praise may feel insulting to the person giving it? When you think about it, there's an element of arrogance involved in the impostor syndrome. After all, what you're really saying is *You people are so stupid you don't even realize I'm inept!* Imagine that you and I met and you told me that you enjoyed my book and I responded with something outrageous like *Really? Then I guess you don't read many books, do you? I mean, do you even get out of the house much or what?* Pretty arrogant, right?

All of us like to have our work noticed and appreciated. But remember, you've got that impostor thing going, which means that the person who most needs to recognize your achievements is *you.* One way you can do this is by giving yourself some kind of reward following the completion of a big project or a win. In addition to being fun, learning to appreciate yourself helps break your old pattern of seeking and then dismissing approval from others. The simple act of rewarding yourself is a concrete way to serve our goal of making that stronger mental connection between you and your achievement.

How you reward yourself is not important. You could treat yourself to a massage, a fancy dinner, even a simple walk in your favorite park. When I finished this book I bought a piece of art for my home. Every time I look at it I'm reminded of all the time and effort I put in. When I told this to a friend, she worried that if the book flopped, the painting would wind up serving as a painful reminder. To the contrary, rewards are not reserved only for the victories. If you gave something your best shot, you still deserve kudos for effort.

Another way you can cement your accomplishments in your mind is to make them more visual. Just because you're not a kid anymore doesn't mean you can't proudly adorn a wall with letters of recommendation, certificates, and other tangible evidence of success. If you don't feel comfortable with such public displays of self-appreciation, take a more private approach and create a success folder you can refer to when impostor feelings creep in.

The Bottom Line

People who identify with the impostor syndrome externalize their success by attributing it to factors outside of themselves. In reality, evidence that you are bright and capable is all around you. In order to feel fully deserving of your success you must learn to claim your accomplishments on a gut, visceral level. This begins with understanding that external factors such as luck, timing, connections, and personality play a valid role in everyone's success—including yours.

What You Can Do

- Create a list of all your achievements large and small.
- Next to each achievement note the role luck, timing, connections, or your own personality may have played in your ultimate success.
- Then write down the specific actions you took to take full advantage of these contributors.
- Make an agreement with yourself that the next time someone compliments your work you will say, "Thank you." Then zip it.

What's Ahead

Hopefully now you see that you really are responsible for your achievements. With that reality check out of the way, it's time to take stock of what is very likely *the* core of your impostor feelings—your personal competence rule book.

[6]

The Competence Rule Book
for Mere Mortals

I have offended God and mankind
because my work didn't reach the quality
it should have.

—Leonardo da Vinci

How will you know when you're "competent"? All achievers want to do
their best. But when you feel like an impostor, "best" includes a host
of self-expectations that go far beyond doing well. Whether you know it or
not, your view of competence is a major contributor to perpetuating your
belief that you are an impostor. Over the years you've adopted notions about
what's required for you to be considered talented, knowledgeable, skilled, or,

in a word, "good" enough. And these notions have everything to do with how competent and confident you feel.

The fact that everyone else sees a highly capable individual where you see an inadequate fraud tells me right there that you operate from a competence playbook that bears little resemblance to reality. It doesn't matter how intelligent or talented or skilled you are right now because I have news for you: You are never going to *consistently* reach that insanely high bar you've set for yourself—ever. That's why if you truly want to beat the impostor syndrome, you *must* adjust your self-limiting thinking as to what it takes to be competent. This redefining process is, bar none, your fastest path to confidence.

What's Your Competence Type?

Every impostor on the planet has a distorted view of competence. However, not all impostors skew it the same way. To show you what I mean, I'd like you to take a moment now to complete the following sentences with the first thing that pops into your head:

I'll know I'm competent at _____
when _____.

If I were really smart, _____
_____.

I should always _____
_____.

If I were really qualified, I would _____
_____.

As you are about to discover, your answers tell a lot about your competence type. They are *the Perfectionist, the Natural Genius, the Rugged Individualist, the Expert,* and *the Superwoman/Man/Student.* Each represents one kind of erroneous thinking about what it takes to be competent—your inner competence rule book.

Competence rules include words like *should, always, don't,* and *never.* For instance, you might be guided by an inner rule that says, *If I were really smart, I would always know what to say.* This way of thinking may in turn drive rules of behavior like *Never raise your hand unless you are 100 percent sure you are right,* or *Don't ask for help,* or *Always overprepare.* At its core, your rule book represents a strong internal expectation that you meet a standard of performance that is rarely achievable and most definitely not sustainable—at least not for mere mortals like you and me.

As you learn about the five competence types, you may recognize parts of yourself in several of them. Typically, though, you'll have one dominant type. A clearer understanding of your own limiting self-expectations will go a long way toward helping you rid yourself of the shame and fraudulence you feel when you fall short.

Once you have a better idea of what you're up against, the next step is to swap your old, unreasonable rules for the *Competence Rule Book for Mere Mortals* you'll receive here. As you'll discover, these new rules represent a profoundly different mind-set than the one that currently fuels your impostor fears. And because your new rule book reframes competence in realistic terms, it offers the opportunity for you to *instantly* feel more confident and competent.

The Perfectionist's View of Competence

For the Perfectionist, there is a single focus, and that is *how* something is done. Your competence rule book is quite straightforward. *I should deliver an unblemished performance 100 percent of the time. Every aspect of my work must be exemplary. Nothing short of perfect is acceptable.* When you fail to measure up to these unrealistically high standards, it only confirms your feelings of impostorism.

Some Perfectionists hold only themselves to these exacting standards, while others impose them on other people. At home the latter might sound like this: *No, honey, that's not how you fold a towel*—this *is how you fold a towel.* There is a right and wrong way to do everything from packing the car for vacation to preparing a project plan. Since no one can measure up to your precise standards, your motto is "If you want something done right, you've got to do it yourself." When you do delegate, you are often frustrated and disappointed at the results.

To be clear, perfectionism is not the same as a healthy drive to excel. You can seek excellence without demanding perfection. More important, non-Perfectionists will attempt difficult challenges and feel okay about themselves afterward—whether they succeed or not. And they're flexible enough to redefine success as the situation warrants. That's not to say they aren't disappointed if they fail. But as long as they gave it their best shot there is no shame. Not so for the Perfectionist.

Indeed, for you just the opposite occurs. Quality-wise, Perfectionists always go for the gold, the A+, the top spot. Anything less and you subject yourself to harsh inner criticism, often experiencing deep shame at your perceived "failure." Precisely because there is such shame in failing, you may avoid altogether attempting anything new or difficult. After all, getting things "right" takes a lot of effort, energy, and aggravation. It's much easier not to even try than to put yourself through those paces and risk the humiliation of coming up short.

Even if you are extremely motivated, success is rarely satisfying because you always believe you could have done even better. You get into a good school but are disappointed because you could have gotten into a better one. You deliver a top-notch presentation but kick yourself for not remembering to make some minor point. You broker a major transaction only to wonder if you could have struck an even better deal.

Perfectionism is a hard habit to break because it's self-reinforcing. Because you do overprepare, you often turn out a stellar performance, which in turn reinforces your drive to maintain that perfect record. *But it's a huge setup.* Because when you expect yourself and your work to always be perfect, it's a matter not of *if* you will be disappointed but *when.*

> Perfectionism is not a quest for the best.
> It is a pursuit of the worst in ourselves,
> the part that tells us that nothing we do
> will ever be good enough—that we should
> try again.
>
> —Julia Cameron, author, poet, playwright,
> and filmmaker

Competence Reframes for the Perfectionist
What you consider to be merely "satisfactory" work probably far exceeds what's actually required. That's why it is so important to reframe your current thinking about things like "quality" and "standards." In the sixteen-plus years that I've been helping people who aspire to be their own

boss, I have found that women are by far more likely than men to wait for everything to be perfect before they launch. They endlessly tinker and tweak and adjust, making sure everything is just so, but they never begin. In the end these high-minded notions of "quality standards" and "getting it right" equal paralysis.

On the whole, male entrepreneurs operate from a very different definition of quality. The mantra repeated by speakers at the numerous Internet-marketing seminars I've attended always comes down to some variation of "You don't have to get it right, you just have to get it going."[1]

One marketing guru went even further, telling procrastinating Perfectionists that "Half-ass is better than no ass." His wording may have been crass, but the fundamental truth remains: If you wait for everything to be perfect, you'll never act. Whether it's a product, a service, or an idea, you have to put version one out there, get some feedback, improve on it, then create a new and improved version from there. You can always course correct as you go. But at some point you must decide it really is good enough.

If you work in the corporate world or in academia, you may be understandably turned off by advice like "Half-ass is better than no ass." So what if we repackage it into something more respectable, like a paradigm? As it turns out, the software-development world not only shares the basic mind-set of my Internet marketer friends, but the concept even has an official-sounding name. Paradigm creator James Bach calls it "good enough quality," or GEQ.

Bach's article "Good Enough Quality: Beyond the Buzzword" appeared in a well-respected publication dedicated to advancing the theory and application of computing and information technology. In it he asserts that GEQ is standard operating procedure in the software-manufacturing world, explaining that "Microsoft begins every project with the certain knowledge that they will choose to ship [a software product] with known bugs."[2] This is not a jab at Microsoft or, for that matter, any software company. Rather, it's recognizing the reality that any manufacturer in the technology sector must operate with a degree of uncertainty.

To be clear: The principles of GEQ—or "Half-ass is better than no ass"—have nothing whatsoever to do with mediocrity. Nor are they about providing the minimum quality you can get away with. None of the seven- and eight-figure-earning entrepreneurs I know got rich selling schlock. And Bill Gates and Steve Jobs did not build the two dominant technology companies in the world by putting out inferior products. For a product to be considered "good enough," Bach insists it must still meet certain criteria. To guide those efforts, his good-enough quality paradigm includes six factors and six "vital perspectives." Notably, being perfect is not one of them.

None of this is to say that you have to relinquish your quest for excellence or do things willy-nilly. What it does mean is, with some obvious exceptions such as performing surgery or flying an airplane, not everything you do deserves 100 percent. It's a matter of being selective about where you put your efforts and not wasting time fussing over routine tasks when an adequate effort is all that is required. If you get a chance to go back and make improvements later, great—if not, move on. There's a reason why scientist and science fiction writer Isaac Asimov is proud to describe himself as a "non-perfectionist," telling fans, "Don't agonize. It slows you down." With five hundred books to his name, I'd say he's on to something.

Reframing perfectionism is also a smart career move. If you work with other people, there's a good chance that your constant need for everything to be just so is a problem for them too. A project manager at IBM told me things got so bad with one perfection-obsessed team member that she finally had to pull her aside to say, "Knock it off. You're slowing the whole team down."

Rather than enabling your success, perfectionist thinking is actually a gigantic barrier. The late author Jennifer White said it best: "Perfectionism has nothing to do with getting it right. It has nothing to do with having high standards. Perfectionism is a refusal to let yourself move ahead." It's that last line that is so powerful.

It will take some practice, but you really can learn to appreciate the virtues of non-perfection. The most beautiful trees are often those that are the most misshapen. Many of the most profound scientific discoveries were the result of mistakes. I once read that in some Islamic art, small flaws are intentionally built in as a humble acknowledgment that only God is perfect. How stupendously boring life would be if every wave was the perfect wave, every kiss the perfect kiss. There is utility, beauty, and grace in non-perfection. Learn to embrace it.

New Competence Rules for the Perfectionist
- Perfectionism inhibits success.
- Sometimes good is good enough.
- Not everything deserves 100 percent.
- Your perfectionism impacts others.
- Non-perfection is to be embraced.

The Natural Genius's View of Competence

The Perfectionist is perhaps the most obvious and familiar of the five competence types. There is an entirely different set of competence rules that is also highly characteristic of impostors typified by the character I've dubbed the Natural Genius. According to Webster's dictionary, *competence* means "having the capacity to function or develop in a particular way."

The operative words here are *capacity* and *develop*. Unfortunately, no one told that to the Natural Genius. Rather, for you *true* competence means having inherent intelligence and ability. Since intelligence and ability are seen as innate, the thinking here is that success should be effortless. If you identify with the Natural Genius, what you care mostly about is *how* and *when* accomplishments happen.

Like the Perfectionist, the Natural Genius has set the internal bar impossibly high. But instead of the key measure being flawlessness, you judge yourself based on ease and speed. You expect to know without being taught, to excel without effort, and to get it right on the first attempt. You think, *If I were really smart, I would be able to understand everything the first time I hear it,* or *If I were a real writer, it wouldn't be this hard.* When you're not able to do something quickly or fluently, your impostor alarm goes off.

The reason Natural Geniuses want to go from novice to expert without having to suffer the in-between stages is not because they're lazy. It's because they don't even realize that an in-between stage exists. You look at people who are at the top of their field, and it all looks so effortless. So as a new job hire you expect yourself to hit the ground running. As a student, you believe you should have emerged from the womb knowing how to do advanced calculus or write a dissertation. You start a business and expect to earn a profit on day one. When learning how to play an instrument or master a sophisticated procedure, you expect to pick everything up right away.

Because you believe a more competent person would be farther along by now, when you do run up against something that is not easily understood, that's difficult or time-consuming to master, you think, *It must be me.* This thinking is reinforced by a culture that has lost the notion of apprenticeship, one that reveres talent over effort and overnight success over slow, steady progress.

If people knew how hard I worked to get
my mastery, it wouldn't seem so wonderful
after all.
—Michelangelo

The Natural Genius's perspective is similar to what Stanford researcher Carol Dweck refers to as a "fixed mindset." In her book *Mindset: The New Psychology of Success,* Dweck summarizes three decades of research that demonstrates the enormous impact your views on intelligence and what it takes to succeed have on how you see your own capabilities.

Briefly, when you have a fixed mindset, your energies are focused on performing well and being smart, both of which require you to continually prove yourself. Succeeding does inspire self-confidence—for a while. When you're faced with a setback, however, your confidence tumbles. And because not performing well evokes such shame, you often go to great lengths to avoid challenge and failure.

To the fixed-mindset person, intelligence and skill are seen as a sum game. Either you can do math or you can't. You're artistic or you're not. You have what it takes to sell or to be a great speaker or you don't. Not surprisingly, Dweck found that people who have a fixed mindset are more likely to rate high on the impostor scale.

Competence Reframes for the Natural Genius

A major reframe for the Natural Genius involves the recognition that innate talent has remarkably little to do with greatness. Not only can you learn how to do any number of things, you can even become great at them—if you're willing to work at it. As extensive research in the United

States and Britain reveals, people who excel in fields from music to sports to chess are the ones who devote the most time in engaged "deliberate practice."[3]

This involves not just repeated practice but repeated practice based on highly targeted measures and goals. Even people who've already reached the top know that *staying there* requires constant practice. That's why just before he's scheduled to appear on one of the late-night shows, comedian and actor Chris Rock readies himself by doing a couple of nights of stand-up.

This emphasis on continuous improvement is indicative of what Dweck calls a "growth mindset." In direct contrast to the fixed mindset we looked at earlier, the growth mindset sees intelligence as malleable and capability as something that can be built over time. Success is not considered a function of being inherently intelligent, gifted, or skilled. Instead the path to mastery is seen as one of lifelong learning and skill building.

And because growth-mindset people know how to learn from mistakes and failure, rather than withdrawing from difficult endeavors or becoming discouraged, they redouble their efforts. When you see yourself as a work-in-progress, you're automatically less likely to experience feelings of inadequacy.

Not only is natural talent not required to be competent, having it does not automatically guarantee success. Dweck cites example after example from the world of sports and art of people who started out with only average abilities but were willing to persevere and wound up doing as well and *often better* than those who are naturally gifted but fail to apply themselves. The good news is that effort is available to anyone willing to use it—and that includes you. With practice you get better, and when you get better, you feel better. Best of all, you'll have the hard-won confidence to prove it.

In the midst of difficulty lies opportunity.
—Albert Einstein

Will you encounter setbacks along the way? Bet on it. The difference is that instead of seeing difficulty and challenge as signs of your ineptness, you now approach them as opportunities to grow and learn. Here's where the power of self-talk and reframing comes in.

Instead of thinking, *I'm unqualified,* think, *I may be inexperienced but I'm fully capable of growing into the role.* In the past, when you were faced with something you'd never done before, you thought, *Yikes, I have no idea what I'm doing!* Now you tell yourself, *Wow, I'm really going to learn a lot.* Words really do matter. Simply changing how you talk to yourself about a difficulty or a challenge changes how you approach it.

Michelangelo said, "Genius is eternal patience." Writing a dissertation or building a practice or doing anything of consequence takes considerable time, effort, *and* patience. Remember that your first draft, first presentation, first painting, or first anything is never going to be as good as your second—or your two hundredth. Swap your false notions of overnight success for the ideal slow, steady progress, and you'll discover the true meaning of genius.

New Rules for the Natural Genius
- Effort trumps ability.
- Challenges are often opportunities in disguise.
- Real success always takes time.

The Expert's View of Competence

For the Expert, your primary concern is how much knowledge or skill you possess—and as far as you're concerned, you can never have enough. This emphasis on knowledge, experience, and credentials leads to self-talk that sounds like this: *If I were really competent, I would know everything there is to know.* Or, *If I were really smart, I would understand and remember everything I read.* Or, *Before I can put myself out there, I need in-depth education, training, and experience.*

Women are especially prone to the Expert trap, some astonishingly so. Mary was valedictorian of her class, had a full academic scholarship to college, and scored so high on the LSAT that the dean of the law school agreed to admit her even without seeing her application. Mary decided instead to pursue a doctoral degree.

She worked at it for a few years until her husband was accepted into medical school in another state. With the move and a pregnancy, she dropped out. A few years later she contacted the university to inquire about her transcripts. That's when an administrator pointed out that she was just shy of completing all of the requirements for a master's degree. He even offered to help her get reinstated. "Oh no," she said, "I couldn't possibly know enough to deserve a master's degree." In hindsight Mary wonders, *What was I thinking?*

Actually, Mary was thinking what a lot of impostors think, namely, that there is a defined threshold of knowledge and understanding that a person must meet in order to be deemed expert "enough." Women don't just fixate on garnering more and more education and credentials, they are also more preoccupied with how much *experience* they have. Among entrepreneurs, for example, experience was found to loom larger in women's estimation of their own success than it does for men.[4]

It makes sense that men would be less rattled. After all, they grew up with the pressure of other people assuming that they know what they're doing. All that time having to act confident while peering clueless under the car hood or at a frozen computer screen forced males to become comfortable with diving in despite a lack of knowledge. As a result, when a man takes on a new job or project he's more likely to be okay having only a basic (or no) understanding because he's comfortable figuring things out as he goes.

Women grew up with a different set of messages—ones that often assume a lack of knowledge or ability. As you learned in chapter 3, the cultural bias against female competence is well documented. So it's not without reason that you've come to believe that you need to know *150 percent* before you consider yourself even remotely up to the task. You read a job description that requires a couple of minor skill sets or some previous experience you don't possess, and you disqualify yourself right off the bat. And in an economy where jobs are being eliminated and the job market is increasingly competitive, this reluctance to jump in and learn as you go has real consequences.

The irony of striving to be the Expert is that even when you really are one, you're probably uncomfortable seeing yourself as such. For a lot of women the title of "expert" feels somehow presumptive. Then there's all that pressure: If you make that kind of public declaration, then you had darned well better be able to back it up. And since you're pretty sure you can't, naturally you're going to worry about what people would think.

This concern about how you're perceived is a frequent theme among women. On numerous occasions Sara Holtz, the former vice president and general counsel for Nestlé, invited me to speak on the impostor syndrome at the practice-building seminars she conducts for female partners of major law firms. In these sessions Sara has participants craft a thirty-second answer to the question "What do you do?"—often referred to as your "elevator talk." It was during this exercise that I met an extremely successful attorney named Stephanie.

Since approximately 60 percent of Stephanie's practice involved representing manufacturers of medical devices, her first instinct was to describe herself as an expert in this type of litigation. On second thought, she worried that it might make her sound "too full of herself." So she ditched the term "expert" and instead decided to say she had a "special interest" in that area of law. You know, like it was her hobby or something. When I told this story to a male attorney who very definitely did not feel like an impostor, his response was, "Sixty percent? I would have said I was a *leading* expert!"

If you identify with the Expert, know that operating out of the mindset that competence requires absolute knowledge has consequences. This idea that you need to know a subject backward and forward keeps you from speaking up or offering an opinion for fear of being wrong. And because you accept the false notion that you need to know everything there possibly is to know before you consider yourself remotely competent, you may not even attempt things you're perfectly capable of doing.

This endless pursuit of ever more information, skills, and experience is also what drives a lot of women to chase after additional and often unnecessary training, degrees, or credentials. Indeed, 2009 marked the first time in history when more women achieved doctoral degrees than men. This is of course great news. But I'll never forget finishing a talk at the University of Pennsylvania when the husband of a woman who was working on her third Ph.D. pleaded with me: "Please make her stop." Easier said than done.

It's hard for the Expert to stop because in her mind there will always be one more book to read, one more class to take, one more experiment to run, one more degree or designation or certification to earn before she dares pronounce herself "expert." Unfortunately, this relentless pursuit to reach the elusive "end of knowledge" can cause you to take months or sometimes even years longer than necessary to achieve a goal.

Obviously, there are professions where testing, matriculating, licensing, and other methods of credentialing are and should be mandatory. But unless your dream is to perform open-heart surgery or design aircraft or something of that ilk, with obvious exceptions, this notion that you need a piece of paper in your hand that "proves" you can do something is nonsense. It's also a serious impediment to success.

I know you feel more "comfortable" when you have a solid grounding in a field or endeavor. However, it's also possible that you're acting in part out of a hyper concern for how your work affects others. The more typically female compulsion to "go by the book" credential-wise is partly a function of insecurity. But it also has to do with not wanting to act irresponsibly. You don't want to go off half-cocked, especially if your actions impact other people. And you certainly don't want to promise something unless you're absolutely certain you can deliver.

All of this is admirable. However, you may think that you're protecting others when you're really just protecting yourself—protection you wouldn't need if you understood that it really is okay to pick up knowledge as you go along and that being an "expert" often comes just as much from doing as it does from degrees.

Competence Reframes for the Expert

Will Rogers once said, "Everyone is ignorant, only on different subjects." For the Expert the main task is to practice being more comfortable with not knowing everything and trusting what you do know. Your obsession with being credentialed and your shame about what you don't know is keeping you from attempting all kinds of things you're perfectly capable of doing. Can you imagine not buying an exquisite piece of art because you found out the artist didn't earn an M.F.A? It's easy to see how silly the preoccupation with formal training is in a subjective area such as art. But what about other fields, like technology, for example?

In an article on the prevalence of the impostor syndrome among women in the high-tech sector, former national director of DigitalEve Canada Jennifer Evans makes the case that a "lack of confidence is a more critical ingredient to women not advancing in technical fields than is their lack of formal education in technology itself."[5] True, the people who head up corporate IT functions often do have impressive degrees after their names. But at the same time, most of the techies Evans knows are self-taught. One of these was a former street kid with little formal education who found some discarded computer parts, began tinkering, became a self-taught computer "engineer," and went on to earn a six-figure income installing firewalls.

Successful people who had the confidence to act on their goals despite a lack of formal training are great role models for the Expert. Take Jean Nidetch. When the overweight homemaker felt her resolve to diet waning, she invited friends to join her for weekly support meetings. Before long she was squeezing forty people into her small Queens apartment. Nidetch's approach of mutual support and empathy coupled with sensible eating was so successful that a few years later she incorporated her business, rented space to hold her first public meeting, and set up fifty chairs. Four hundred people showed up. As you may have guessed, Nidetch went on to found what is now a multibillion-dollar international empire called Weight Watchers.

Notice, she did not have a degree in nutrition or exercise physiology. Nidetch was a high school graduate whose work experience consisted of raising her sons while helping support the family selling eggs door-to-door for an aunt who owned a chicken farm in New Jersey. Her credentials were her success stories.

Finally, there's the unlikely story of a *self-taught* weapons-system expert named Jeff Baxter. Baxter was initially interested in learning about the technology behind music-recording equipment and in the process discovered that it used hardware and software originally developed for the military. With his curiosity sparked, Baxter began to study weapons systems and ultimately wrote a five-page paper proposing a missile-converting option.

Despite having zero formal education on weapons systems, Baxter went on to chair the Congressional Advisory Board on Missile Defense and become a highly paid consultant to such military contractors as General Atomics and Northrop Grumman. What was his previous job? "Skunk" Baxter, as he used to be known by his fans, was a guitarist with rock bands Steely Dan and the Doobie Brothers. If a former rock star with no formal training is good enough for the Pentagon and major aeronautics companies, then trust me, you can become a self-made expert on just about anything!

The reason I'm sharing these stories is not to deter you from getting an education. It's because I want you to know that there are many paths to expertise. You can get multiple degrees and never have the same knowledge as what can be gained from your own firsthand experience. If your approach works, then it's just as valid as anyone else's. If you have no track record or if there is no recognized path from where you are to where you want to be, then design your own "degree" program, minus the degree.

Think about the course topics you'd include, the books that should be required reading, the publications you'd subscribe to, and the field trips or internships that could provide valuable experience. If you need to establish a track record or credibility before applying for a job or hanging out your shingle, then volunteer, run a pilot project, or offer a few freebies to prospective customers or clients in exchange for feedback, testimonials, and referrals.

On the flip side is the famous Clint Eastwood line in *Magnum Force:* "A man's got to know his limitations." And so do you. Having a healthy respect for the limitations of your own knowledge and expertise is also a sign of competence. You don't want your financial advisor dispensing your medications or your pharmacist managing your investments. Why should you expect yourself to know it all? Instead of judging yourself, respect where your expertise ends and someone else's begins.

As coaching legend John Wooden said, "It's what you learn after you know it all that counts." There is no "end" to knowledge. When you try to know everything, especially in such fast-moving and information-dense fields as technology and medicine, it's like trying to get to the end of the Internet. It's simply not possible. The quest for ultimate knowledge is based on a delusion. Instead relax and just do the best you can.

Besides, you don't need to know everything. You just need to be smart enough to figure out who does and take it from there. Once you reframe knowledge this way, you no longer need to apologize or to judge yourself or to fret when you don't understand something. Instead you know you have just as much right to ask questions or to not understand as the next person. Gone are the days where you sit in a group feeling hopelessly lost only to be totally relieved when someone else asked the very question you didn't out of your fear of appearing "stupid."

From now on, you're going to confidently raise your hand and say, *Can you explain what you mean by that?* or *How would that work exactly?* or *I'm not following you; can you go over that again?* And if someone asks you a question about which you have no clue, channel Mark Twain, who said confidently, "I was gratified to be able to answer promptly. I said, 'I don't know.'"

New Competence Rules for the Expert
- There are many paths to expertise.
- There is no end to knowledge.
- Competence means respecting your limitations.
- You don't need to know everything, you just need to be smart enough to find someone who does.
- Even when you don't know something you can still project confidence.

The Rugged Individualist's View of Competence

As a Rugged Individualist you've spent years quite literally laboring under the misguided notion that true competence equals solo, unaided achievement. Don't confuse this with the Perfectionist, who prefers to do things herself as a means of quality control. The reason the Rugged Individualist likes to go it alone is because she believes she shouldn't need help. The misguided thinking here is, *If were really competent, I could do everything myself.*

In your mind, the only achievements that really count are those you reached all on your own. If you acted as part of a team or were engaged in any sort of collaborative effort, then it somehow diminishes the achievement. Similarly, if you were admitted to college as a so-called legacy student or if someone so much as put in a good word for you with a potential employer or client, it doesn't count. You see ideas the same way. If you are a writer or a scholar or a budding entrepreneur, you expect your work or idea to be totally new and original. If someone else got there first, you're crushed.

The stereotype is that men don't ask for directions because it's a sign of weakness. The Rugged Individualist feels equally vulnerable. After all, what if you do ask and it's perceived as a sign that you really *don't* know what you're doing? That was Diane's big fear. Shortly after a promotion into a role and at a level that were *both* firsts for a woman in her company, Diane was assigned to head up a major project three hours away from the home office. Complicating the situation was the fact that she worked in a very male-dominated field. Diane knew that, at least in the minds of some, asking for assistance may have been viewed as "proof" that women weren't fit for the job. So she didn't.

Seven days a week Diane left her house at four in the morning and often returned past midnight. This madness went on for months. Everyone could see that both Diane and the project were floundering, but still she refused to ask for help. The impossible hours and workload finally took a physical toll, to the point where Diane was forced to take a medical leave.

In her absence the project was assigned to a man named John. John took one look at the job and said, "I'm not going to do that job. That job will kill somebody! I want an apartment near the new facility, four more staff members, and complete access to all of the division heads back in the home office." And he got it. Was it because he was a man? Maybe. Especially when you consider the work environment. However, Diane's belief that the only true achievements are those accomplished entirely on her own certainly played a role as well.

On some level you really do know that all of the things you are being asked to do cannot be done—at least not as fast as is expected or as well as you'd like, and definitely not all by yourself. Even if you didn't feel competence was contingent on doing it all yourself, women don't want to be a bother or put anyone out. So you knock yourself out sacrificing your health or personal life in order to perform miracles. And when you do somehow manage to pull it off, you think, *What a fraud I am. If they only knew I'm just holding on by a thread, they wouldn't think I was so great after all.*

Competence Reframes for the Rugged Individualist

Of course the major competence reframe for the Rugged Individualist is to reject the myth that in order for an accomplishment to "count," you have to do it completely on your own. That's why I wanted you to meet Diane. Her story contains a powerful lesson for counteracting the go-it-alone mentality. The truth is that Diane *couldn't* handle the job. But under the same circumstances neither could John or anyone else. The critical difference is that he knew it, which is why he felt perfectly entitled to ask for what he needed in order to do it.

Even taking double standards into account, the real story here is that John understood a cardinal rule of competence: *Competence doesn't mean knowing how to do everything yourself. Instead, competence means knowing how to identify the resources needed to get the job done.* Whenever I tell that to my female audiences, every woman in the room reaches for her pen.

Resources come in different forms. For example, you may need

- additional time to complete a project
- access to content experts or decision makers
- additional information before you can fully assess a situation, make a recommendation, or proceed to the next stage
- hands-on assistance to carry out certain tasks
- physical space—meeting rooms, a laboratory, technology—or equipment
- a bigger budget or other financial resources

In addition to recognizing what to ask for, you need to know *how* to ask for what you want. Obviously, having a confident demeanor helps. But you also always want to frame your request in terms of the requirements of the project and not your needs as a person. In other words, *"I'll never meet the deadline without help"* could be construed as a personal deficiency rather than an objective analysis of the situation. Instead take yourself out of the mix with, *This is what's required to meet the deadline,* or *In order for X to happen, the project requires Y.*

> I use not only all the brains I have, but all I can borrow.
> —Woodrow Wilson

Recognize too that only a true impostor would be afraid to ask for help. Years ago I heard Secretary of State Henry Kissinger nonchalantly tell a reporter about a potential nuclear crisis he didn't know how to handle. What did he do? He picked up the phone and called the guy who'd held his job before him. Not only did Kissinger see no shame in seeking outside counsel, he seemed downright tickled with himself for thinking of it. "I make progress by having people around who are smarter than I am—and listening to them. And I assume that everyone is smarter about something than I am," he said.

As the nature of the work becomes more complex, sometimes all you need is someone to help you think things through. If confidentiality is an issue, hire a consultant or a coach to serve as a sounding board. You also need to be cognizant of where *not* to seek help. As the thirteenth-century poet Rumi warned, "When setting out on a journey, never consult someone who has never left home." If your dream is to license an invention or you want to quit your job to attend cooking school in Paris, don't seek advice from your well-intentioned but uninformed friends and family. Instead ask for counsel from people who have done it.

Truly competent people not only ask for advice, but they delegate wherever and whenever they can. In some cases it really does take less time to just do it yourself than to train someone else. In the long run, though, delegating will save you time and stress, and if you are self-employed, delegating saves money as well. The rule of thumb is to assign a task to the lowest level in the organization at which it can be performed competently—not perfectly, competently. If you don't have the option to delegate, see if you can tap some coworkers now and then.

And what about all that stuff that's been delegated *to you*? Now that you understand that your being competent does not hinge on being a combination of the Lone Ranger and a miracle worker, you may want to practice the art of "delegating up." The next time another major project, client, or function is added to your already overflowing plate, put the ball back in your boss's court by asking which deadlines need to be completed first so you'll both know which will have to wait. Better your boss put some deadlines on the back burner than you knock yourself out.

Finally, not only don't you have to do everything yourself, but you don't have to come up with everything yourself either. Students, aspiring entrepreneurs, and writers are particularly prone to thinking their work or idea has to be totally groundbreaking and original to be of consequence. This belief that *If I didn't think it up first, then it's too late* is utter nonsense. Whether it's coming up with a new cookbook or doing scholarly research, there is always more to say on any subject.

Competent people (scholars included) are always building on the work of other competent people. Dale Carnegie wrote one of the bestselling books of all time. Where did he get all those great techniques he included in *How to Win Friends & Influence People*? "The ideas I stand for are not mine," said Carnegie. "I borrowed them from Socrates. I swiped them from Chesterfield. I stole them from Jesus. And I put them in a book." Even Einstein understood that "the secret to creativity is knowing how to hide your sources." (If you are a student, I hasten to add that he was not talking about plagiarism!)

New Competence Rules for the Rugged Individualist

- To get the job done, you first need to identify the resources required.
- Competent people know how to ask for what they need.
- Smart people seek out people who know more than they do.
- When seeking advice, it's important to ask the right people.
- Your work does not have to be groundbreaking to be good.
- Competent people know it's okay to build on the work of other competent people.

The Superwoman/Man/Student's View of Competence

It's easy to confuse the Superwoman/Man/Student with the Perfectionist. The major distinction is that a Perfectionist really can be content to perform flawlessly chiefly in school or on the job. But for the Super Woman/Man/Student competence rests on the ability to juggle multiple roles masterfully. Although you likely have some perfectionist tendencies, for you competence has as much to do with how *many* things you can handle as it does how well you do them.

Unlike the other competence types, the Superwoman in particular is largely a cultural creation. It came into being when the traditional roles of mother and homemaker were extended to accommodate the additional role of full-time paid worker. Suddenly "having it all" became "doing it all." With help from Madison Avenue and the now famous seventies Enjoli perfume commercial that celebrated the modern woman's ability to "bring home the bacon, fry it up in a pan," and still have the energy and desire to "never let you forget you're a man," a collective bar had been raised for women everywhere.

Think of the Superwoman as the Perfectionist, the Natural Genius, and the Rugged Individualist on steroids. Instead of seeing the pressure to have the looks of Halle Berry, the ambition of Anita Roddick, the financial savvy of Suze Orman, the munificence of Mother Teresa, and the domestic flair of Martha Stewart as societal in origin, you tell yourself, *If I were really competent, I would be able to do it all.*

Increasingly I hear from students—male and female—who relate to trying to be the "Superstudent." You may not be concerned with domestic prowess but you may feel pressure both internal and external to overextend in other ways. You play sports, serve on student government, spearhead any number of civic or charitable activities, maintain a perfect grade-point average—and make it all seem effortless to boot. You can do it for a while, but sooner or later you're bound to drop a ball. And when you do, you're extremely hard on yourself. Even if you can keep up, you never feel satisfied because you think you could do more.

And when the Superstudent meets the Superwoman/Man—look out! After a presentation at Duke University I was approached by two doctoral students who were managing to meet rigorous academic demands while simultaneously holding down full-time jobs. That would be impressive enough, but they were also raising young children who had their own overly full roster of extracurricular activities. I was exhausted just hearing about their overextended lives. I assumed that they approached me for advice on how they could offload some responsibilities. Instead these women wanted to talk about how guilty they felt about not having time to do volunteer work in their community.

Competence Reframes for the Superwoman and Superstudent

Perfection is impossible to sustain in even one area. To shoot for it in all aspects of your life is a recipe for failure—and disappointment. By striving to be the best student, worker, spouse or partner, mother, friend, homemaker, hostess, and more, you've succeeded at only one thing—setting yourself up to fall short in multiple roles.

The major reframe for the Superwoman/Man/Student is that competence is not a function of how many things you can do. In fact, rather than make you feel better about yourself and your level of competence, your constant striving to be everything to everybody can make you feel even more inadequate. Plus there's a good chance that sooner or later you'll hit a wall in the form of illness or exhaustion, and possibly resentment.

On the bulletin board at my post office hung a quote from the Women's Theology Center in Boston. It read: "We must go slowly, there's not much time." Instead of attempting to operate at warp speed packing ever more into your already jammed schedule, experiment with what it feels like to ease up now and then. Years from now no one will remember all the extra projects you took on or your meticulously organized garage. What they—and you—will recall is the time you said no to a work assignment to take your kids to the science museum or when you ignored household chores to enjoy the sunset.

The major behavioral change for the Superwoman/Student can be summed up in two words: Do less. One reason why it's easier for men to say no is because their interpretation of competence keeps them from taking on more than they need to in the first place. Just like the Rugged

Individualist, you need to ditch the guilt and recognize that truly competent people delegate whatever and whenever they can.

If you live with anyone over the age of five, chances are you can delegate more on the home front. In addition to saving you time, you also instill in your children a strong work ethic and give them the opportunity to learn how to function as part of a team—both of which will serve them for the rest of their lives. Not a parent? You can still offload more tasks at home. Delegate the holiday planning to a sibling, set up online bill paying, or, if you can afford it, hire someone to clean the house, paint the living room, or mow the lawn, and use the extra time for yourself.

I know you pride yourself on your ability to multitask, but just because you *can* do something doesn't mean you *need* to. There are some things on your to-do list that you can eliminate altogether. If you like the idea of gardening more than the backbreaking reality, grass over your garden and support your local farmer instead. Instead of baking holiday cookies yourself, buy them from the PTA fund-raiser. Use the saved time for more important things like catching up with an old friend, reading, or any activity that renews you.

Once you've shed some nonessential roles and responsibilities, recalibrate your success measurements by establishing attainable goals and realistic due dates. Things always take longer than you expect. If you think the project will take a week, give yourself three. Having a realistic picture of how long things really take will help you say no when new requests come along.

I understand that it may be hard for you to lay down your cape for your own sake. If that's the case, I invite you to consider the message you're conveying to the next generation, a message that can only contribute to ensuring a never-ending stream of capable females growing up to feel like they're never good enough. Not that they need your help, mind you. A study titled "The Supergirl Dilemma" reports that 60 percent of girls grades three through twelve say they often feel stressed. As one ninth-grader puts it, "Girls are very pressured today to get good grades, look good, have a lot of friends, do a majority of the chores, and still have time for family."[6] Sound familiar?

New Competence Rules for the Superwoman/Man/Student
- It's okay to say no.
- Delegating frees you and gives others the chance to participate.
- When you slow down and cut out unnecessary tasks, you get to focus on activities that really matter.
- Being a Superwoman sends an unhealthy message to your daughters and sons.

Banishing Competence Extremism

In their own way, all five competence types hold an extreme view of competence. Whether you are a Perfectionist, a Natural Genius, an Expert, a Rugged Individualist, or the Superwoman/Man/Student, for you there is no such thing as a competence middle ground. Instead, from moment to moment you judge yourself based on where you think you are on a continuum represented by dazzling brilliance on one end and a dimly lit bulb on the other.

If you're not operating at the top of your game 24/7, then you're incompetent. Since your view allows for no in-between, you are left with the belief that *If I don't know everything, then I know nothing. If it's not absolutely perfect, it's woefully deficient.*

It's understandable that you constantly teeter on these extremes. After all, you *really do know* what it's like to feel brilliant. Like everyone, you've experienced those exhilarating times when your brain is firing on all cylinders, when everything just seems to click, when you think, *Damn, I'm good!* Of course, being human, you also know what it's like to not be able to think to save your life. To feel like you are wearing a big sign that says, Sorry, brain closed for the day.

And herein lies the problem: Because you know you're *capable* of brilliance, if you're not there all the time, you automatically thrust yourself to the other end of the continuum. And once there, you're very unforgiving of yourself.

To be clear, it's not that extremes don't exist; they do. In fact, when it comes to achievement, extremes go with the territory. Whether you're conducting a scientific experiment, creating art, managing a project, starting a business, or doing anything of significance, it's always an exercise in extremes. Clarity and confusion, deficiency and mastery, knowing and not knowing, all are part of the creative actualization process. However, once you recognize these extremes for what they are, you'll be able to accept your own low points without self-incrimination.

Regardless of your competence type, you can and should strive to do your best. Just stop expecting yourself to remain in a constant state of extreme brilliance. Instead strive to feel comfortable with being fabulously adequate. The reality is, even the brightest and most talented among us spend the majority of their waking hours smack in the middle of the competency scale. Just like me—and you.

When you feel yourself sliding into competence extremism, recognize it for what it is. Then make a conscious decision to stop and really savor those exhilarating mental high points and forgive yourself for the inevitable lulls. That's what Tina Fey does. "The beauty of the impostor syndrome," says Fey, "is you vacillate between extreme egomania and a complete feeling of: 'I'm a fraud! Oh God, they're on to me! I'm a fraud!' So you just try to ride the egomania when it comes and enjoy it, and then slide through the idea of fraud."[7]

Few things are black or white, and that includes your competence type itself. Obviously, your old rule book has enormous downsides. However, you don't have to ditch it entirely. For example:

- As the Perfectionist you are welcome to hold on to your pursuit of high standards, but shed the shame you feel when you fall short.
- As the Natural Genius you can keep your desire for mastery, as long as you recognize the time and effort that's required to get there.
- As the Expert you can still value the importance of knowledge, but ditch the unrealistic expectation that you should know it all.
- As the Rugged Individualist you can take pride in the knowledge that you can go it alone if you have to, just stop thinking you must.
- As the Superwoman/Man/Student you can honor your desire to be the very best you can on multiple fronts, but abandon the idea that you have to do it all.

The trick is to make a conscious choice to hold on to these positive aspects of your type while letting go of the far-more-numerous unrealistic and self-limiting tendencies that are fodder for impostor feelings.

The Bottom Line

Everyone has a personal definition of competence. The extreme and unrealistic notions of what it takes to be competent only perpetuate the lie that you are an impostor. If you continue to measure yourself using this same warped yardstick, it will not just be harder to beat the impostor syndrome, it will be impossible.

Fortunately, there is a solution. Lower your internal bar by adopting the healthy rules in the *Competence Rule Book for Mere Mortals.* The quicker you can "right-size" your unsustainably high performance standards, and the more effort you make to integrate this new way of thinking into your life, the more competent and confident you will feel. Guaranteed.

What You Can Do

- Identify your primary competence type.
- Pick one of the new realistic rules for your competence type, ideally the one that would give your confidence the biggest boost, and start there.
- Spend the next few weeks consciously looking for opportunities to put your new rule into action.

What's Ahead

At the heart of each of the competence types is a fundamental fear of failure. In the next chapter we'll explore how your response to failure, mistakes, and criticism contributes to your fraud fears and how learning a new response can boost your confidence.

7

Responding to Failure, Mistakes, and Criticism

Treat a male student badly and he will think you're a jerk. Treat a female student badly and she will think you have finally discovered that she doesn't belong in engineering.

—Dr. Sheila Widnall, professor of aeronautics and astronautics at Massachusetts Institute of Technology and former secretary of the U.S. Air Force

No one *likes* to fail. Impostors positively hate it. The fact that researchers have found a strong link between fear of failure and the impostor syndrome is hardly surprising.[1] In one way or another you've spent your entire adult life trying to avoid stumbling. In the impostor world there is no such thing as constructive criticism—there is only condemnation. To not make the grade in some way only serves as more proof that you're a fraud. And to receive less-than-positive feedback from someone else—well, that just makes it official.

The Competence Rule Book for Mere Mortals you received in the last chapter will help for sure. But taken together, failure, mistakes, and criticism constitute another piece of the competence puzzle. How you think about and handle these inevitable parts of life has an enormous impact on how competent and confident you feel. See for yourself:

Answer yes or no

- When things go wrong, I automatically blame myself.
- When I make a mistake, I have a really hard time forgiving myself.
- I often walk away from conversations obsessing over what I said—or "failed" to say.
- I remember every dumb thing I ever said or did.
- I take even constructive criticism personally, seeing it as proof of my ineptness.

If you answered yes to the majority of these statements, you are most definitely not alone. And by *you* I mean you and practically every other woman in the world. Of course, male impostors struggle with these issues too. However, in regard to failure, mistakes, and criticism, there really are some notable gender differences that shed light on why impostor feelings are so much more prevalent in women.

"It Must Be Me"

Perhaps the biggest difference has to do with where males and females ascribe blame. It's well known, for example, that despite doing better academically in the early school years, girls have less confidence in their intellectual abilities.[2] Partly this has to do with the tendency for females to blame failure on a lack of ability. Males do just the opposite. They credit themselves for their accomplishments and point to outside reasons for failure—the teacher didn't give us enough time to study, the test was too hard, the referee was unfair.[3.]

It's known as self-regarding attribution bias. Basically it's the difference between thinking that rises in your stock portfolio are a result of your savvy financial instincts and blaming losses on bad luck. A cartoon I once saw said it all. A woman struggling to zip her pants says, "Yikes, I must be getting fat!" A man in the same predicament says, "Hey, there must be something wrong with these pants!"

It's easy to laugh. But if you happen to be the one constantly pointing the finger at yourself, you've got a major problem. For starters, *where* you place the onus of responsibility for a failure directly impacts your options for managing it. Say you deliver a presentation and it bombs. It's one thing to assume ownership of the failure by admitting that you skimped on prep time. It's quite another to believe that you performed poorly because you're incompetent. In the first scenario the solution is clear: Prepare more next time. If, however, you believe things went badly because you are fundamentally inept, then you have no recourse for improvement. It's why when faced with the prospect of failing a course, female engineering students are likely to leave the program altogether, while their male peers are more likely to repeat the course and continue to pursue their degree.[4]

When you personalize failure or criticism in this way, you also allow them to mean more about who you are as a person. So when your boss or your advisor tells you that your work is inadequate, what you hear is "*You're* inadequate." You may be so accustomed to reading too much into things that even kudos can be interpreted as criticism. Like the graduate student who after successfully passing her oral exam was told by her advisor, "You couldn't have done any better." At first the student took it for the compliment it clearly was. On further reflection, though, she decided that what he really meant was, "Given your limited intellectual capabilities I guess that's the best we could expect from you."

Obviously, the more personal ownership you assume for your failures and mistakes, the harder you're going to be on yourself when they do happen. Berating yourself in the privacy of your own mind is one thing. But when other people judge your performance as lacking, it's another thing entirely. After all, now you have outside confirmation that you are indeed deficient. You think, *They ought to know—right?*

After Tony DiCicco's U.S. Women's National Soccer team clinched the 1999 World Championship, *Today show* host Matt Lauer asked the coach to clarify past statements that he coached women differently than men. DiCicco began by stating that the similarities are more common than the differences. But, he said, there *are* differences. Research shows that women tend to respond to criticism with shame or sadness, while men are more inclined toward anger. That certainly mirrored DiCicco's experience.[5]

Of female athletes he said, "I can go into a room of women, and I can say, 'We have some players that aren't fit,' and they all think I'm talking about them individually. . . .[But] if I did the same thing with men . . . the men on the team would go, 'Coach is right, I'm the only one fit here. The rest of these guys better get it together.'" As DiCicco put it, "Women internalize everything."

There are those who attribute men's tougher skin to the fact that they grew up playing sports. Exposure to constant critiquing by no-holds-barred coaches early on helps you learn that everyone has his mistakes pointed out. You realize that it's a vehicle toward greater competency and not personal indictment. Of course, Title IX opened the doors for many more girls to engage in sports under the same conditions. Even though he was coaching elite female athletes who have been involved in team sports since childhood, DiCicco still found that the "getting in your face type of coaching just doesn't work with women. Being overly critical in front of their peers doesn't work."

True, men do different things with criticism. But that doesn't mean they're always more confident or that their way of handling it is better. When they do take in the criticism, men are more apt to assume a defensive posture. On numerous occasions in my own workshops I've observed men who identify with the impostor syndrome deal with negative feedback by invalidating the messenger, insisting, *That guy was a moron,* or *What does she know about good design work anyway?* For that reason there are some who maintain that when delivering corrective feedback to men, a more public approach may be required. "When coaching men, you're coaching their egos a lot of times," said DiCicco. "So sometimes you have to address them in front of everyone, to make sure that they know, and everyone knows, where their shortcoming is."

It's possible you grew up being sheltered from failure. In chapter 2 you were asked to recall an early "failure." When Kim did this exercise, she immediately recalled the time she tried out for the high school basketball team. She was so confident she'd made it that she took a uniform home after the tryouts. Not only did Kim *not* make the team, she was the only girl to get cut. The coach sent her best friend home to deliver the bad news and retrieve the uniform.

How did Kim feel? Devastated, embarrassed, humiliated, disappointed, confused. How did those around her respond? The way Kim told the story, everyone knew how crushed she was, so family and friends alike went out of their way to be supportive. They reminded her of all the other things she was good at, and for the entire next week she enjoyed special attention from her parents—she even got to pick out a new outfit.

Kim's parents *were* supportive. But it's what I like to call the "Don't you worry your pretty little head" form of support reserved for girls. The message is subtle but clear: If it's too hard, you don't have to try. How else might Kim's parents have supported her after she failed to make the team? Well, along with all the nurturing, they could have said something like "That was a really tough break, honey. But if you really want to make the team, then you have to try again. And when you do we'll support you one hundred percent." Then they could have backed up their promise by putting up a hoop in the driveway, driving her to the local basketball court, or signing her up for a youth league. The point is, like Kim, too many girls don't learn to lick their wounds and then quickly get back out there and try again.

At the same time, if there are relatively few women in your workplace or at your organizational level, then a hypersensitivity to failure and mistake making should be seen in its larger social context. We know there are still those ready to magnify women's mistakes and sell them as proof of being underqualified. In other words, when you succeed, you succeed on your own as an individual. But when you screw up, you do so as a woman.

"I Can't Stop Thinking About It"

There's little danger of criticism rolling off you. Couple the tendency to internalize failure with the superior memory often ascribed to women, and a harsh review can become permanently seared in your brain. The same slight you can't stop thinking about may barely register for a man. It's the same with failure. Women will hold on to memories of transgressions long after their usefulness as a learning tool has passed. You can turn the same scene over and over in your mind grappling for answers to the unanswerable *How could I have been so stupid? Why did I say that?* Depending on the magnitude of your alleged offense, an incident that took all of ten seconds to occur may take you days or even months to get over.

Whether it's male bravado, denial, or, as some have argued, brain hardwiring, men generally don't hold on to their failures and mistakes the way women do—at least not with the same intensity or longevity. The good news/bad news is that you have easier access to emotions that men more often compartmentalize. It's also why so many women in my workshops report that when they do endlessly revisit some unsettling incident or something they did—or that they wished they'd said or done—their husband or boyfriend responds with things like *Just don't think about it,* or *Let it go,* or *Forget about it.*

He thinks he's being helpful. But to a lot of women, his seemingly more "rational" knack for externalizing things only makes you feel worse about your own more visceral response. Instead of feeling better, you wind up thinking, *If I were really competent, I wouldn't let this get to me this much.*

It's easy to take his being less rattled to mean he's more competent— or at least more confident—which to the untrained eye is often mistaken as one and the same. More likely you're seeing the effects of socialization. Girls are raised to believe it's their job to please others. You've grown up assuming that if someone isn't happy, it must be something you've done.

Boys got other not necessarily healthy messages. For example, one reason men may be more resilient to criticism is that they grew up hearing more of it. When Stanford researcher Carol Dweck and her team observed grade schools, they saw boys receive eight times more criticism for their conduct than girls.[6]

Boys grow up criticizing one another more too. They call it "razzing." Girls don't tend to do that. Communication experts tell us that females will make themselves the brunt of the joke, while males make fun of others. You're never going to hear a woman tease another woman about her expanding waistline—even in private. But men think nothing of publically razzing another man about his receding hairline or reminding him of the time he blew the big sale. Insult humor is a way to bond. In the workplace it's also a way to establish the pecking order, since (like other things) humor always flows down the organizational chart, not up.

Criticism also raises the prospect of abandonment, something that females tend to be more sensitive to than males. Which raises another point. This tendency for females to internalize and dwell on criticism and for males to tune out or lash out may actually be a reflection of how the two genders manage stress. To withdraw or attack in the face of criticism are both characteristic of the fight-or-flight stress response more typical of men. However, when a woman has been criticized, her first instinct is probably going to be to talk about it, a phenomenon UCLA stress researcher Shelley Taylor famously dubbed the "tend and befriend" response.

Communication is a tool that can be used in different ways. Generally speaking, men use it to create solutions and fix problems whereas women use it as a means to express thoughts and feelings. So when a man tells you to "stop thinking about it," he probably is trying to help. The problem is that "Stop worrying about it" also means "Stop talking about it," and that's not going to fly with you because when you're anguishing over some unsettling experience, you aren't actually looking for a "solution"—at least not in that moment. What you need to hear is "I feel that way too sometimes." Not because you're any less competent or confident. But because for you, talking it out and getting support *is* the solution.

How to Win at Failing, Making Mistakes, and Receiving Criticism

The reason I've been talking about failure and mistake making in tandem is that I know that in your competence rule book the two are synonymous—to make a mistake is to fail. In reality all mistakes do is make us human. There will be days when you turn out a top-notch performance and days when you bomb miserably. One day the critics—your professor, advisor, boss, clients, readers—love you, and the next day they pan you. Sometimes you'll nail it the first time, and other times you'll need to do multiple retakes.

> It's better to explore life and make mistakes than to play it safe. Mistakes are part of the dues one pays for a full life.
> —Sophia Loren

You think you're "supposed" to consistently bat a thousand. But if you know anything about baseball, you know it's not even statistically possible. A .333 batting average is considered outstanding, which means that for every ten pitches the batter only has to hit the ball three times. Even the legendary Babe Ruth batted "only" .342. You can't hit every ball that comes your way, and neither can anyone else. Remember, you can be at the top of your game and still strike out more often than not.

As real estate guru Robert Kiyosaki says, "Sometimes you win and sometimes you learn." When you change your mind-set about failure, both you and your confidence level will grow exponentially. You may have bombed, but if you're wise, you'll actually wind up being more competent.

Why do you think engineers spend so much time engaged in the process of failure analysis? They recognize that you can learn just as much from studying what went wrong as you can from what went right. It's what led Thomas Edison to famously remark, "I have not failed. I have successfully discovered twelve hundred ideas that don't work."

You can't change what happened. But you can use what happened to affect the future. It's why athletes go back and study the game tape, especially if they lost. You need to do the same. You know what it's like to hang up the phone and think, *I sounded like such an idiot.* Instead of beating yourself up, force yourself to take a moment to mentally rehearse a better response. Not in the regretful, self-berating way you normally do. But in the way athletes use visualization to improve their performance.

When you imagine a different way to handle the conversation, you essentially prepare yourself to know what to say—or not to say—as similar occasions arise. Plus a mental do-over helps you to depersonalize the situation. When you focus on what you can learn, you automatically make it less about you and more about growth and moving forward. This is important, because when you internalize failure, there's a greater chance that you'll give up following a setback. Don't. Instead study famous "failures" who pressed on despite the odds and the critics.

Creativity icon Walt Disney was fired from a newspaper job for "lacking ideas." Rowland H. Macy's store failed seven times before it caught on. Michael Jordan was cut from his junior varsity basketball team. Abraham Lincoln suffered repeated failures on the road to success, including losing in his first bid for Congress, when he sought the appointment to the United States Land Office, and when he ran for the United States Senate. From time to time everybody makes bad decisions. We all get egg on our face sometimes. The key is to see failure for what it is—a curve in the road, not the end of it. Like Billie Jean King said, "Be bold. If you're going to make an error, make a doozy."

Besides, it's how you handle failure that matters. Imagine literally taking a tumble with no fewer than a billion people watching. That's what Miss USA Crystle Stewart did when she fell during the 2008 Miss Universe pageant. She handled the fiasco by putting on a radiant smile, picking herself up, and clapping her hands over her head as if to say, "Let's have a round of applause." This was not the first time Stewart had to pick herself up after a failure. It took her five tries before being crowned Miss Texas. Failure is a given. You can't control what other people think. You can only control your own response—which begins with giving yourself permission to literally and figuratively fall as flat on your face as the next person.

Because it's coming from the outside, learning to think about and respond to criticism differently will probably be more challenging than dealing with failure. There will be times when no matter how thick-skinned you are, when someone criticizes you or your work it will take all of your emotional strength to quiet the relentless critic in your head. Precisely because criticism does pack an emotional punch, depersonalizing it requires a major shift in thinking.

Here again sports analogies can be useful. In international competitions, for example, judges recognize that even supposedly objective assessments involve a certain amount of bias. That's why they routinely throw out both the high and low scores and instead go with the average. You need to apply the same filter yourself. Hillary Clinton says she's "heard the nastiest of smears about myself [and] the most inflated and overheated praise." Which is why, she says, her general rule is to "disregard comments that are at either extreme and focus on what I believe to be true of myself. I try to take criticism seriously, but not personally."[7]

The next time your work is subjected to unflattering remarks, step back and ask yourself, "How would a person who took criticism seriously but *not* personally respond?" Then proceed to assess what's useful, what's not, and toss out anything that's not true to you.

> Do what you feel in your heart to be right,
> for you'll be criticized anyway.
> —Eleanor Roosevelt

Better yet, what if you were able to see critical feedback as a form of compliment? That's not to say it doesn't hurt, because it does. Once you've licked your wounds, remind yourself that those whose opinions matter are not going to give you feedback if they didn't think you were competent enough to use it. That's what Walter Cronkite did. While he was writing for his high school newspaper, the fourteen-year-old's confidence was badly shaken when his mentor sat him down and told him a story he'd written was "simply terrible." That one comment could have completely squashed his journalistic dreams. Instead, Cronkite says, as he gathered up his article and headed for the door he consoled himself by thinking, "Well, he couldn't be that mad at me if he's suggesting ways I could do better."[8]

Your best defense against criticism may be to go on the offense by proactively seeking it out. In decades of observing negative feedback in various work environments, Boston University psychologist Peter Gray found the most constructive and amiable interactions were those in which an individual reached out to an older mentor or peer for advice. Gray says its human nature not to want unsolicited advice. However, advice you ask for, even when corrective, is apt to be perceived as more helpful and less personal.[9]

Some of the feedback you'll receive in your life will be dead-on. But that doesn't mean there aren't plenty of critics who will get it wrong. Jack Kerouac, George Orwell, Anne Frank, and Sylvia Plath are just a few of the authors whose books were turned down—all by a single publisher.

After Elvis Presley's first—and last—appearance at the Grand Ole Opry, a producer advised him to go back to his previous job as a truck driver. And following dance legend Fred Astaire's first audition, a producer famously observed, "Balding, skinny, can dance a little." Let's face it, you don't like everyone else's work, so why should you expect everyone to love yours?

A certain amount of criticism and rejection are inevitable. Why not have a bit of fun with it? Wallpaper a room with your rejection letters, write a rap song about all of your bad reviews, or craft an imaginary future award speech in which you thank all the admissions officers, hiring managers, casting directors, or whoever turned you down (won't *they* feel embarrassed)! Whatever you do, don't burn those rejection letters or bad reviews. After all, they'll make for great reading when your biography is written!

If you still need help depersonalizing things, try this approach I learned from a couple of Coast Guard Academy graduates. In advance of their first deployment, a senior female commander offered the female cadets some final words of wisdom and a Q-tip to serve as an acronym: Quit Taking It Personally. Try it yourself. Tape a cotton swab to your bathroom mirror, tuck another inside your desk drawer or bag to use as a visual reminder.

Realize too that just because you *feel* inadequate doesn't mean you *are* inadequate. I can practically guarantee that sometime in the next twenty-four to forty-eight hours you will have the opportunity to feel stupid just like the rest of us. It's called life. Again, the words you use really do matter. You'll be amazed at how differently you feel simply by changing your response from "I am so stupid!" to "Boy, did I feel stupid."

There's no quick fix for ruminating. Just as with a song you can't get out of your head, stopping those pesky recurring thoughts begins with becoming aware of what's happening. Sharing your feelings does help.

When you talk things through, you'll probably see that whatever you were obsessing about is not as big a deal as you thought. You can also practice using what psychologists refer to as stop-thought techniques. The moment you realize what's happening, silently shout STOP! Repeat this as often as necessary. You can also try techniques like tapping on a table or deep breathing.

When the self-blame game begins, consciously call upon your more logical self for a "second opinion." In other words, the instant the thought *My proposal was so lame* enters your mind, check in to see what the "other side" thinks. With emotions out of the picture, allow your rational mind to counter with *I'm sure it was better than I'm giving myself credit for.* Even if by objective standards your proposal was weak, counter the impulse to blame yourself with the rational reminder *The more I write, the better I'll get.*

The Bottom Line

It's well known that from a young age females are more likely than males to internalize failure and personalize criticism. Women blame themselves more when things go wrong, take criticism personally, and have a hard time mentally letting go of both. By comparison, men's more tempered response can make them appear more confident and, presumably, more competent. In reality what we're seeing are the effects of socialization. Regardless of how we got here, a key to ditching the impostor syndrome is to learn a new, self-affirming response to failure, mistakes, and criticism—one that recognizes these things as both inevitable and offering priceless lessons on the road to success.

What You Can Do

Add these rules about failure to the *Competence Rule Book for Mere Mortals* you received in the last chapter:

- No one ever bats a thousand; if you connect three out of ten pitches, you're a star.
- Failures offer valuable lessons—and opportunities for growth.
- Failure is just a curve in the road.
- It's how you handle failure that counts.

What's Ahead

In the next chapter we look at how other people factor into your achievement experience, which may point to yet another reason why the impostor syndrome is more prevalent among women.

8

Success and the Female Drive to Care and Connect

I'm so glad I never feel important;
it does complicate life!
—Eleanor Roosevelt

Throughout life we are all presented with the opportunity to say *yes* to success. *Yes* to applying to school. *Yes* to moving far from home in search of that big break. *Yes* to hanging out your shingle or showing your work. *Yes* to a huge promotion or another chance to prove your mettle. *Yes* to changing careers or changing course entirely. Part of you is excited, perhaps even giddy. And why wouldn't you be? You've just put yourself one step closer to achieving your goals and realizing your full potential. Life is good.

But then the impostor syndrome kicks in and with it all the self-doubt and fear. Suddenly, merely *entertaining* the thought of saying yes makes you anxious—maybe even terrified. That's when the second-guessing starts. You worry, *Can I really handle it? Do I know enough? Am I smart enough?* Obviously the fact that you feel like you fooled people all these years complicates matters right off the bat. If only you felt surer of yourself, saying yes to success would be so much easier. Or would it?

Believing in yourself will certainly get you far. But shoring up your confidence alone may not be enough to completely squelch the anxiety you have about saying yes to success. That's because even though you are achieving as an individual, you're not in this success game alone. Simply put, to grow up female means that other people's feelings, needs, well-being, affiliation, acceptance, and opinions matter. Not just a little bit—they matter a lot.

And the fact that you *do* care means there will be times when it's hard for you to know where the fear is coming from. Are you hesitant to forge ahead because you don't think you *can* do it—or because on some level you understand that saying yes to success has implications for your relationships with others? This is your chance to find out.

It's Not All About You

It was the work of social psychologist Carol Gilligan that introduced me to the central role that care, concern, and connection for and with others plays in women's lives and choices. Her 1982 book, *In a Different Voice*, broke new ground when it challenged the prevailing theory of developmental psychology that said girls were largely incapable of achieving the same level of moral reasoning as boys. Rather than being lesser, she argued, women's moral reasoning is simply different and has at its core an "obligation to exercise care and avoid hurt" and to avoid isolation.

The reason this matters is because the road to success is nothing if not a series of choices. Choose to attend a local college or move halfway across the country or the world. Pick this major or career path or that. Take the job or turn it down. Negotiate for more or take what's offered. Share your accomplishment with others or keep it to yourself. Not coincidentally, these are also the very decision points where your impostor feelings get triggered.

Women in my workshops speak often of the real or perceived consequences of their achievement choices. These consequences play out in seven distinct ways, what I refer to here as "success scenarios." Two involve possible consequences of success *on* others, while the other five speak to the potential of success to impact your connection *with* others. Here's a summary.

Potential Consequences of Success

On Other People

- If I win, someone might feel badly.
- If I'm too successful, my family will suffer.

With Other People

- If I'm too successful, I may feel isolated at work.
- If I stand out too much, I'll feel isolated.
- If I'm too successful, I'll lose connection with my family, friends, or community.

- If I'm too successful, it may hurt my getting or keeping a man.
- If I act too smart, self-serving, or bossy, people may not like me.

Before exploring each of these success scenarios, there are a few things you need to know. For starters, if one situation jumps out more than the others, feel free to start there. However, to understand the larger picture I recommend you read all seven. Also, even though in some cases I do offer advice on dealing with certain scenarios, in the end there are no one-size-fit-all solutions to what are often personal situations and decisions. Instead, at the end of each scenario are questions to help you decide if you're dealing primarily with a confidence issue or if your reaction is more relationship-based.

Next, although these scenarios depict a primarily female experience, some may resonate equally with men from working-class backgrounds and men of color. Also, just because the ethos of care, concern, and connection is central to female culture doesn't mean every woman will identify with the more typically female responses described here. In addition, the message here is not that success is bad or is something to be avoided. To the contrary, I want you to go as far and as high as your dreams take you.

Finally and most important, the message is most definitely *not* that there's something wrong with your caring so much about others. Empathy, compassion, sensitivity, and thoughtfulness are valuable traits. So valuable, in fact, that not only do companies with the highest representation of female executives experience better financial performance, but as Gloria Feldt points out in *No Excuses: 9 Ways Women Can Change How We Think About Power,* Ernst & Young, Catalyst, the World Bank, and McKinsey have "all discovered over the past few years that once parliaments and corporate boards reach 30 percent female representation, the quality of decisions improves, the guys behave better, and there is less corruption."[1]

Empathy is also one of six aptitudes Daniel Pink cites as necessary to flourish in the new world economy. In *A Whole New Mind: Why Right-Brainers Will Rule the Future,* he makes the case that companies can move functions like customer service, tech support, and reading X-rays overseas. But you can't outsource empathy. Once diminished as "touchy-feely," empathy is now reshaping how training is conducted in fields such as medicine and law. These trends bode well for women, who more naturally tune in to other people's pain and apologize when mistakes are made—behaviors, says Pink, that can be a stretch for a lot of men.

Success at the Expense of Others

To be a woman is to experience a certain tension between your personal ambitions and wants and the image you have of yourself as an unselfish person who cares about others. In fact, in her quest to uncover what women themselves think about ambition, psychiatrist Anna Fels found that most shunned the very word. "Ambition necessarily implied egotism, selfishness, self-aggrandizement, or the manipulative use of others for one's own ends," says Fels.[2]

And why wouldn't it? From a young age, girls learn from their mothers to sacrifice themselves by putting others' needs first. This notion that being virtuous lies in self-sacrifice, says Gilligan, "has complicated the course of women's development by pitting the moral issue of goodness against the adult questions of responsibility and choice." These first two success scenarios depict this core dilemma.

Scenario 1: If I Win, Someone Else Loses

Even as girls, females are highly sensitive to the feelings and needs of others, and achievement situations are no exception. If you got an A and your best friend got a C, you may have lied about your grade to protect your friend's feelings. Caring is commendable. However, often what you're also seeing is the belief that your success will somehow diminish others—a belief that can cause you to feel more guilt than pride. As the British actress Rachel Weisz told a reporter, "Any success—getting a good degree, getting an agent, getting on TV [makes me feel guilty]. As if somehow by doing well, I was depriving someone else of something—it could be anyone, sister, mother, friend."[3]

The idea that if you win, someone else has to lose reveals itself in subtle ways. There are women, for example, who will remain with an employer even when it's clearly in their long-term interest to move on. You may be staying in your comfort zone to keep your impostor fears at bay. However, it's also possible that you stay because you believe they "need" you. Loyalty is admirable, just not when it's always at your expense.

Competitive success can be especially loaded for females because winning violates the code of caring. Sports psychologists tell us that boys will battle their best friend tooth and nail, beat them, and then shake hands. But if relationships are central to your life, competition can be fraught with inner conflict. It certainly was for National Spelling Bee contestant Zoe Londono, who at age twelve was called "the Human Dictionary." In an NBC *Dateline* segment Zoe went head-to-head with her best friend, Sheila, and beat her. The victory was bittersweet. "We're best friends," said Zoe. "I just beat my best friend. I'm sorry."[4]

Obviously, there are women who thrive on competition, and you may well be one of them. Yet even seasoned competitors and epic tennis rivals Martina Navratilova and Chris Evert struggled to strike a balance between competition and connection. The two would share bagels an hour before a match, go out and battle tooth and nail, then return to the locker room, where the winner would console the loser. Not because the winner was *sorry* she'd just trounced her opponent. But because each knew what it felt like to lose.

Martina especially struggled to figure out how to care and compete at the same time. Her onetime fitness coach and partner, basketball star Nancy Lieberman, felt that in order for Martina to reach the top she had to hate Chris. "[Martina] tried that for a while," says former athlete and author Mariah Burton Nelson, "but it didn't work for her so she went back to sharing bagels and laughter with Chris in the locker room. The two remain friends."[5]

Empathizing with the loser or with the underdog is fine. The problem comes in when you routinely suppress any pride or excitement about your own achievement in order to spare another person's feelings. In her work with gifted elementary school girls, Dr. Lee Anne Bell found that this tension between empathy and achievement can cause females to want to change the rules altogether. When she asked a group of girls to role-play a hypothetical situation in which one girl won a science prize but then dismissed her accomplishment in front of a friend who was envious of her win, the girls were able to act the scene out with ease.[6]

Next Bell instructed the girls to find ways the winner might respond that would enable *both* girls to feel good about themselves. This task proved considerably more daunting. At first the girls came up with options like "tear the trophy in half," "give it to the teacher," "leave it in school," or "give the trophy away, it's just a piece of metal." Although all of these strategies did preserve the relationship, they still sacrificed the winner being able to feel good about her achievement. Finally the group arrived at a solution focused *not* on individual achievement but on changing the system of judging altogether. If students got to work cooperatively in teams rather than competing as individuals, the girls surmised, everyone would get to do creative, high-quality science projects, and *everyone* could win.

The female desire to change the system from "I won and you lost" to "We all won" is a powerful reflection of what clinical psychologist Georgia Sassen refers to as women's "heightened perception of the 'other side' of competitive success . . . [a sense] that something is rotten in the state in which success is defined as having better grades than everyone else."[7] It also casts the difficulty women have in claiming credit for their achievements in a different light—one that, according to Dr. Peggy McIntosh, speaks to other dimensions of the impostor syndrome that can't be addressed by raising confidence.

McIntosh sees a lot of authenticity in feelings of fraudulence, wondering if perhaps those who really think they are the best and the brightest are the real frauds. "When women apologize or falter in public, or refuse to take individual credit for what they've done, I think we should listen twice," she says, because these behaviors may help us to "question the myth that those who have power individually deserve it." She adds, "When women feel fraudulent, often they are trying to share power, privilege and credit in ways that have not yet been recognized."[8]

If you identify with this success scenario, ask yourself:

- Does your ability to feel and express empathy toward others prevent you from feeling or expressing pride in your accomplishments?
- If yes, what would you do differently if you were not concerned with how your success made someone else feel? Be specific.
- How can you be sensitive to others and feel good about your achievements at the same time?
- If you are in a situation you know you've outgrown, how much has to do with fear of stepping out of your comfort zone and how much is out of concern that they "need" you?

- Are you using loyalty as an excuse to avoid challenging yourself?
- If so, are there ways you can achieve your own goals while also being considerate of others, like going out of your way to help find a suitable replacement or offering to stay on to train that person?

Scenario 2: If I'm Too Successful, My Family Might Suffer

If you have a family, any career advancement that requires you to spend more time at work is going to trigger concerns about the impact of your success on loved ones. If moving up in the organization also entails a physical move, it can mean disrupting your partner's career or children's education or being away from aging parents. These decisions are difficult enough. Feeling like an impostor makes it that much harder to parse relationship considerations from your usual self-doubt.

One thing that can help is to at least recognize that your guilt is not entirely self-generated. No one raises concerns about a man's ability to work and raise children at the same time. Even at the highest levels, no one assumes he's not up to the job. But society is quick to sow these seeds of doubt about you—*seeds that, if you're not careful, can take root in your own mind.* After all, success enhances a man's likelihood of being a good provider and makes him deserving of the title "family man." There is no comparable term to describe a woman who provides financially for her family because she's seen as pursuing her career at the *expense,* not for the *sake of,* her family.

If you feel selfish or guilty for being driven, remember that to have children is to experience a certain amount of parental guilt—period. Thinking of others first is admirable. At the same time, there's a reason flight attendants tell you to put your oxygen mask on first before helping children. Rather than see your success as coming at the expense of your family, make sure you give equal weight to the ways your success *serves* them. Of course there is the obvious financial contribution you make. In addition, though, consider how your children benefit from having an accomplished role model, one who is pursuing her goals and utilizing her talents.

If this success scenario speaks to you, ask yourself:

- How much of your reluctance to take on more responsibility or to relocate is because you feel inadequate, and how much is a genuine concern about what it might mean for your family?
- Is it possible that you are using your family as an excuse to stay inside your comfort zone?
- If you knew your family would be okay, would you have the same level of doubt about your ability to take on a new challenge?

We just looked at two scenarios that have to do with the impact of success *on* others. Now it's time to explore the ways that saying yes to success can factor into your relationship *with* others.

How Success Can Impact the Connection Between You and Others

One of the exercises in my workshops involves asking participants to generate a list of self-expectations or inner rules that contribute to their feeling like impostors. Two rules that invariably come up for women are *Don't act too smart* and *Always downplay your accomplishments*. No surprise there.

Next I ask them to name the perceived consequence of breaking these rules. The most obvious, of course, is that other people might find out that you're a fraud. After all, if you act like you know the answer or that you're "all that," and you turn out to be wrong or average, people will know you're an impostor. But that's not all that's going on here. When asked why they care what people think of them a more fundamental female fear is revealed, namely, *People may not like me.*

This is not just insecurity. Females learn young that being "too" anything not associated with traditional notions of femininity can put you at risk of not being liked—a well-documented dilemma that led Facebook COO and mother of two Sheryl Sandberg to tell an audience, "I want my son to have a choice to contribute fully in the workforce or at home, and I want my daughter not only to succeed but to be liked for her accomplishments."[9]

This is important because when connection is paramount in your life, any decision that holds the potential to lessen the connection between you and others can be disconcerting. As Gilligan observes, in achievement women recognize "the danger [of] isolation, a fear that in standing out or being set apart by success, they will be left alone." To different degrees, the next four scenarios speak to this core issue of isolation.

Scenario 3: The Higher I Go, the More Isolated I'll Be

The last thing most male executives worries about is being the only man at his level. You, however, are keenly aware that the higher up the organizational chart you climb, the more male and pale the landscape becomes. And for women, it really is lonely at the top. According to *Fortune* magazine, in 2010 only eleven of the Fortune 500 companies were run by women, down from fifteen the previous year. Among Fortune 1000 companies, a total of fourteen women had the top job. The isolation is even more profound if you are also a person of color who is expected to leave her—or his—racial identity at the door.

You don't have to occupy the executive suite to know that a promotion can incur jealousy and even resentment from people who were once your peers. Men have to deal with this too, of course. But even in tightly knit work groups men tend to relate to coworkers more superficially—or at least in a less familial way than do women. Guys might bond over a drink after work or on the golf course. But it's the women who organize the office parties, collect the money for the baby-shower gift, and decorate for the holidays. The more familylike the atmosphere, the tougher it can be to leave work pals behind, especially if your former coworker is now your direct report.

Women will often attempt to minimize the discomfort by trying to still be one of the gang. The problem with this strategy is that organizations are based on the more hierarchical relationships men prefer. So even if your former peers embrace you as one of them, your behavior has violated an unwritten rule that managers are supposed to mainly socialize with people at their level. It's okay to occasionally lunch with your former work pals, but it's considered a bad career move not to shift primary allegiance to the new management level.

If you identify with either example, use these questions to parse what you're really dealing with:

- Is your apprehension about advancing into senior ranks a function of confidence, or is it the stress of knowing you'll be the only one who looks like you?
- If you knew you would not feel isolated, would you experience the same level of fear about advancing?
- How much of your hesitation to vie for promotions stems from self-doubt, and how much has to do with maintaining relationships with coworkers?

- Would you experience the same level of fear about being promoted if you weren't worried about alienating people you work with?

Scenario 4: If I Stand Out Too Much, I'll Be Isolated

Feeling isolated is not just a function of job level. It can happen any time you work in an overwhelmingly male-dominated environment—something that you learned in chapter 2—and can easily contribute to self-doubt in women. Think about how you feel when you walk into a networking event where you're the only woman: Do you feel confident and in control? Or do you feel self-conscious, perhaps even a little intimidated? If you chose the later, you're not alone.

Psychologists wanted to understand the possible effects of gender-imbalanced settings on advanced math, science, and engineering students. So they had them watch videos portraying a summer leadership conference. One video showed a conference where men outnumbered women three to one, and another portrayed a conference with equal numbers of men and women. Not surprisingly, women who watched the first video reported a lower sense of belonging and less desire to participate.

What is significant was the finding that just *watching* the gender-imbalanced video caused these elite female students to experience faster heart rates, perspire more, and be more easily distracted—all indicators of stress.[10] Knowing this can help in those real-life situations where you might judge yourself for letting your minority status get to you in the first place. Now instead of thinking, *If I were really competent, I wouldn't be so unnerved*, you understand that you can be perfectly competent and still experience stress in these situations.

If you identify with this success scenario, ask yourself:

- Am I anxious about being in a male-dominated environment
  because I really don't think I'm competent enough, or am I
  experiencing the normal stress that comes from feeling isolated?

Scenario 5: If I'm Too Successful, I'll Lose Connection with Family, Friends, and/or Community

Gender is not the only factor that can lead you to worry about the alienating effects of success. If you are a person of color, you may experience cultural pressure to downplay your academic or professional success in order to avoid being accused of "acting white." Similarly, if you are a first-generation professional, your success may alienate you from the people you grew up with—sometimes to a painful extent. Even if you want to talk about your work with family or friends, it's not always easy. If they don't ask you about your work, you feel hurt. If they do ask, it's obvious they don't really get what it is you do. Rather than trying to bridge this new divide, you may attempt to circumvent it altogether. You avoid mentioning that prestigious college or job around hometown friends lest they assume you think you're "better" than them.

The loss of connection may be so intolerable that some people deliberately choose a job below their training or abilities. I once met a Ph.D. in business who had taken a job as a bookkeeper. The impostor syndrome had something to do with her lowering the occupational bar, but it was also a way to close the connection gap. "When people find out I have a Ph.D.," she said, "I can immediately feel this gulf widening between us."

Sometimes the distance caused by a career decision is more physical than emotional. It's scary enough to move far from home; feeling like an impostor only adds to the anxiety. If you also happen to belong to a religious, racial, or sexual minority, then this can further complicate your decision. Not only are you leaving friends and family behind, but depending on the demographics of the new locale, you may cut yourself off from your larger social network as well. When you are forced to decide between advancing in your career and experiencing social isolation or in some cases even the risk of physical violence, it's that much harder to separate legitimate misgivings from impostor fears.

Any kind of major change or transition will trigger impostor feelings. If you identify with this success scenario, ask yourself:

- How much of your reluctance to say yes to success is related to self-confidence, and how much comes from wanting to avoid feeling alienated emotionally from family and friends?
- If you're hesitant to move, would you still be reluctant to go if you knew you would be welcome and happy in the new location? If the answer is yes, then your impostor fears probably outweigh the relationship concerns.

Scenario 6: If I'm Too Successful, It Could Hurt My Chances of Getting or Keeping a Man

You might think accomplished women worrying about not finding love is a thing of the past. In reality the women in my workshops speak often about the challenges they face on the relationship front. There is a reason MIT professor Sheila Widnall includes on her list of *10 Reasons Why Women Don't Go into Engineering* the concern that a female with the highest math score won't get a date to the prom. The dating scene has never been easy for "nerdy" guys, but it's probably not because women are threatened by a smart man. At least not in the way some men feel about being "outsmarted" by a female—especially on their own turf.

Even if you personally brush off such nonsense, every heterosexual woman who's ever studied in a male-dominated field such as math or science knows that the response to the question "What's your major?" is not exactly a dude magnet. One female physics major was actually coached by a male friend to lie and tell prospective dates that she was majoring in early-childhood education. Apparently he thought other males would be less intimidated by a woman preparing to command a classroom of five-year-olds than by one who might someday run a laboratory of fifty-year-old men.

There aren't a lot of men who worry that being "too successful" will hurt their love life. But depending on your age, I bet you remember the famous 1986 *Newsweek* cover-story prediction that "a single, 40-year-old woman had a better chance of being killed by a terrorist than getting married." *People* magazine fanned the fear when it featured photos of Diane Sawyer, Linda Ronstadt, Donna Mills, and Sharon Gless with the headline "Are These Women Old Maids?" and warned: "Most single women over 35 can forget about marriage." Years later the terrorist line was introduced to a whole new audience when it showed up in the 1993 movie *Sleepless in Seattle.*

As it turned out, there were no such dire consequences for women who put off marriage to focus on their career. In fact, twenty years later *Newsweek* admitted it had misrepresented an obscure demographic finding, tossed in a terrorist reference that was intended to be a joke, and generally created a scenario that had little basis in reality. But a powerful seed had been planted in the minds of many single women: You can be highly successful or you can have love, but you can't have both.

Even women who have found love admit to worrying about the consequence on their relationship of advancing *too* far in their career. Of course, most couples realize that a middle-class lifestyle requires two paychecks. However, if you happen to be one of the estimated 40 percent of women in the United States who outearns her spouse, unconsciously you may be concerned with the effect of your success on the male ego—something that's even more of an issue for couples who work in the same organization or industry.

If you identify with this success scenario, ask yourself:

- To what extent are you letting concerns that you'll be less desirable to a man impact your career decisions?
- How much of your reluctance to say yes to success is a lack of confidence, and how much has to do with concerns about the impact on intimate relationships?

Scenario 7: If I'm Too Smart, Self-Serving, or Bossy, People May Not Like Me

The value you place on being liked can also impact how you behave—or, in some cases, don't behave. According to New York University professor Clay Shirky, even when the situation calls for it, his female students "aren't just bad at behaving like arrogant, self-aggrandizing jerks. They are bad at behaving like self-promoting narcissists, antisocial obsessives, or pompous blowhards, even a little bit, even temporarily, even when it would be in their best interests to do so." He adds, "Whatever bad things you can say about those behaviors, you can't say they are underrepresented among people who have changed the world."[11]

His comments were made in a blog post titled "A Rant About Women." As you can imagine, they caused quite a buzz, even catching the attention of National Public Radio and the BBC. Shirky's rant was prompted by a male student who asked him to write a job recommendation. When he asked the student to elaborate on what the letter should say, the professor received a draft full of superlatives. It was only after sending off a toned-down version of the letter that Shirky realized that because of that over-the-top draft, the student got a much better recommendation out of him than he would have otherwise.

It also caused him to worry that most of his female students couldn't write a letter like that, explaining, "I'm not concerned that women don't engage in enough building of self-confidence or self-esteem. I'm worried about something much simpler: not enough women have what it takes to behave like arrogant self-aggrandizing jerks." And what it takes, he argues, is *not caring what people think about you.* That's a problem. Because women *do* care what people think about them—and as it turns out, with good reason.

Shirky went on to predict that more of his male students will go on to become famous for no other reason than that "men are just better at being arrogant, and less concerned about people thinking they're stupid (often correctly, it should be noted) for trying things we're not qualified for." Here we agree.

However, the really big boat that Shirky missed was his initial failure to recognize the backlash for women who *are* self-aggrandizing. What we're really seeing here is not so much female modesty or insecurity as women's internal responses bumping up against certain social realities. Namely, even if a woman *wanted* to behave like an arrogant self-aggrandizing jerk, and even if she didn't give a hoot about being judged or ostracized or isolated, if she does care about being considered *competent,* she can ill afford not to care.

This is important to understand because it would be easy to assume that the reason you're hesitant to do things like negotiate for more money or take on a leadership role is that you lack confidence. And that may well be true. However, as you are about to learn, for females, being *too* smart, or *too* bossy, or *too* self-serving, has consequences.

IF I ACT TOO SMART, PEOPLE MAY NOT LIKE ME

If you grew up near the top of your class you may have experienced at a young age the conflict between being smart and being liked. This is true of course for boys too. People who specialize in working with academically gifted students, however, will tell you that gifted girls often presume that boys do not like intelligent girls. Sadly, with good reason: Of the four categories of gifted and nongifted males and females, gifted girls were deemed least popular.[12] When you consider the strong social pressure to fit in, it's easy to see why a lot of gifted girls learn to downplay or devalue their abilities in order to avoid ostracism by their peers. It's a lesson that may well be carried into adulthood.

Being self-effacing or dismissing your abilities or accomplishments as "no big deal" in front of others sure sounds like the impostor syndrome. However, if you sense in certain settings that your superior intelligence is costing more points than it's winning you, then you may unconsciously hold back.

There is a difference between minimizing an achievement to guard against "bragging backlash" and believing you're not actually responsible for it. In other words, you may be perfectly comfortable, even proud of your smarts. But if you believe you'll be thought less of if you *talk* about your accomplishments, you may either (a) stay mum, or (b) downplay your success with statements like "It was nothing" or "I was just lucky." After all, you don't want people to think you're "full of yourself." Such behaviors look and sound like impostorism when, at least in part, they may represent a social strategy designed to maintain relationships.

After all, if you care about what people think of you, then you're also going to go out of your way to protect the other person's feelings. And being modest helps you do that—that is, if you're a woman. In one study, college students who scored higher on an intelligence test were asked to disclose their scores to students who did not perform as well. When women shared their scores with another woman in a modest (i.e., non-bragging) way, they assumed that the other person liked them more. They also thought that by being modest, they allowed the other person to feel more intelligent and confident. For men the opposite occurred: Men who bragged about doing well assumed that women liked them *more* and that the other people felt *better* about themselves.[13]

Finally, for some females the concern is not that people won't like them for being too smart but for not being smart enough. After fourteen-year-old Melissa Rogers tied for twenty-second place at the 1999 National Spelling Bee, her hometown held a parade in her honor. When she made the competition again the next year, the pressure was on to at least improve on last year's performance. While cramming for the contest, Melissa says she "had a breakdown. . . . I was thinking, you know, *What if I just totally spell my first word wrong and then I'm out in the first round?* I was, like, *Then nobody in my town will like me anymore.*"

IF I ASK FOR TOO MUCH, PEOPLE MAY NOT LIKE ME

Make no mistake about it: A lack of confidence is a huge reason why most women undervalue themselves in salary negotiations. At the same time, a reluctance to ask for more money may also be based on a keen understanding of the social realities for women who do ask.

For instance, observers who watched videos of men and women in mock job interviews not only perceived the women who asked for more to be "less nice" and "more demanding," but also said they'd be significantly less willing to work with a female candidate who attempted to negotiate her salary than with one who did not.[14] It's worth noting that while the men in this study penalized female candidates who asked, women penalized *both* male and female candidates who attempted to negotiate.

Just because you may be judged more harshly doesn't mean you should walk away empty-handed for lack of trying. What it does mean, say the researchers, is that while a collaborative approach benefits all negotiators, for a woman it may be crucial to make an extra effort to be liked during negotiation.

IF I'M TOO BOSSY, OTHER WOMEN MAY NOT LIKE ME

Earlier you learned that impostors sometimes attempt to skirt detection by keeping a low profile. If that rings true for you, it may explain a reluctance to step into the role of leader. However, it may be that you're simply weighing the benefits of being in charge against the interpersonal repercussions of being seen as too "bossy." In a 2008 survey by the Girl Scouts, a third of girls aged eight to seventeen who indicated a desire to be leaders worried about making people mad at them, being laughed at, not being liked, or coming across as bossy.[15]

Typically we think it's men who label female leaders as bossy. What you hear less about is the negative response women have to other women whom they perceive as bossy. For all the progress we've made, management experts Pat Heim and Susan Murphy observe, "women are somewhat more comfortable with a powerful woman who plays down her importance than one who does not."[16]

After all, women are used to men exerting power. It's the reason a male executive can drop a file on his female assistant's desk with a curt "Have this ready in an hour" and get away with it. But if you do that to another woman, it's going to cost you major points on the likability scale. It has to do with an unspoken dynamic between women that Heim and Murphy call the "Power Dead-Even Rule." The Power Dead-Even rule says that in order "for a positive relationship to be possible between two women, the self-esteem and power of one must be, in the perception of each woman, similar in weight to the self-esteem and power of the other."

That's why your male counterpart can head off to his meeting confident that his demand will be met with no real consequences to the boss-assistant relationship. But if you want to maintain a good relationship with your female assistant, then the two essential elements of self-esteem and power must be kept "dead even." This means that before you can delegate you need to first invest time and energy chatting about the weekend, the family, or otherwise psychologically balancing the relationship.

This desire to keep things even is one reason that women issue so many more apologies then men—something that can make you both look and *feel* less capable. You probably apologize for things that aren't your fault. Not because you really think you're to blame but as a leveling device. For example, let's say a coworker named Deb sent you the wrong information. You don't want Deb to feel bad, so you start out by apologizing for not being clear about what you needed. At which point Deb probably offers her own apology for misunderstanding. Since you both apologized, everything is "even." With the balance restored, the relationship is intact and you can get back to the business of getting the correct information.

But if Deb's name is Dave and Dave doesn't understand the game, he might respond to what was a purely ritualized apology on your part with *Well, obviously you weren't very clear, because I sent you exactly what you asked for.* Okay, now you're pissed because you weren't *really* sorry! You were just trying to help him save face and preserve the relationship.

If you identify with this success scenario, ask yourself:

- How much of your being afraid to say yes to success is because you think you're an impostor, and how much comes from learning to act less intelligent and knowledgeable than you really are in order to fit in?
- Do you downplay your accomplishments because you feel undeserving, or are you trying to make the other person like you?

- How much of your reluctance to ask for more is your impostorism, and how much is your concern that you'll be disliked if you do ask?
- Is it possible that one of the reasons you think people won't like you if you negotiate is because, like the women in the negotiation study, you don't like it when others negotiate?
- How much of you not taking on leadership positions is your lack of confidence, and how much is a desire to maintain positive relationships with other women?
- How much of your apologizing has to do with actually believing you did something wrong, and how much is a ritualized mechanism to help the other person save face?

The Bottom Line

There are significant benefits to the female culture of care, concern, and connection. At the same time, being other-oriented can complicate the decision to say yes to success. That's because on some level you understand that in different scenarios, your success can have an impact on your relationships with others. As a result, when you're faced with a career decision it can be difficult to tell whether you're dealing with a confidence issue or a connection one.

It's unlikely that you'll totally stop caring about what people think of you or about the effects of your decisions on others. And that's okay. Instead, strive to not be so consumed with other people's needs and opinions that it keeps you from moving up, speaking up, or otherwise saying yes to success.

What You Can Do

- Review the seven success scenarios to see which, if any, you identify with, and answer the related questions.
- Moving forward, when success anxiety strikes, pay attention to how much is the impostor syndrome and how much has to do with a finely tuned and often realistic awareness of what may lie on the other side of success.

What's Ahead

Success is complicated for everyone, and even more so for women. As you are about to discover, there are additional factors other than the impostor syndrome that may cause you to hesitate in the face of success.

[9]

Is It "Fear" of Success or Something Else?

It is our choices . . . that show what we
truly are, far more than our abilities.

—J. K. Rowling

f you've done well in the past in work or in school, then it would be rea-
sonable to expect that you will continue to be successful in the future.
At least that's how it works for most people. But you're not most people.
You're someone who believes that the achievements you've managed to
pull off until now have been on a wing and a prayer. So naturally the idea
of becoming even *more* successful is going to be stressful. There's more

responsibility. More people will be counting on you. The stakes are higher. There's farther to fall. And of course with each new success, the chance increases that they'll find out you're really not that competent or talented after all.

On a day-to-day basis you may not think a lot about success per se. That is, until either you decide to raise the bar or something happens to raise it for you. It was the latter scenario that caused my friend Sharon to call me in a panic. She was being recruited for a great position at a significantly higher level. The new job would put her in charge of more people and a larger operation. It also came with a huge salary bump.

Sharon was excited—and anxious. I'd been in enough of these conversations to know that my job was to talk her down off the impostor ledge. I was supposed to remind her of how normal it is to feel nervous when faced with a new challenge. That she was more than capable of handling any challenge that came her way. How she'd be crazy not to take what was clearly an incredible opportunity. But that's not what happened. Instead I said simply, "Maybe you just don't really want it."

In seconds Sharon went from shock to relief. Make no mistake about it, my friend *was* afraid to take the job, although not totally because she didn't think she could do it. What happened to Sharon happens to a lot of impostors. You become so used to those niggling voices of self-doubt that you totally forget to heed other voices. Voices that may have far more to do with *who you are* and *what you want* than with how much you know or what you can do.

Personally I hardly ever talk about impostors being *afraid* of success. That's not to say that success can't be intimidating or even downright terrifying, because it can, and all the more so if you think you're a fraud. However, I believe everyone has a powerful inner desire to succeed. And that includes you. At the same time, I've met hundreds of women who, like Sharon, find themselves standing hesitantly at the crossroads of success.

In the last chapter you learned that there are other reasons you might hold yourself back that can easily be confused with a lack of confidence. Here the focus is on whether there are aspects of success itself that may be causing you to pull back. By bringing to your consciousness some of the legitimate reasons for your success anxiety, you'll be in a better position to decide for yourself: *Am I afraid because I don't think I can do it—or is it because I don't want "it"?*

Are There Downsides to Success?

There are so many obvious benefits to success that they hardly require mentioning. And I certainly do not want to go on record as advocating that you or any woman not take her rightful place at the table or in any way contribute to the already diminished economic status of women. In fact, further into this book, I'm going to encourage you to shoot even higher.

At the same time, you really are allowed to define success for yourself. Which is why I'd be remiss if I didn't point out some of the less talked-about aspects of success that may be giving you pause. For instance, hopefully when you began in your career it was because you had a passion. Maybe you loved solving complex programming issues or working directly with kids or doing in-depth research. The problem is that organizations are famous for taking people who are happy as individual contributors and turning them into managers or bureaucrats, and for pulling them away to serve on committees or perform other good-citizen functions. All of which only takes you farther away from what drew you to the work to begin with.

Being considered a specialist can bring challenges as well. This one can catch you off guard because your whole life you were told to "just pick something" and specialize in that. But after reaping the rewards of your hard-won expertise, you may be surprised to discover that the more narrowly focused your work becomes, the more your success can funnel you into increasingly specialized and repetitive roles. Over time, the work can lose the excitement it once held, so naturally the idea of becoming even more specialized will be disconcerting.

More success also generally means more complexity. If you thrive on running a large operation, managing lots of people, and juggling multiple projects simultaneously, this is a nonissue. But if you've always been the keep-it-simple type or if you started out loving the fast track only to find yourself wistfully watching the gardener who cares for the company plants, then the more complicated things get, the more averse you'll be to advancing.

Success Female-Style

It's impossible to talk about women's greater susceptibility to the impostor syndrome or for that matter about women's supposed fear of success without looking at how women tend to *view* success. The fact is, hardly anyone talked about women being afraid of success until the 1980s when they began entering the traditionally male work world in large numbers. Once they did, it was naturally assumed that women would aspire to achieve the traditional measurements of success—status, money, and power. Plenty of women have. But not everyone got on board, or at least not to the exclusion of other priorities.

Whether you embrace the money/power/status model or not, it is no coincidence that situations where these elements are in play—salary negotiations or being singled out for recognition in your field or being tapped for a promotion—are the very times when you wonder, *Do I really deserve it?* or *Can I really handle it?* You assume it's the self-doubt talking. And maybe it is.

However, it's also true that women have always had a more layered definition of success, which means it's just as likely that your anxiety could be signaling a mismatch between the social definition of success and what matters most to you. It's not that status, money, and power aren't important. For you they may be paramount. Overall, though, women place—and it should be said, have been *allowed* to place—a higher value on the quality of their personal and work lives. It's one of the reasons, for example, that women-owned businesses tend to be smaller than businesses owned by men. Instead of being motivated by the opportunity to be the "boss" and to grow the enterprise as big as possible, more women report starting a business to be personally challenged and to integrate work and family.[1]

To be clear, having different priorities is not the same as shooting low. Even high-achieving women often share a more expansive view of what success looks like. When asked to define it, female medical school students, residents, and faculty alike described the need for "career efficiencies that allow individuals to excel professionally while also honoring their personal values and responsibilities."[2] In plain English: They want a successful career and they want a life.

There are, of course, more than a few men who would love to forgo obligatory golf outings or to log fewer hours on the job in order to spend time with their family. Unfortunately, men are more confined by a view of success measured exclusively in work and material terms. We know, for instance, that male business owners are more than twice as likely as women to cite family or financial pressures to keep a steady, traditional job and be the breadwinner as the main challenge to being able to make it as an entrepreneur.[3] And a study exploring male-female attitudes about success found that many men who had pursued it to the detriment of their family later looked back at their lives with a sense of regret.[4]

For many women, success also has a lot to do with the nature of the work itself. We know that income plays a smaller role in female self-esteem. So when given the choice between making a lot of money and doing work that is personally enjoyable or meaningful, a woman is more likely than a man to choose the latter. It's the reason why efforts designed to attract more women into the fields of science, technology, and engineering must go to great lengths to emphasize the social value of the work to female candidates. Ideals are so important to women that in an experiment where college students who were enrolled in an introductory physics class were asked to reflect, even briefly, on their most closely held values, the women showed a significant improvement in their academic performance. The exercise had no effect on the male students.[5]

If the work you do does not reflect your authentic self, you can become a different kind of fraud. You were cast as an attorney or an accountant when deep down you long to dig in the soil, help find a cure for autism, or be the next Jane Goodall. But rather than heed your calling, you go to job interviews and tell them you love doing this or that knowing full well that you're lying through your teeth. One day you wake up and wonder, *How did I get here?* It's a different kind of fakery for sure. Still, it can make it tougher to distinguish whether what you're feeling is intellectual fraudulence or vocational inauthenticity.

It's not only women who get tripped up here. Just yesterday I received an email from a fellow named Frank with the subject line "What if I really *am* an impostor?" After recently completing his Ph.D. in physics, Frank was admitted into a postdoctoral program. By all outside measures Frank is a success. He should feel great about what he's achieved. Instead the guy is so miserable he is seriously considering giving up his fledgling career. Frank writes:

I can't shake this feeling that I really am a fake. I'm not really good in the field I'm supposed to be an expert in, and that's not talking bad about myself, that's an actual objective assessment. I know what I am capable of, and I know what I should be capable of, and there is a huge difference.

Make no mistake about it, Frank *was* faking it. But perhaps not in the way he thought. True, he did offer clues that he suffers from impostor syndrome: He certainly was hampered by the false belief that his being considered competent requires that he come up with "original ideas" (thinking, you may recall, that is indicative of the Natural Genius competence type whom you met in chapter 6). At the same time, I couldn't help but notice that there was nothing in Frank's letter that remotely suggested a passion for physics. In fact, he ended by saying:

I'm really depressed, and I have no idea what it takes to make me feel good again. I've given up basically all my hobbies "thanks" to science, and now I'm stuck in a rut, where I get the impression I'm not wanted/ needed/useful.

Obviously if Frank's hobbies and the need to know that his work matters weren't important to him, he wouldn't have bothered bringing them up. The fact that he did suggests that his main problem was not that he lacks the intelligence to succeed in his field. The problem is that he is either in the wrong field altogether or in the right field but applying his training in the wrong arena.

It's something I see more often than you might think, especially among well-educated people. You invest six, eight, twelve years of your life and in some cases well over a hundred thousand dollars in training to become a lawyer or a surgeon or a professor only to wind up feeling conflicted and anxious. You think you're just worried that you still don't have the intellectual goods to succeed in your field when in fact it may be that in your heart of hearts, you know you're on the wrong path. Given everything you've invested, you feel tremendous pressure to not "waste the degree."

If that rings true for you, first know that nothing is wasted. You can't always fully see it now, but every experience you've ever had in some way contributes to your own unfolding story. Look at me. It was only after investing a lot of blood, sweat, and tears to earn my doctorate that I realized I didn't need the degree to perform the work I do. But I don't regret the experience for a moment.

That experience is what inspired me to become an adult educator, which led me to be a professional speaker and workshop leader, which gave me the credentials to snag a position in the training and development department of a Fortune 200 company, which, once I was on the inside, allowed me to move into management in a marketing function, where I gained the knowledge and skills that enabled me to go on and launch my own business, which, sixteen years later, brought me to write this book using firsthand knowledge of my three main audiences: students, people in the corporate world, and entrepreneurs. My point: No experience is wasted.

American author and journalist Christopher Morley once said, "There is only one success, to be able to live your life in your own way." How you define success matters, and even more so if you feel like an impostor. The question you need to ask is *If the work I was doing and the environment in which I was doing it reflected my gifts and priorities, would I still question my competence to the same degree?* If the answer is no, then a career shift may be in order. You don't have to walk away tomorrow. But at least when the anxiety sets in you'll know what you're dealing with. If you do decide to change course, start by giving yourself permission to move in whatever direction your natural gifts and interests take you.

Instead of trying to force yourself into a certain definition of success, imagine what it would be like if we all lived in a society that placed as much value on work-life balance and on pursuing work that reflects our authentic self as it does on who has the most money, power, or status. There are the obvious solutions that everyone would benefit from, like having the same six-plus-week vacations enjoyed by most of the rest of the industrialized world or easing the burden on women's time by enlisting men to help out more at home.

But what if there were other, more outside-the-box ways to allow people to enjoy some of the benefits of traditional success *and* more meaningful balanced lives? I'm thinking here of things like finding a way to make job-sharing arrangements work at higher organizational levels the way they do at lower levels, or encouraging young people to take time between high school and college to explore various interests before choosing a career path.

I've thought a lot about different ways to help women entrepreneurs find a way to achieve financial success and still live life on their own terms. We already know that the money part is seriously lacking. In the United States there are half as many majority women-owned businesses with over $1 million in annual revenues as ones owned by men. Current efforts to encourage more women to grow microbusinesses into seven- and eight-figure enterprises emphasize strategies such as hiring and managing staff, raising capital, and creating the infrastructures necessary to support a larger-scale operation. I love that these programs exist and believe that they're absolutely vital in helping women overcome both structural and attitudinal barriers to growth.

Having spent the last decade and a half working with women in small solo businesses, I know many of them have operations that really could be scaled up. Many hold back because they lack either the confidence or the skills to go after capital, or both. However, there are others who really *do* know that they have what it takes to build an empire but who have zero desire to manage people or systems. In fact, a big reason a lot of women business owners fled the corporate world to begin with was to get away from all that.

As Albert Einstein once said, "The problems that exist in the world today cannot be solved by the level of thinking that created them." So what if there were a way to catapult more women-owned businesses to the seven-figure mark that was not contingent on "fixing" these steadfast lifestyle entrepreneurs? What I'm thinking here is that there is no shortage of experienced executives who feel stymied in their efforts to reach the top—individuals who've demonstrated acumen for managing and growing large-scale operations and who are drawn to entrepreneurship but don't have a viable idea of their own.

Another way to encourage more financially successful female-owned businesses might be to match talented but complexity-averse business owners with female execs who really *would* enjoy the challenge of growing a multimillion-dollar enterprise. Should the new venture hit its financial target, the result would be a win-win-win . . .

- It's a win for the people hired to fill the new jobs required of a larger operation.
- It's a win for the former executive who gets to utilize her skills in a more autonomous fashion than she could in a corporate job.
- It's a win for the company founder, who gets to continue working in the parts of the business that drew her to start it in the first place.
- And of course, assuming the partnership works, everyone wins financially.

You don't need to be an entrepreneur or an executive to affirm your own definition of success. When you do, though, it's just possible that old fears about whether you're "smart enough" or "good enough" or, for that matter, "successful enough" will be cast in an entirely different light. You may find that what up until now you've thought of as your fear of success may instead be a healthy reluctance to succeed on *someone else's* terms.

Are You Wise to Feel Like a Fraud?

You can be extremely ambitious and still be uncomfortable being a rising star in a system in which you know that the best and brightest do not necessarily rise to the top. One where hiring and promotion decisions are just as likely to be based on petty considerations like insider politics, age, even height and weight as they are on a person's merits. If you do make it, you can feel like a fraud. Not because you doubt your competence but because you see the game for what it is—a point raised by Dr. Peggy McIntosh decades ago.

In fact, whereas the vast majority of researchers zeroed in on family dynamics as the source of fraudulent feelings, McIntosh saw something very different. In her thought-provoking series *Feeling Like a Fraud*, she put forth a very different explanation for why the impostor syndrome is more common in women.[6]

[Women feel like impostors] because we know that usually those who happen to get the high titles and the acclaim . . . are not "the best and the brightest," and we don't want to pretend to be either. When we entertain nagging thoughts about whether we belong or are deserving to be at the podium, or in the boardroom, or tenured, or giving an interview to a newspaper, or earning a good salary for what we like to do, we may be deeply wise in feeling anxious and illegitimate and fraudulent in these circumstances.

When you are achieving in a system that is at odds with who you are—one that too often values style over substance, face time over productivity, competition over cooperation, there's bound to be a certain amount of inner tension. If that rings true for you, then know that what you experience as fraudulence may at times be a healthy reaction to the low-grade deception and fakery that traditional success requires *of all of us.*

There's a reason it's said that the truth is rarely told between the hours of nine and five. It's hard to feel real when you're wearing a mask. And that's exactly what happens when you're trying to win at someone else's game or when you're fulfilling someone else's dream. Seen in that light, ambivalence about success may be a wise choice.

"Stressed for Success"

The most obvious reason you or any woman may be apprehensive about advancement is the time factor. Responding to a question about the lack of women in technology, Oracle Corporation co-president and CFO Safra Catz told her female audience, "You have to be better. You have got to work harder, work longer, be louder."[7] If you aren't exactly leaping at the chance to work harder and longer, it may be because you know that nine-to-five has already morphed into eight-to-late. Add to that the expectation that you be constantly tethered to your work by technology.

Even if do you covet that top spot, you understand that it's a lot easier to log ten- to fourteen-hour days, travel for business, and attend after-work functions when someone else is taking care of things at home. If you don't know, just ask the 75 percent of male executives who have a spouse who stays home full-time. Then compare their answers to those of the 74 percent of women executives who are married to someone who also works full-time.[8]

Women at all organizational levels know what it's like to feel constantly caught between a clock and a hard place. It's precisely this dilemma that led psychiatrist Anna Fels to conclude that the majority of working women today are "stressed for success." "As contemporary women evaluate their goals, they must decide how much of the stress and discomfort that comes with ambition they are willing to tolerate," says Fels. All the more reason it's important that you take time to sort out for yourself: Are you shying away from success because you feel inept? Or is it because you understand the sacrifices required to get and stay at the top?

On the Money

To really explore women's complex relationship with money would require a whole book. Instead we'll quickly touch on a few aspects of money that speak to the qualms many women have about financial success—qualms that can be easily confused with fear of success.

For starters, despite what you see in the media, financial success is not necessarily a sign of greater confidence. In fact, not only has materialism been found to arise from self-doubt, but increases in self-doubt also heighten materialistic orientation. The connection between materialism and poor psychological functioning led psychologists to conclude that materialism is a "precarious basis for judging self-worth."[9]

If being highly money-oriented is a turnoff, it's probably because you've seen what money can do to people. Obviously money can be used for enormous social good. But you also know it can turn people into jerks. In fact, psychologists found that just *reminding* people of money made them both less willing to help another person and more likely to put more physical distance between themselves and others.[10] You may think, *If that's what money does to people, count me out.*

The fact is, money really *does* bring happiness. Just not in the way you were probably led to think. As it turns out, it's what you *do* with money that matters. When given the chance to spend money on other people or on themselves, those who spent money on others felt happier.[11] Instinctively you know this. It's just that we live in a society that celebrates people who measure their success by their ability to amass a fortune. You hear far less about the people who measure their success by how good they are at giving it away. But that's what Rosie O'Donnell does. Over the years the entertainer has donated over $50 million to various charities, explaining, "When I started making the money, I said to the money person, 'If I'm ever on the *Forbes* list of richest people, you're fired.'"[12]

You don't need to be a multimillionaire to have a more socially oriented approach to money. In their interviews with minority women entrepreneurs, Babson College professors Mary Godwyn and Donna Stoddard discovered that having an outsider status can lead to better business practices. These entrepreneurs see business values as an extension of their personal values and profits as something to be balanced with social good and environmental sustainability. "This pattern is repeated in statistical evidence from around the globe that women contribute a much higher percentage of their earnings to social good than do men," say the authors."[13]

If money alone is not enough to inspire you to advance, it may be because you're sensitive to the hidden *cost* of money. If you're living a middle-class lifestyle, you know that money can both free you and trap you. You spend money to buy services and the latest time-saving devices. Yet in order to afford these devices, you must maintain a heavy workload. In his book *Time and Money,* Gary S. Cross sums up the dilemma this way: "The choice to consume more is the choice to be more exhausted. You make a decision to have weaker family ties, to have fewer friends. There are all sorts of things that go into the decision to have more goods."[14]

Still, it's confusing when all you've ever heard is people singing the praises of financial success. I mean, who *doesn't* want to be a millionaire? Money, as the song goes, does make the world go around. It's also what pays the rent, buys the food, clothes us, and keeps the lights on. If you already make good money, you may feel pressure to maintain the lifestyle your success has afforded you. At some point, though, you may ask, how much is enough? "Buy now, pay later" takes on new meaning when you gauge the true price of working more hours to make more money so you can buy more things. "If you spend your life energy on stuff that brings only passing fulfillment and doesn't support your values," write Joe Dominguez and Vicki Robin in *Your Money or Your Life,* "you end up with less life."

After you reach a certain financial threshold, even money can lose its appeal. If you find yourself wanting to hop off the fast track (or you resisted getting on it in the first place) or are content in middle management or running a small self-sustaining business, it may not necessarily be that you lack the confidence to do more. Rather the attitude I see in some women is *I'm making good money where I am. Who needs all the added grief?*

This "less is more" attitude typically associated with women is remarkably similar to that of a majority of New Zealand business owners. But not everyone is happy about it. According to an article in *Inc.* magazine, "At a time when American entrepreneurs aspire to improve their work-life balance, New Zealand—as a matter of public policy—is trying to coax its lifestyle entrepreneurs into spending a little less time enjoying life and a little more making money."

The "problem," as the government sees it, is that the country's business owners work just enough to buy a second home and a boat and to send their kids to school. After that the incentive to keep enhancing their personal fortune at the cost of sacrificing work-life balance seems to vanish. Most are so keen on keeping things simple that they avoid hiring employees. By one count, the entire country, with a population of 4 million, has just 240 businesses that employ more than 500 workers.[15] When you come from a culture like the United States, where people live to work rather than work to live, that's pretty remarkable.

Yet there are signs that even those who have money are starting to redefine what it means to be rich. As Chris Rock told CBS's Harry Smith, "Being rich is not about having a lot of money. Being rich is about having lots of options."[16]

Maybe your self-worth is not as dependent on your bank statement as it is for a man. But you also live in a status-oriented society. There may be times when you judge yourself for not being as financially driven as you think you *should be*. That's why it's so important to get clear about exactly what's going on. If the reason you earn less money than you *know* you really *could be* earning is that you feel like an impostor, then it makes sense to focus on bolstering your self-confidence. However, if the reason you're reluctant to go higher is that you know that achieving greater financial success will require an unacceptable demand on your time or because you believe making money is self-indulgent or evil, then no amount of confidence building will help. If that rings true for you, stop defining yourself as someone who is afraid to succeed and recognize instead that you may simply embrace a different definition of success.

What about you? If you are not motivated by money, what does inspire you to work harder or otherwise achieve your dreams? Do you have certain attitudes that prevent you from achieving financial success—attitudes that result in guilt or shame? Do you look at rich people with contempt, envy, or maybe a little of both?

Think too about how much money you make now and how much you'd like to earn. If you're like most women, you will probably shoot lower than you deserve—and less than you'll practically need in retirement. If so, know that there truly is no nobility in poverty. Whatever number you come up with, keep adding to it until you feel anxious. Then double it. You can give the other half away if you like. Just the act of thinking bigger will cause you to stretch your thinking about what's possible.

Find Your Own Success Comfort Zone

Any of these success scenarios can easily masquerade as fear of success. That's why it's so important that you step back to see what's really going on. Are you afraid to take that next big step because you genuinely don't believe you're intellectually or otherwise up to the challenge? Or are you apprehensive for any of the reasons cited here? Chances are it's not a simple either/or, but from situation to situation it's probably more one than the other.

One way to tell the difference is to imagine yourself as the confident, fully capable person you would like to be. If the supremely competent you was faced with the exact same decision, how would she feel? If you're still averse, then you know something other than confidence or lack thereof is at play, and you have an opportunity to explore what it is.

If pausing only briefly to affirm their values can cause women to do better on a physics exam, imagine what taking some time to reflect on what you care most about can do for you. Take a moment to explore what success means to you. Is it standing out in your field, being recognized or respected in your organization? Being promoted or elected? Being famous? Raising a healthy family? Making policy? Making money? Making a difference? A combination of the above? Remember, there is no right answer, only the right answer for *you*. As writer Anna Quindlen says, "If your success is not on your own terms, if it looks good to the world but does not feel good in your heart, it is not success at all."

The reason I'm pushing you to be crystal clear here is because as legitimate as your concerns about success may be, let's not forget that you also struggle with the impostor syndrome. And there's nothing quite like a good challenge to induce a full-blown crisis of confidence. I've seen how lifestyle or money issues can also be used as an *excuse* to continue to play small.

I saw this firsthand at a recent presentation I delivered to 150 managers and executives at a multinational technology company. Toward the end of the program a woman currently in middle management raised her hand to say she'd seriously considered senior management but held back because she saw how many more hours executives had to put in. The time demand is a valid consideration. Yet in the exchange that followed it also became clear that despite an impressive track record, the impostor syndrome caused her to question her ability to perform at that level. In other words, both things were true.

You may be of two minds about going after success as well. If so, I'll tell you the same thing I told her. Why don't you go be an executive or build a megabusiness or run for public office or go for the Oscar—and *then* decide if you don't like it? After the presentation I was swarmed by four women who wanted to know one thing: *Do you really think she should go for it, or did you feel like you had to say that?* The fact that they asked speaks to how difficult sorting out these issues can be.

The Bottom Line

When faced with the opportunity to achieve greater levels of success, indifference can easily be confused with fear and self-doubt. In fact, there are any number of non-confidence-related factors that can make you reluctant to move ahead, including a mismatch between your definition of success and what is expected, the additional demands that come with success, and your relationship with money. Once you're aware of these things you can sort out for yourself, are you anxious because you don't think you can do it, or do you just not want it?

What You Can Do

- Explore other reasons why you may be anxious or ambivalent about moving ahead, such as being in the wrong career, managing increased complexity, suffering the pitfalls of specializing, or having diminished time to do the work you enjoy.

- Your natural skills and talents are bound to be less leveraged if you're in a job that does not involve much, or enough, of what you most love to do. If you think a career change is in order, spend less time worrying about what you think you *should* do and ask yourself instead, *"What do I really love to do?"* If you're still not sure, consult a traditional career coach; if you are interested in self-employment, find a coach who specializes in helping people see ways they can profit from their passions.

- Take fifteen minutes to capture *in writing* what success means to you. If you get stuck, flip the question around and ask instead, *What am I not willing to sacrifice in order to have money, status, and power or to otherwise succeed?*

- Examine your relationship with money and how it impacts your desire to advance.

What's Ahead

In this chapter and the previous one you learned how factors
like relationships and how you see success can confuse the
confidence picture for women. Now it's time to switch gears.
Next we turn our attention to a challenge that all impostors face,
and women especially: the challenge to act more confident
than you really feel.

Why "Fake It Till You Make It"
Is Harder for Women—and
Why You Must

I'm very good at pretending that I know
what I'm doing when I don't.

> —Christian Siriano, *Project Runway*
> clothing design competition winner

You're finally starting to see yourself as the bright, competent, successful individual everyone else sees. But not completely. Despite all your progress, there are bound to be times when you still feel a little (or a lot) shaky. This is when you need to heed the often issued advice to newbies and impostors alike: *Just fake it till you make it*. The idea is that you don't have to wait until you feel sure of yourself before you step up your game. In other words, it's perfectly normal to be nervous as heck, just as long as you *act as if* you expect to be an unqualified success.

This strategy may strike you as being at odds with the challenge you're already facing. Here you've spent a lifetime pretending to be more confident than you really feel, and all it's ever done is reinforce your belief that you're an impostor. It's only natural that you'd think, *I already feel like a phony and you want me to pretend even more?* I know it sounds like a contradiction. But the short answer is: Yes, I absolutely *do* want you to start acting like the bright, competent person you really are, even when you don't always feel that way.

The premise behind "acting as if" is that you become what you do. It worked for James Taylor. The Grammy Award–winning singer-songwriter once said, "I started being a songwriter pretending I could do it, and it turned out I could." Seeing that you really *can* do the thing you didn't think you could do in turn generates real confidence.

Fake it till you make it is more than a catchphrase. It's actually been proven that pretending to act differently than you feel can cause you to feel differently. When scientists at Wake Forest University asked fifty students to act like extroverts for fifteen minutes in a group discussion, *even if they didn't feel like it,* the more assertive and energetic the students acted, the happier they felt."[1] It works the same way with confidence. You can still have serious doubts about whether you have what it takes to get elected, earn an advanced degree, or achieve any number of goals. What matters is that you do it.

I am fully aware that acting self-assured when you feel anything but is not easy, especially for women. Even when you see the merits of the fake-it-till-you-make-it strategy, you may fail to employ it. But not necessarily for the reason you might think. True, it is harder to feign confidence when you already feel like a big phony. However, even if you didn't identify with the impostor syndrome for any of a host of reasons we'll explore here, you may be uncomfortable faking confidence.

"Fake It Till You Make It" on Steroids

Bertrand Russell once said, "The whole problem with the world is that fools and fanatics are always so certain of themselves, and wiser people so full of doubts." Part of the reason you resist acting as if is because you know that sometimes those who are the most confident have the least reason to be.

On one end of the confidence continuum is the impostor syndrome. Fully capable people like you who have every reason to feel confident but don't. On the other end is a lesser-known but arguably far more dangerous condition known as irrational self-confidence syndrome (ISC)—a wonderfully apt term coined by former *Rocky Mountain News* reporter Erica Heath to describe the unjustifiably confident. If you've ever watched contestants audition for shows like *American Idol* or *America's Got Talent*, then you've seen people who seem unable to recognize the true limitation of their talents.

On television it's comical. But it's not so funny if you've ever had to work with or under a poor performer who can talk a good game. "Big talk and supreme self-confidence have landed many jobs in fields such as sales, marketing and elected office," writes Heath. "Once he's on the inside, the ISC patient can be difficult to spot if he plays the game right." Over time, she says, ISC employees move up the ladder, acquiring bigger budgets and more support staff, and frequently reorganizing their departments to avoid detection. "The best of the bunch can pull off this sleight of hand several times before sensing that it's time to pull up stakes. Just in time, they talk their way into a new, better job, leaving behind a mess and angry ex-colleagues."[2]

To be clear: This is not the same as the healthy confidence that comes from accepting that you can't possibly know everything but jumping in anyway. As you'll soon discover, that kind of confidence is not only a good thing, it's *essential* in overcoming the impostor syndrome. What we're talking about here is the danger of those arrogantly confident people who really do *think* they know everything.

The problem, says entrepreneur and self-identified impostor Steve Schwartz, is that [such people] "have a tendency to make others think they know what they're doing, which makes others tend to rely on them. It causes others to put them in charge of things it *seems* like they know how to handle. And, of course, since these people legitimately think they know how to handle these things, they are likely not to look it up or defer to people who actually know."[3]

Research bears out that people who do things badly are usually supremely confident in their abilities, while the better performers tend to make more humble predictions and therefore more accurate self-assessments. To be clear, not everyone who is confident (deservedly or otherwise) is either inept or reckless. Still, we've all run into people whose self-assurance far exceeds their actual base of knowledge.

There are hundreds of studies on the impostor syndrome—90 percent of them conducted by women. Oddly, there's been scant attention paid to another phenomenon that disproportionately strikes untold numbers of men. It's called "male answer syndrome." The term first appeared in a 1992 *Utne Reader* magazine article by Jane Campbell, who used it to describe the "chronic answering of questions regardless of actual knowledge." Not all men feel this compulsion, of course. Although, she says, there are not many men who like to say "I don't know," preferring instead to say things like "That's not what's important here." Campbell offered this tongue-in-cheek yet accurate description of male answer syndrome at work:

> [Men] try not to get bogged down by petty considerations such as, "Do I know anything about this subject?" or "Is what I have to say interesting?" They take a broad view of questions, treating them less as requests for specific pieces of information than as invitations to expand on some theories, air a few prejudices, and tell a couple of jokes. Some men seem to regard life as a talk show on which they are the star guest. If you ask, "What is the capital of Venezuela?" they hear, "So tell us a bit about your early years, Bob."

Psychologists at Southwestern University sought to determine whether such a thing as male answer syndrome actually exists. Through a series of studies they found three things. One: Men and women alike are indeed aware that when faced with a difficult or ambiguous question some people feel compelled to generate a rational-sounding answer rather than admit that they don't know. Two: Everyone believes that this tendency is much more common in men. Three: They're right.[4]

When you combine the bluster of irrational self-confidence syndrome with the false authority of male answer syndrome, you get yet another more typically male tendency. This one involves a small but vocal minority of uninformed men who nonetheless feel compelled to go out of their way to "enlighten" others, and women especially. And if you're unaware that it's happening, it can knock your confidence for a loop.

In a compelling essay in the *Los Angeles Times* titled "Men Who Explain Things," award-winning author Rebecca Solnit reflected on the many times men had explained things to her, "whether or not they know what they are talking about."[5] In it she recounts this exchange between herself, her friend Sallie, and their pompous party host:

He . . . said to me. "So? I hear you've written a couple of books."

I replied, "Several actually."

He said, in the way you encourage your friend's seven-year-old to describe flute practice, "And what are they about?"

They were actually about quite a few different things, the six or seven out by then, but I began to speak only of the most recent on that summer day in 2003, my book on Eadweard Muybridge, the annihilation of time and space and the industrialization of everyday life.

He cut me off soon after I mentioned Muybridge. "And have you heard about the very important Muybridge book that came out this year?"

So caught up was I in my assigned role as ingénue that I was perfectly willing to entertain the possibility that another book on the same subject had come out simultaneously and I'd somehow missed it. He was already telling me about the very important book—with that smug look I know so well in a man holding forth, eyes fixed on the fuzzy far horizon of his own authority. . . .

So, Mr. Very Important was going on smugly about this book I should have known when Sallie interrupted him to say, 'That's her book.' Or tried to interrupt him anyway.

Their host was undaunted, and so it took Sallie three or four more tries before he finally took in what was being said. At which point he was stunned speechless by the fact that she was indeed the author of a very important book that as it turned out he hadn't even read but had only read *about*. After a brief moment, Solnit writes, "he began holding forth again. Being women, we were politely out of earshot before we started laughing."

Of course, men like this explain things to other men too. And there are certainly women who can, in Solnit's words, "hold forth on irrelevant things and conspiracy theories." But, she says, "the out-and-out confrontational confidence of the totally ignorant is, in my experience, gendered." It's a lot of other women's experience too.

Unfortunately, rather than distrust the expounder of misinformation, women often doubt themselves instead. Look at Solnit. She's an accomplished author of half a dozen well-regarded books. If a woman with this level of success can even for a moment be, in her own words, "willing to believe Mr. Very Important and his overweening confidence over my more shaky certainty," it's not hard to imagine the tamping effect the superior tone of presumed greater knowledge can have on someone who perceives herself as having far less under her belt. If you've ever been on the receiving end of this kind of "confrontational confidence," you know how intimidating it can be, and all the more when the man who is explaining things to you is older, has a bigger title, exercises power over you, or all of the above.

Solnit says it best: "It's the presumption that makes it hard, at times, for any woman in any field; that keeps women from speaking up and from being heard when they dare; that crushes young women into silence by indicating, the way harassment on the street does, that this is not their world. It trains us in self-doubt and self-limitation just as it exercises men's unsupported overconfidence."

Certainly the occasional encounter with an egotistical man who explains things is unlikely to affect your confidence in any lasting way. However, if you were raised by, study under, or work for the terminally pompous, your view of "acting as if" may be permanently tainted. You think, *If that's what it means to fake it till you make it, then count me out.*

When you do meet an explainer, the first thing you need to do is to see the situation for what it is. First, don't immediately assume that the person knows what he's talking about. And definitely don't question your own knowledge or your better judgment. If your instinct tells you that someone is full of hot air, trust it. This sort of uninformed bluster can be infuriating. If you feel your blood pressure rise, it may help to shift from anger to pity for someone who is so sadly self-important. Most important, remind yourself that what's happening has everything to do with the explainer's insecurity or narcissism and nothing to do with you, your intellect, or your abilities.

When an uninformed man is explaining things to you, you have two choices. You can walk away or you can engage him. If you decide to reply with accurate information, recognize that the odds of any sort of admission on his part are next to nil. However, if the situation in any way undercuts you or your work, especially in a public forum, you should push back. You don't need to be confrontational in order to stand firm in the face of someone else's confrontational confidence. Instead, calmly but firmly set the record straight and in no uncertain terms.

What about you? Have you ever been on the receiving end of an uninformed man or woman explaining things to you? If so, how did you feel about yourself at the time? To what extent has this experience affected what you think about faking it till you make it? Knowing what you know now about the sometimes false authority of the overly confident, what do you think you might feel, say, and do differently in the future?

The kind of blustery confidence on steroids you've just seen is off-putting and potentially dangerous. So it makes sense that you'd have misgivings about anything that seems to suggest you need to become "like them." Pretending to know more than you really do feels deceptive, phony. It's the stuff of scoundrel politicians, unscrupulous used-car salesmen, home-repair contractors, and others fairly or unfairly associated with "bullshitting."

Ted Koppel Changed My Life

He doesn't know it, but I can honestly say Ted Koppel changed my life. Or at least his words did. The broadcast journalist and longtime host of the award-winning late-night news program *Nightline* spent the better part of his career interviewing world leaders, scientists, and leading experts from a myriad of fields. In a 1985 special student edition of *Newsweek,* senior editor and columnist Jonathan Alter turned the tables on Koppel by asking, "Do you ever feel you don't know enough about a subject to ask the tough questions?"

Koppel's answer forever changed how I looked at the world. He said: "No. When I can, I'd rather go into a program knowing as much as possible about the subject, but I don't consider it a handicap [when] I know next to nothing." Part of the reason is that Koppel saw himself as a conduit for the audience. If he didn't understand, he figured, his audience probably didn't either. Even with this explanation, when you're accustomed to disqualifying yourself from applying for jobs because you lack one or two minor requirements, the idea that someone could be unperturbed at knowing "next to nothing" is both stunning and illuminating.[6]

But that wasn't even the part that changed my life. What changed my life was the reason Koppel gave for being so unfazed: "[I figure I can] pick up enough information in a short period of time to be able to bullshit my way with the best of them." And that, ladies and gentlemen, is a key difference between *most* women and *most* men. When I made this point during a talk at Cornell University, a professor in the audience piped up to concur: "Not only do males consider bullshitting to be a skill, but if you're really good at it," he said, "you're considered a bullshit artist!"

Obviously there are plenty of men (my father among them) who either couldn't or wouldn't BS to save their own life. Still, on the whole, males really are more comfortable with this kind of winging it—a difference that goes a long way in explaining why the fake-it-till-you-make-it strategy comes more naturally to men. It also makes you wonder whether everyone is even on the same page about what it means to be an impostor.

After all, one of the statements researchers use to gauge whether a person identifies with the impostor phenomenon is, I *can give the impression that I'm more competent than I really am.* A high score on this question would ordinarily indicate the shameful impostor feelings talked about here. But what if by answering this question in the affirmative what the person really means is *Sure, I can give the impression that I'm more competent than I really am, and it's pretty great that I can pull it off!* The reason I ask is because I've met more than a few men who see it exactly this way. I'm not referring to the blowhards you met earlier. I'm talking about honorable men who readily and, like Koppel, proudly admit to occasionally faking it but who don't experience faking as a problem. When viewed in this light, the notion of being an impostor takes on an entirely new meaning.

Neither perspective is right or wrong. That said, you should at least be aware that the distinctively female bias against faking it can hold you back. Because while you're waiting until you've got it all together, dotting every *i* and crossing every *t,* getting more and more credentialed, a lot of your male colleagues are taking full advantage of the healthy benefits of the fake-it-till-you-make-it approach.

The Real Poop on Bullshitting

People who do make it up as they go along are often considered "bullshitters." But what exactly does that mean? Answering that question requires you and I to wade knee-deep into a big old pile of, well, bullshit. I've met a lot of women who have a strong aversion to the notion of bullshitting. If you do too, then the first thing I'm going to urge you to do is to frame it in a way you *can* live with. The reason I want you to replace one word or phrase for another is not to obscure what's happening, it's to clarify what's really going on.

Remember, part of the reason Ted Koppel said he "does not consider it a handicap when [he] knows next to nothing" is because he knows he can "pick up enough information to be able to bullshit his way *with the best of them.*" I've emphasized these last few words so you understand what he's really saying. The guy is a distinguished broadcast journalist. Was he talking about lying or deceit or manipulation? No.

Okay, then what are some ways of describing what Koppel meant that you would feel more comfortable with? What about *winging it . . . holding your own . . . rolling with the conversation . . . being in the moment . . . trusting your instincts . . . improvising*? What you call it doesn't matter. What is important is recognizing that there are times in life when you have to be able to fly by the seat of your pants—and that this kind of going with the flow can be very freeing. But unless you're open to rethinking BSing as it relates to the fake-it-till-you-make-it approach, you may never get to experience that kind of freedom.

To help us understand some of the reasons it's harder for you and a lot of other women to make it up as you go along, we're going to turn to someone who has distinguished himself as the leading authority on, what else, bullshit. His name is Harry G. Frankfurt and he's a professor emeritus of philosophy at Princeton University. A short essay Frankfurt wrote in 1986 called "On Bullshit" went on to become a pint-size book and a surprise bestseller. Frankfurt's observations about the nature of bullshitting provide a useful jumping-off point for exploring some common female misgivings about faking it in general and BSing in specific.[7]

Before we begin, I want you to read my lips: You absolutely do not have to become "a bullshit artist" to overcome the impostor syndrome. But you do need to understand any unconscious resistance you have to the advice to "Fake it till you make it." That way you can decide for yourself whether you see some advantages to acting as if.

"It Feels Too Much Like Lying"

By far the loudest objection I hear from women is that faking it feels dishonest. Obviously, if you think bullshitting is just another word for lying, and authenticity is important to you, then the very idea of faking it is going to be a turn-off. However, Frankfurt invites the reader to consider a line from Eric Ambler's novel *Dirty Story*, in which a character recalls a lesson he learned as a boy from his father: "Never tell a lie when you can bullshit your way through."

In other words, unlike the liar, Frankfurt maintains, the bullshitter "is neither on the side of the true nor on the side of the false. . . . He does not care whether the things he says describe reality correctly. He just picks them out, or makes them up, to suit his purpose." Often that purpose is to cover for some sort of error, mishap, or lack of knowledge. Clearly, talking your way out of a serious breach of ethics or the law is objectionable. But some situations really are harmless and the quick thinking it takes to get out of a jam can actually be to humorous effect.

Shortly out of college, Tom worked as a recreational counselor at a YMCA. He was only a few weeks into the job when the director asked him to teach a cross-country ski class. There was just one problem. Tom didn't know how to cross-country ski. But he did know how to read. So he bought a book on cross-country skiing for beginners and within days was leading his first class. All things considered, Tom did quite well. That is, until they came to the first hill. Tom went first to show how it was done and upon reaching the bottom promptly wiped out. When I asked if he was embarrassed Tom positively beamed. "Not at all! I just leapt up, turned to my students and said, 'And *that's* how you get out of a fall!'"

You'd think that after spending decades studying differences in male-female communication, Georgetown professor Deborah Tannen had seen it all. Yet even she was amazed by her attorney's response to a disconnected conference call caused when he accidently bumped the phone with his elbow. Once the other party was back on the line Tannen just assumed he'd apologize and move on. But that's not what happened. Instead he said, "Hey, what happened? One minute you were there, the next minute you were gone!"[8]

As she thought about her attorney's "knee-jerk impulse not to admit fault if he didn't have to," Tannen decided it could be "a very adaptive strategy in many settings." It's also an approach women rarely use. As importantly, we tend to judge those who do. In her review of Tannen's book, *Newsweek* contributor Laura Shapiro's response was, "Knee-jerk? or just plain jerk?" before voting for the later. You may agree. As tempting as it may be to lay claim to superior ethics, the research as to whether females are more ethical than males is mixed.

Boys grow up learning how to exaggerate. More happened in the backseat of the car with the girl than really did. The fish was "this big." Other things are larger than life. When you grow up playing sports, you learn that bluffing and exaggerating are part of the game. You learn to fake a pass, to fool the other team by changing up your play, and to use bravado to psych out your opponent and "get inside his head."

There are no comparable lessons in traditional girls' games. No one tries to bluff her way through dolls or fake a move in hopscotch. That's not to say girls don't argue over whether a player stepped outside the line or went out of turn. But if there is a disagreement over the rules, girls will stop and renegotiate for the sake of the relationship. To girls, rules are flexible and can be adjusted depending on the players or the situation. But in traditional boys' games, rules are sacred. Players never change the rules to accommodate a less skilled player, for example.

Cover-ups aside, the reality is that there are times when you need to appear calm and collected even when you're nervous as heck. To do that really does require that you pass yourself off as something you're not. In other words, you have to be able to bluff. It may seem like a fine point, but Frankfurt says that bullshitting is actually "closer to bluffing than to telling a lie." It's not so much about trying to deceive, he says, as it is an attempt to convey a certain impression of yourself.

You see this kind of impression management all the time in the business world, especially early in one's career. After all, everyone has to start somewhere, and that includes you. "Even if you haven't encountered great success yet," says Donald Trump, "there is no reason you can't bluff a little and act like you have." Doing this involves a certain amount of posturing—something that definitely comes more naturally to males. Even in the animal kingdom, survival of the fittest often means that the male of the species has to appear bigger than he really is. "Display behavior," as it is known, is used to attract females and ward off rival males. Two-legged males also recognize the value of such behavior.

Drawing on his animal instincts, Pierce Brosnan told a reporter, "You've got to be a fighting rooster, man. You've got to get out there and preen those feathers and look like you know what you're doing and hope you know what you're doing and have a good time."[9] That's not to say Brosnan or anyone who knows how to bluff is insensitive to failure. When he was unexpectedly replaced as the lead in the James Bond movies, he too had to deal with "the punch and the pain of being passed over or rejected." Nor is he fearless. The idea of singing and dancing in the film *Mamma Mia!* made him "terrified to my core."

Still, men are more likely not only to exaggerate their abilities but to fabricate them altogether when necessary. Partly it has to do with the awareness that the door of opportunity can close quickly. That's why, Brosnan said, "[you] have to be as tough as old boots." When they ask, "'Do you sing?' Of course I sing. 'Do you sky-dive?' Of course I do. 'Do you fight?' Yeah. 'Are you a lover?' Are you kidding?" It's not so much about "faking it," he said, as it is about being "prepared"—and, once again, trusting in your ability to figure it out as you go along.

As you learned in chapter 6, the assumption that you have to know everything before you can consider yourself competent is a big reason why you (and a lot of other people) walk around feeling like a clueless fraud. Nothing could be further from the truth. In a spot-on blog post titled "No One Knows What the F*ck They're Doing (or 'The 3 Types of Knowledge'),"[10] Steve Schwartz breaks down knowledge into three categories (he's since added a few more, but these are the basics):

1. Sh*t you know
2. Sh*t you know you don't know
3. Sh*t you don't know you don't know

The people who you're certain are so much more confident and able are actually no more knowledgeable or capable than you are, says Schwartz. It's just that instead of dwelling on the second category, non-impostors have figured out that most knowledge falls into the third category, stuff you don't know you don't know. The big difference between you and them, he says, is that "they realize it's okay to not know everything, but strive to nonetheless." In other words, they're comfortable with not knowing. If you know you have the basic ability to figure out what you don't know, then there's no reason not to raise your hand. In other words, it's not lying if you know there's a better-than-average chance you can ultimately back it up.

What about you? Are there situations where you could benefit from engaging in a bit of harmless posturing? Assuming you see the value in "acting as if" in these kinds of situations, can you pinpoint what stops you? Is it fear of breaking the rules? Worry that you really don't have what it takes to back it up? Afraid they'll find you out?

Obviously, for someone to call your bluff about something you purport to know or do only heightens the precariousness you already feel. But if you really embraced the idea that you are both *capable* of figuring things out as you go along and that with obvious exceptions it really is *okay* to do so, it would change everything.

All you have to do is think of a situation where the ability to fake it till you make it would come in handy. Now imagine what it would be like if you really believed that you don't have to know everything ahead of time. How would you feel if you enjoyed unlimited faith in your ability to wing it a bit? What would you do differently? If you still can't imagine it, then run, don't walk, back to chapter 6 and reread the Natural Genius and Rugged Individualist portions of the *Competence Rule Book for Mere Mortals*.

"It Feels Like Getting Away with Something"

While BSing is not, by definition, synonymous with lying, Frankfurt says that the bullshitter *is* trying to get away with something. Here again, men may have an advantage. Even though they respect the rules, males are always looking for new and creative ways to test the rules without getting caught by the official. Breaking the rules without getting caught is considered part of the fun of the game. So if you're playing a game and the ball is a little bit out, if you think you can get away with it, you can call it in. This tracks with what a male coworker once told me: "Some mistakes really only matter if you get caught," he said. "It's like sports. If the official didn't see you step on the line, then it didn't happen."

Girls are socialized to be concerned with fairness and openness. If you do something wrong, you apologize. Boys get a different message. They learn that saying "I'm sorry" is a sign of weakness. With women it's just the opposite. In fact, it doesn't matter if no one catches us, because we'll turn ourselves in! Over the years I've heard scores of stories from women about these kinds of "true confessions." One had cowritten a book with her husband. At the start of every book signing she'd announce that they'd found some typos and the book was being reprinted. "The third time I did it my husband pulled me aside and said, *'Stop telling them that!'*"

Then there was the researcher who told of being flabbergasted to receive a call congratulating her on being singled out for an award. "There must be some mistake," she said. Believing there were so many more "worthy" candidates to choose from, she actually suggested that the selection committee might want to reconsider. When the caller assured her that they'd spent months arriving at their decision, she replied, "Then a few more days won't hurt anything."

You certainly don't have to adopt the more male model of covering for yourself. Be aware, though, that this other extreme is not exactly ideal either. I'm not suggesting that you hide mistakes as a matter of course—especially not ones that have serious consequences for other people or your organization. However, there really are some harmless foul-ups that are just not serious enough to warrant blowing the whistle on yourself. For males, this ability—whether on the ball field or the dating field—is considered a badge of honor. Women, on the other hand, tend to like to go "by the book," especially on the job. For you, breaking the rules is going to provoke guilt, not pride.

You may also be wary that someone is trying to pull a fast one. On the consumer level, women are more suspicious of anything they consider marketing hype. I've seen many female business owners fail because they self-righteously refuse to take advantage of perfectly legitimate marketing tactics, for example, creating the appearance of success, for fear of being seen as misleading. To fake it till you make it feels like you're somehow cheating (something it's been found that people with the impostor syndrome are actually less likely to do). You think, *Better to avoid any kind of fakery than to risk being accused of getting away with something.*

Here too, cheating is in the eye of the beholder. The same behavior men consider a skill you're apt to see as evidence of your inadequacy. "People raved about my presentation," said one ad executive. "But all I could think was, 'If they only knew that was really just a bunch of bullshit I threw together at the last minute, they wouldn't think I was so great.'" If you work well under pressure, rather than responding to kudos by thinking, *Fooled them again*, instead think, *I'm really good at pulling together useful information in a short period of time.* That really is a skill and that's no bull. In fact, in the next chapter you'll meet some people who've launched their entire career by bending the rules.

As an achiever you may be bothered by the fact that there's a certain degree of *laziness* in acting like you know more than you really do. More than simple carelessness or inattention to detail, Frankfurt says, it's the idea that in trying to get away with something, one isn't really trying. If you are a perfectionist, a workaholic, or a by-the-book type, then not bothering to put in the effort can be a turn-off in and of itself.

At least it was for National Public Radio senior news analyst Daniel Schorr. As a college student in New York City in 1930, he aspired to be a music critic. On his way to meet the renowned *New York Times* music critic Olan Downes, Schorr read a review Downes had written of the previous evening's New York Philharmonic concert. Of the soloist Joseph Segetti, Downes wrote, "Segetti's tone was his usual impeccable but the profile of the tone left something to be desired." Schorr panicked. "What the hell does that mean? I mean, this guy has a level of [understanding of] music I'll never reach." So he asked his new mentor what his critique meant. That's when, Schorr said, Downes "put his hand on my shoulder and said, 'Boy, don't let that kind of thing worry you. That's the bullshit that you write when you're on deadline.'" That's the day, Schorr laughingly said, that he decided, "music criticism was not a respectable career."[11]

What about you? Have you ever gone to the other extreme and volunteered more information than was necessary? Perhaps you've pointed out flaws in your work no one would have otherwise noticed, or you focused everyone's attention on what you don't know rather than on what you do. If so, stop unnecessarily turning yourself in. Instead, the next time you're tapped for something that feels out of your league or someone compliments your work—even if you know it could be improved—say "Thank you." Then zip it.

Are you letting a concern that you might be "getting away with something" prevent you from occasionally pretending to know more than you do? If so, look for contradictions in your belief system. It's easy to take a strong stand against faking it when men do it. However, is your opinion about "getting away with things" more flexible when it occurs in a more classically female context, like trying to appear thinner, or younger, or otherwise presenting an image of yourself that is not entirely true?

Are You a Confidence Snob?

It's easy to be critical of self-important jerks and male confidence run amok. At the same time, you may also have a built-in bias against people who are "too" confident, even when they can back it up. And it doesn't take much to trip women's anti-ego meter—including mine. Some years ago I consulted with the CEO of a company that sold day planners. Sheila's major competitor at the time was Franklin Covey—Covey being Stephen Covey, who wrote the mega-bestselling book *The 7 Habits of Highly Successful People*. The CEO had been approached by an up-and-coming speaker named Jim who was pitching himself as her company's spokesperson. I'd actually seen Jim present, and he really was quite good but not yet spokesperson material. He'd also self-published a book, but his few hundred sales were no comparison to Covey's millions.

None of this dissuaded the supremely confident Jim as he repeatedly painted his competitor as a fading star and himself a rising one. "He's like Jack Nicklaus and I'm like Tiger Woods," he crowed, a declaration that instantly prompted Sheila and me to trade "Oh, brother" glances. The third time Jim compared his minor record to that of a publishing icon, it was all I could do to not go all Lloyd Bentsen on him.[12]

Unfortunately for Jim, this kind of über confidence typically doesn't play well with female audiences. Had he been making his pitch to a couple of men, it's entirely possible that Jim would have gotten the job. But he wasn't, so he didn't. As it turned out, the real joke was on us. While women like Sheila and me sit on our high horses, men like Jim are off to the races. I know because ten years later the supremely confident Jim has a new book that's selling like gangbusters. And among the impressive celebrity book endorsements is one from his old rival Stephen Covey!

What about you? Are you similarly intolerant of any behavior that strikes you as "too confident"? If so, you may want to check your anti-ego meter. You certainly don't need to cultivate a supersized ego to beat the impostor syndrome or to fake it till you make it. But what if you bumped it up just a notch? True, Jim is still not a household name. Yet somehow his vision of being the next Stephen Covey is not as far-fetched as it once sounded.

Of course ego alone will take you only so far. The rest comes down to hard work. However, I have to believe that Jim's effort was propelled by his belief that he was a rising star. You're probably never going to let yourself become an egomaniac, so why not allow yourself to fake a little more confidence than you feel and see where it takes you?

Faking it till you make it does not mean you have to choose between self-doubt and self-righteousness or modesty and puffery. You can speak with measured confidence without being self-important. Indeed, after you sift out the arrogance, condescension, and presumptiveness that are such turn-offs to women, you may find, as Jane Campbell suggests, that there are certain aspects of male answer syndrome that women can actually learn from.

For example, there's something appealing, she says, about being able to bring a kind of "expansiveness" to what the questioner is actually asking. Whereas a woman may "shrug helplessly, acknowledging that some things are simply unknowable," Campbell says, "a man, on the other hand, will come up with a few theories." She adds, "Men have the courage and inventiveness to try to explain the inexplicable."

It's the same way with "bullshitting." Frankfurt too used the term "expansive," explaining that the creativity that goes into bullshitting is less analytical and deliberate than what's required to come up with a lie. The reason men enjoy getting together to "shoot the bull" in the first place is that everyone knows not to take anything that's said too seriously. It's hard not to smile when you hear that American frontiersman Daniel Boone once insisted, "I have never been lost, but I will admit to being confused for several weeks."

At the Very Least, Know It When You Hear It

It bears repeating: You absolutely do not need to become a bullshit artist to overcome the impostor syndrome. But at the very least, I want you to know it when you hear it. Otherwise you will walk around thinking everyone but you has a clue. It happens far more often than you may think. Incredibly capable individuals falter in their careers because they don't recognize BS when they see it. It almost happened to Angela.

The bright but insecure Guatemalan American was the first person in her immigrant family to graduate from high school. When I met her, Angela was studying for a Ph.D. in a new form of math so obscure that there was no known application for it yet. For those of us who struggled with basic geometry, this alone is bewildering. But Angela was not the typical math student. Her highest-level math class in high school was Algebra II. Yet here she was, only one of two students in the entire university studying in this area. "Math always came easily to me," she told me. "I could just see the answers in my head."

Apart from their shared aptitude for math, Angela and the other student could not have been more different. He was as confident as Angela was hesitant, evidenced by his penchant for explaining his calculations by saying things like "Of course" and "As we all know" and "Obviously." One day when it was Angela's turn to present, her professor began peppering her with questions. Most she could answer but some she could not. Heat rushed to her face. She couldn't think clearly. Finally she burst into tears and bolted out the door. That was the day Angela decided she was not graduate school material and promptly called her family to announce that she was dropping out.

She would have too had her professor not bothered to track her down. "What's going on?" he asked. Angela tried to explain how inadequate she was compared with her clearly more capable counterpart. That's when the professor stopped her cold. "Wait a minute," he said. "You don't actually think he always knows what he's talking about, do you? Half the time he's bullshitting." (If you had no clue it's possible to fake it in math, you're not alone!)

Angela's story is a painful reminder of how easy it is to confuse confidence for credibility. Fortunately for Angela, someone took the time to provide an alternative view that would prove perspective shifting. When I tracked Angela down some years later, she said, "Where I thought I looked bad for admitting when I failed to grasp a concept, my professor made the distinction between the other student skirting a question and my maintaining intellectual integrity. I now listen very differently."

Even highly educated people joke that "Ph.D." really stands for "piled higher and deeper." Still, if you work with the well educated or in an occupation where you just expect a certain kind of professionalism, then you may not be on the lookout for it. You may assume that the more a person knows, the less he might need to rely on bullshitting as a means to get by. But to hear Harry Frankfurt tell it, the opposite may be true. "Not only do more highly educated people have the linguistic and intellectual gifts that enable them to create bullshit," he said in a videotaped interview, "but also I think that a lot of people who are highly educated acquire a kind of arrogance that leads them to be negligent about truth and falsity. They have a lot of confidence in their own opinions."[13]

And where better to find large groups of highly educated people than in higher education, where, some believe, intellectual arrogance rises in proportion to institutional prestige. Indeed, it was while studying for her Ph.D. at Harvard University that Martha Beck suffered from a severe bout of impostor syndrome. In her autobiographical book, *Expecting Adam*, she shares a story that changed everything.

One day on her way to class she stopped off at a friend's laboratory. Beck watched fascinated as her friend conducted an experiment involving rats attached to electrodes swimming in a plastic "kiddie pool" decorated with those funny little blue Smurf cartoon characters. When she arrived late to her own class Beck apologized, explaining that she'd gotten sidetracked in the psych lab watching rats swim in a Smurf pool.

"I see," said the instructor. "Yes, I believe I've read about that."

A professor, one of the visiting dignitaries, chimed in. "How is Smurf's work going?" he inquired. "I understand he's had some remarkable findings."

"Yes," said a graduate student. "I read his last article."

It went on that way for a few moments more. As the reality of what was happening became clear, Beck's initial confusion turned to delight:

I was giddy with exhilaration because after seven years at Harvard, I was just beginning to realize that *I wasn't the only one faking it*. I had bluffed my way through many a cocktail party, pretending to know about whichever scholar or theory was the current topic of conversation. I had always wondered how I survived among the staggeringly intelligent people lurking around me. Now I was beginning to understand.

"He's a good man, Smurf is," said the instructor solemnly.

The next time you find yourself in one of those situations where you think everyone else is smarter, more interesting, and more informed than you, check your assumptions. Rather than let the situation knock you off base, realize that on some level or another everyone is faking it. And when you find yourself in one of those moments I want you to smile and say to yourself, "Good man, Smurf."

The Bottom Line

As you continue to whittle away at your impostor feelings, you'll probably have to wing it a little—or a lot, especially in the beginning. The key is to not wait until you feel confident.

Change your behavior first and allow your confidence to build. That's where it helps to "fake it till you make it."

There is no right or wrong way to feel about BS or faking it. At the same time, it's important to be aware that your feelings are probably shaped to a large degree by gender. More important, know that your thinking on the subject can impact your ability to feel as confident as you deserve to.

Whether you call it bullshitting, bluffing, winging it, holding your own, flying by the seat of your pants, or just plain chutzpah is not important. What matters is that you start to act as capable as you really are, even—no, make that *especially*—when you don't always feel it. Don't let the more objectionable aspects of male hyperconfidence lead you to miss out on what remains one of the most powerful impostor-busting strategies there is— acting confident despite your very human self-doubts.

What You Can Do

- Explore how your current attitudes about things like male answer syndrome, irrational self-confidence syndrome, posturing, bluffing, covering up, getting away with things, and bullshitting in general affect your ability to fake it till you make it.

- If the idea of "bullshitting" is a deterrent, reframe the phenomenon in less offensive terms, such as improvising, winging it, holding your own, or going with the flow.

- Seek out low-risk opportunities to "act as if" you are more confident than you feel. Once you have a few of these under your belt, up the ante by pursuing larger goals you may have previously shied away from.

- As you do, remind yourself that (1) you don't always have to feel
  confident to act confident; (2) in most situations it really is okay
  to figure things out as you go along; and (3) the more you act on
  behalf of your goals, the more success you will have.

What's Ahead

One element of faking it till you make it that we haven't yet
touched on is risk taking. In the next chapter we'll explore ways
you can build your risk-taking muscles. Plus you'll meet some
individuals who can serve as powerful and fun role models for
the fake-it-till-you-make-it approach.

Rethinking Risk Taking
and Cultivating Chutzpah

There is a microscopically thin line
between being brilliantly creative and
acting like the most gigantic idiot
on earth. So what the hell, leap.

—Cynthia Heimel, author and playwright

W hen it comes to risk taking there are two types of impostors. One copes with a sense of inadequacy by playing it safe. The other compensates by taking more chances. Which are you? Both types set and achieve goals. If you tend to err on the side of caution, then your goals may be more modest—or at least safer. If you're more comfortable flying without a net, you probably have both bigger goals and the success to show for it.

Either way you picked up this book because you want to feel different. To feel different, though, you have to do things differently, and that includes taking risks. As management guru Tom Peters says, "Unless you're willing to walk out into the unknown, the chances of making a profound difference in your life are pretty slim."

If you're already a risk taker, then you're used to walking into the unknown. Now you need to do it without all the impostor baggage. For you the focus needs to be on using what you learned here to credit yourself for the gambles that do work and learn from the ones that don't pan out. Once you do that, you'll find the courage to seize bigger and better opportunities.

However, if taking risks does not come naturally, your first task is to build your risk-taking muscles. The more risks you take, the more courage you'll have and the more successful and competent you'll feel. A good place to start is by understanding why you avoid risks in the first place and why others don't.

Why Do Men Take More Risks?

For all the reasons we've talked about here, on average men significantly overestimate their abilities and women underestimate theirs.[1] It stands to reason, then, that women take fewer risks than men.[2] But it's not entirely a confidence issue. Partly we're looking at differences in socialization.

It's known, for example, that parents treat girls more gingerly while allowing boys more latitude around adventure seeking. Up until about age eight girls and boys are encouraged to explore their surroundings equally. After that universally boys are allowed a greater "home range" for independent travel and activities.[3] Even if you were raised in a relatively enlightened environment, you may have gotten mixed signals. Aspiration-wise, you may have been told that the sky's the limit. You can grow up to be anything you want, you can fly to outer space like Sally Ride . . . but don't go outside of the neighborhood.

There are some who see a biological explanation for men's propensity to engage in more risky behaviors. Women have long been mocked for their supposedly flighty, out-of-control hormones. Perhaps that's why there was so much buzz about research linking higher levels of testosterone with high-risk behavior by Wall Street traders. The study was conducted by former Wall Street trader John Coates, now a senior research fellow in neuroscience and a finance researcher at the University of Cambridge.

Looking back at his own trading days, Coates recalls how, when his male coworkers were making money, they displayed almost physical symptoms of mania, punching the air and yelling and generally working themselves into a frenzy. He remembers thinking it was like they were on some kind of drug. In a way they were. Long observed in animals, the phenomenon is known as the "winner effect." Decades of experiments have shown that succeeding at a task floods the brain with testosterone, causing lab animals to make decisions faster, try harder to win, and be willing to take more risks.

The same behavior happens among males in the wild. When two stallions fight, the loser's testosterone plummets while the winner's surges, making him more confident and aggressive. This can go on for several days, and then one day the victor essentially suffers from actual testosterone poisoning. Hopped up on hormones and less able to assess risk, the winning horse ventures farther outside his territory, taking on bigger competitors and generally putting himself in danger.

Coates wondered whether testosterone was having a similar effect on traders. What he discovered was that traders who started their workday with high levels of testosterone were making more money. And a hot day on the market sent their levels of the natural steroid up even more. Remember, as long as you're winning, confidence remains high; too much testosterone, though, can include feelings of omnipotence and carelessness. Under the swagger of their own hormones, male traders started to take bigger risks in hopes of bigger rewards, which, as with the stallion, led to reckless behavior.

This biologically puffed-up confidence led *New York Times* columnist Nicholas Kristof to ask, "Would we have been better off had it not been Lehman Brothers, if it had been Lehman Brothers and Sisters?" It's an excellent question when you consider that being overly confident can be just as risky as being overly cautious. There's reason why the billionaire Warren Buffett's patient, research-intensive approach has been likened to "investing like a girl." In certain situations a less impulsive, more measured approach can be a big plus. A 2009 report found that hedge funds run by women, for instance, fell only half as much during the financial crisis as those managed by men. Also during that time the value of female-managed funds dropped by only 9.6 percent, compared with 19 percent for the rest.[4]

There's another reason why the two genders may approach risk differently. When researchers at Columbia University looked beyond the surface data, they discovered that men weren't necessarily more risk-seeking but rather that they placed a greater value on the perceived *benefit* of taking a risk than women did.[5] In other words, for women certain risks just aren't considered worth it. This may explain the finding that female "impostors" who are risk takers also exhibited a strong desire to show that they can do better than others and therefore compete harder.[6] If it's important to you to prove yourself, then it's going to be worth it to you to take a shot.

You Are Already a Risk Taker

Whether you embrace risk or run from it, you're probably defining risk too narrowly. The fact is, women take chances every day. It's just that society doesn't recognize and appreciate them as such. Once you expand your notions about what constitutes risk, you may discover that you're a bigger thrill seeker than you thought.

The risks I'm referring to are easy to miss because, as you learned earlier, it is society that determines which traits get valued and rewarded. When people think of risk in a career context, most picture behaviors that have do with the quest for power, money, or status, all of which occur in the public arenas historically associated with men. Yet in the private realm of relationships, long the domain of women, risk taking happens every day. We just don't often think of it that way.

When it comes to spending and investing money, women are generally more conservative than men. Yet on the relationship front, women take calculated financial risks all the time: putting all their eggs in one basket by expecting a man to be a retirement plan, interrupting a career to raise children, or supporting a spouse/partner through school with the promise of future reciprocity.

You don't have to bungee-jump to engage in physical risks. In the developed world, childbirth is considered relatively safe. But women in poor countries routinely put their very lives at risk to bear children. If men did that, they'd erect shrines to those who have lost their lives in the line of duty.

Then there are emotional risks. In four out of five types of risk—financial, health and safety, ethical, recreational, and social—women were found to be more risk-averse than men. The exception was in the social arena. This includes things like voicing your opinion about an unpopular subject at a social occasion or admitting that your tastes are different from those of a friend. Society may not always value the ease with which you share your innermost feelings, but it really does takes courage to make yourself vulnerable like this.

Emotionally speaking, women take death-defying leaps, plunges, and falls all the time—risks that would terrify most men. Just as men consider shooting the bull to be a fun pastime, you may feel the same about sharing. Opening up is so much fun for some women that some are actually holding "shrink parties" complete with a guest psychologist brought in to help guests work through their "stuff" over a few cocktails. This may not feel high-risk to you, but to a lot of men it's scary as hell. As former Major League Baseball player Mark McGwire once remarked, "It's probably harder for somebody to open up and show their sensitive side than to hit a baseball."[7]

The reason I want you to recognize just what a big deal having easy access to your emotions really is, is so that you don't miss the opportunity to reap the benefits. The new buzzword in business and government sectors is "transparency." Being able to speak frankly, to share weaknesses and admit mistakes, is suddenly all the rage. To be credible today, business leaders and entrepreneurs must demonstrate vulnerability, humility, intuition, and sensitivity, all things that come more easily to women. As you assess your own appetite for risk, give yourself extra competence points for your willingness to be vulnerable, transparent, *and* on the cutting edge.

Finally, one thing all risk takers share is a zest for intensity and uncertainty—in a word, they love the thrill. Temple University psychologist Frank Farley even coined a term to describe them: the type T personality, with the *T* signifying *thrill*. Just because you're not into extreme sports or you aren't going after venture capital doesn't mean you're not a thrill seeker. Farley cites women such as Margaret Mead and Helen Keller as famous female risk takers who were thrilled with the adrenaline rush of their original thinking. Keep that in mind the next time you're going full creative throttle in a brainstorming session!

Bold and Bolder

Why be content with taking your garden-variety risks when you can experience the even greater benefits that come when you take bold action on behalf of your dreams? In the last chapter you learned three things that relate to risk taking. One: You don't always have to feel confident to act confident. Two: There's actually an element of creativity, play, and expansiveness in being able to "fake it till you make it." And three: Some people who identify as impostors see the ability to wing it a bit as a skill. Convincing other people that you know what you're doing is only a problem if you see it as such.

On this last point, the American essayist and journalist H. L. Mencken once said, "All men are frauds. The only difference between them is that some admit it. I myself deny it." All truly competent people know that to a certain extent they're "impostors." In other words, the difference between them and you is that they don't see it as a problem. They know they may have to fake it a bit, especially in the beginning, and they're fine with that. They feel comfortable bending the rules a little, relying on gut instinct, and having faith that they can learn as they go.

It's called chutzpah [*hoot*-spuh]—a wonderful Yiddish word originally used to register indignation over someone shamelessly overstepping a boundary. Yiddish, and later English, put a more positive spin on it to mean gutsy audacity. "That took chutzpah" is frequently used admiringly to describe a display of "guts" with flair and boldness.

You are about to meet some famous and not-so-famous "chutzpah artists," people who have a very different take on what it means to "fake it," who understand that the ability to wing it a bit (or a lot) is a valuable skill. At their core, none of these stories are about deception. Rather, they are examples of believing in one's inherent capacity to succeed. All of these individuals, in their own way, saw a problem or recognized an opportunity and had the boldness to act, no matter how insecure they may have felt. The fact that they did it with more than a bit of creative flair is what makes them chutzpah artists! Their stories are meant to inspire you to add a bit of fun to your future risk-taking endeavors.

For example, someone who was undaunted by risks was Estée Lauder, who built what would become a multibillion-dollar cosmetics empire from scratch. Mostly she did it the same way any successful entrepreneur does—through enormous amounts of grit and hard work. But Lauder was also not above a few shenanigans. In his book *Profiles of Female Genius: Thirteen Creative Women Who Changed the World*, Gene N. Landrum tells how Lauder managed to land an important buyer for her first perfume:

> By 1960, the ever-aggressive Lauder had launched an international program and personally broke the prestigious Harrods account in London. She was forced to resort to some sales creativity to break the prestigious Galleries Lafayette account in Paris. When she could not get the manager to agree to stock her products, Lauder "accidentally" spilled her Youth Dew (her first fragrance) on the floor during a demonstration in the middle of a crowd. The appealing scent was pervasive and aroused customer interest and comments. The manager capitulated and gave her an initial order.

For a particularly audacious example of chutzpah in action, we turn to a teenager with a passion for moviemaking. The tale beings when a seventeen-year-old visiting relatives in Canoga Park, California, went on the studio tour of Universal Pictures. The tram didn't stop at the soundstages, so he snuck away on a bathroom break to find them and watch. When a man asked what he was doing, he explained about the 8-millimeter films he'd been making in his parents' living room since he was practically old enough to hold a camera.

As luck would have it, the guy was the head of the editorial department. He invited the fledgling filmmaker to bring in his films and gave him a one-day pass to get onto the lot. The department head was genuinely impressed but had to get back to work, so he wished the teenager good luck and said good-bye. As it turned out, he wouldn't need luck, just the chutzpah to break a few rules.

The next day the young man donned a business suit, tossed a sandwich and two candy bars into one of his father's old briefcases, and returned to the studio. With a wave to the guard intended to convey the message "I belong here," he strode confidently onto the grounds of Universal Pictures. This went on all summer. The teenager in the suit who dreamed of being a director got to hang out with actual directors, writers, editors, and dubbers. He even found an office that wasn't being used and became a squatter. Since he was there every day, people just assumed he worked for the studio. And in an even more incredible show of chutzpah, the kid bought some plastic letter tiles, which he used to add his name to the building directory. It read: STEVEN SPIELBERG, ROOM 23C.[8]

As audacious as Spielberg's stunt was, it was hardly original. Clare Boothe Luce was equally bold some thirty-five years earlier. After graduating first in her class at the age of sixteen, Boothe Luce looked forward to a bright future. However, ten years later she found herself divorced from a cruel alcoholic. With little job experience and the Great Depression just beginning, anyone would have found it hard to get work; being a woman and a single mother only made it more challenging.

But Boothe Luce was no ordinary woman. She'd met Condé Nast, owner of *Vogue* and *Vanity Fair* magazines, through mutual friends. When she ran into him at a dinner party, she saw her opportunity. According to biographer Stephen Shadegg, "She approached the publisher with a directness which must have been disarming and asked him for a job on one of his magazines." Nast gave her the brush-off. "My dear girl," she later recalled him saying. "I've had many like you come and ask for jobs, but you won't stick it out. You won't have any capacity for work."[9]

Undaunted, Boothe showed up at the *Vogue* offices three weeks later only to find that Nast had left for Europe. What others might have viewed as a setback Boothe recognized as an opportunity. "She noted through the open door another editorial office where there were six desks. Two of them were vacant. She popped into the office and asked about the empty desks," Shadegg writes. "Someone told her that two caption writers had left to get married. [She] took off her coat and gloves and settled herself at one of the desks with the brief explanation that she was ready to go to work." By the time Nast returned, she was already on the payroll, proving herself.

Boothe continued to prove herself. Four years later she became managing editor of *Vanity Fair*. That was in 1933. From there she went on to write six plays, three books, and an Oscar-nominated screenplay, to work as a foreign correspondent for *Life* magazine in Europe and in China during the early part of World War II, to become the first congresswoman from her home state of Connecticut, then ambassador to Italy, receiving the Presidential Medal of Freedom for her service. Boothe used a bit of fakery to make it, but there was nothing false about her competence or her success.

Companies do this kind of thing all the time. In the early days when cash was tight, the owners of Home Depot had employees stack up empty boxes to create the illusion of a fully stocked store.[10] As new business owners, Claudia Jessup and Genie Chipps also recognized the value of appearing bigger than you are. In 1972 the two out-of-work actors started a creative personal-assistant company with ninety dollars and a catchy motto: "We'll do anything that's not illegal, immoral, or already being done." They knew it would be hard to make the right impression when their world headquarters was a tiny Manhattan studio. So they bought a record of background noises called *Sounds of the Office,* complete with ringing phones and busy typewriters. And voilà, problem solved![11]

Our last chutzpah artist is a children's book writer named Starr Hall. By the time she was twenty-one, Hall had written three books. Despite positive reviews, every time she tried to set up a reading at one of the major bookstores she was met with the same response: "It sounds great. Have your publicist call us." "Even if I could find a publicist," said Hall, "I couldn't afford one." That's when she hatched a plan to take on the persona of "Holly Grant, publicist." "Holly" even had her own phone line and business cards.

Hall didn't know the first thing about being a publicist. So she did what any resourceful chutzpah artist would do—she learned "on the job." "Each time I called on a new bookstore I'd discover something more about being a publicist," she said. "When they asked about the media release, I'd think, 'Okay, time to figure that out.'" It worked. Kids lined up outside Barnes & Noble for story time, and once she even got a reporter from the *Los Angeles Times* to show up. And in one final act of boldness, when one bookstore manager innocently pointed out how much Holly sounded like Starr, Hall/Grant replied, 'Oh yes, and people tell us we look a lot alike too!"

Awakening Your Inner Chutzpah Artist

You have been held hostage to your impostor feelings long enough. It's time for you to set yourself free. And as Robert Frost said, "Freedom lies in being bold." If you are already a risk taker, congratulations! You join a long line of women who have taken bold action in the face of uncertainty. Women such as Madam C. J. Walker, Andrea Jung, Dara Torres, Jessica Watson, and Julie Taymor remind us how satisfying and fun it can be to go for it. Chances are, though, you'll need some help getting there.

For the record, no one is asking you to trespass your way into a career or make up a fictitious persona. But you do need to start acting like you deserve a place at the table—whether that's space on the bookshelf, in an elite school, the corner office, or a prestigious art gallery. None of the people you just heard about are any smarter, more talented, or deserving than you. Being bold is not about being right, being perfect, or knowing it all. Rather it is about marshaled resources, information, and people. It involves seeing problems as opportunities, occasionally flying by the seat of your pants, and ultimately being willing to fall flat on your face and know you will survive.

Building your risk-taking muscles begins with the recognition that new challenges will always create a certain amount of inner tension. But that doesn't mean you aren't up to the task. Not only should you expect to feel afraid, you should worry if you *don't*. Two-time Oscar winner Denzel Washington certainly never took his starring role in the Broadway hit *Fences* for granted. "That last five minutes before we go on that first [Broadway] preview, if you don't have that 'what the hell am I doing here [feeling],' . . . if you don't have that, then they say it's time to quit."[12]

Next, when performance jitters strike, you need to practice reframing the situation. That's what Elizabeth Alexander did. When President-elect Obama tapped Alexander to be the inaugural poet, there was a flurry of interviews leading up to her big performance. One question everyone had was "Are you nervous?" (a question I would venture to guess was not put to the first inaugural poet, Robert Frost). Each time she was asked, Alexander spoke of feeling excited, thrilled, honored, humbled—but never scared. Why? The way she put it: "To be scared would not be helpful."[13]

The second you feel fear kick in, take a deep breath, then calmly remind yourself, *This is not helpful right now.* Then decide which emotion *would* be helpful in the situation. How about exhilaration, anticipation, wonder, joy, pride, enthusiasm, or determination? There's a reason why famed psychologist Fritz Perls describes fear as "excitement without breath." Think about it. Your body has the same physiological responses to both fear and excitement—nervous stomach, sweaty palms, dry mouth. And since your mind only knows what you tell it, it doesn't know the difference.

Say, for example, that you have a fear of public speaking. You should still expect to have some butterflies as you head to the podium. Just make sure you keep telling yourself, "I'm excited . . . *I'm* excited . . . *I'm excited!*" From there you can do things like increase your volume and use gestures that support your message. Not only will you be a more engaging speaker, but both techniques offer the bonus of burning off nervous energy.[14]

Taking risks is like any other skill. The more you do it, the more comfortable you get. Eleanor Roosevelt's advice was to "do one thing every day that scares you." Try it for a week. Sign up for a singing or a fencing class. Submit your poem or an article to a magazine. Raise your hand for a challenging assignment. Naturally you'd like things to turn out well, but the outcome is not so important. Really! What is important is that you stepped outside of your comfort zone and learned something in the process.

As you ponder different risks, make sure you put the perceived consequences into proper perspective. A bright midlevel manager at an international cosmetics conglomerate told me she'd spent her entire career erring on the side of caution because she didn't want to be responsible if something went wrong. That is until her boss told her, "Look, there is no single thing you could possibly do that is going to bring this company down, so go for it." Decisions do of course have consequences, but rarely are they as dire or as permanent as you think.

Going for it comes down to having faith that, despite your insecurities, you'll be able to figure it out along the way. And what if your plan goes awry? Well, in the words of Admiral Grace Murray Hopper, "It's much easier to apologize than it is to get permission."

Recognize too that playing it safe can be the riskiest move of all. If you don't take chances or ever put yourself or your work out there, you will avoid failure. But you also need to consider what all that safety is costing you. In her book *Perseverance*, Margaret Wheatley writes, "Security is not what creates life. Safety, safe havens, guarantees of security—none of these give life its capacities. Newness, creativity, imagination—these live on the edge."

Stop now and think of a challenge or opportunity you could go after but have been afraid to. Name three things you'll miss out on if you continue to play it too safe. It could be anything from a financial cost to the chance to get valuable feedback to the pride of knowing that win or lose, at least you tried.

If you can't "see" yourself doing something, it probably won't happen. Using any of the chutzpah artists you met here as inspiration, picture yourself with more chutzpah. Go back in your mind to a specific situation where even a small amount of chutzpah would have come in handy. Replay the scene in your mind, but this time add a dash of creative boldness. What would you do or say differently? What would that feel like?

Now that you have a mental image, just as a scientist would, I want you to set up some experiments and then evaluate what happened. Maybe you can't imagine bluffing your way into a job, but if you knew it might keep you from being taken advantage of by an unscrupulous auto mechanic, would you feel all right about giving the impression that you know more about cars than you actually do? In other words, I want you to find your own chutzpah comfort zone—and then to stretch a bit further.

Come up with two or three ways you can practice chutzpah where there is not a big price tag. What if, for example, you went into a Jaguar dealership and took a test drive? It doesn't matter if you can't afford a Jaguar or that you wouldn't want one even if you could. The point is to see what it feels like to pretend a bit. Were you sufficiently convincing? Too bold? Not bold enough? Most important, how did you feel?

Remember, the thing all risk takers have in common is that they love a thrill. If you've played the icebreaker game Two Truths and a Lie, then you know how fun—even thrilling—it can be to pretend. Here's how the game works: Each person takes a turn telling a group of strangers two things that are true about himself, and one outlandish lie. Then everyone has to guess which one is false. So you might say something like I took a cooking class in Paris, my mother delivered me on the way to the hospital, and I used to be a competitive archer. Take a moment now to think up your two truths and a lie—the wilder, the better!

You could try it with friends or, if you really want to practice "acting as if," you might try it when you strike up a conversation with a stranger on an airplane or while on vacation thousands of miles from home. You can still be from Cleveland and have two kids. But instead of being Teresa from accounting, be a freelance writer who gets paid to travel the world reviewing health spas or an internationally recognized expert on the history of beer. Don't know a thing about either subject? Make it up as you go along! You'll be amazed at what comes out of your mouth when the person asks you how you got into that. What have you got to lose? In the worst case a person you'll never see again thinks you're delusional. Remember, it's all in the name of building confidence and seeing what life is like in the "bold zone."

In her autobiography, *I'm Wild Again: Snippits from My Life and a Few Brazen Thoughts*, Helen Gurley Brown wrote, "People think chutzpah is in the genes. It isn't . . . it's in the needing and longing and being willing to fall on your face. It isn't fun . . . who wants all that rejection, but life is sweeter if you make yourself do uncomfortable things."[15] Fortunately, not only do you have a choice about how you handle failure, you also have a huge say in what *kind* of failures to have. You can have relatively mundane ones like flunking a class or losing a big client. Or you can take the advice Garrison Keillor offered in a commencement address when he urged graduates to "have interesting failures."[16]

Let those words sink in for a moment. Have *interesting* failures. Each one of the chutzpah artists you met here could have just as easily failed. Lauder could have ended up building a mere multimillion-dollar cosmetics company versus a multi*billion*-dollar one—or she could have fallen flat on her face. Spielberg could have taken home only one Oscar instead of four—or he could have not won any. The point is, life is short. And since a certain amount of failure is inevitable, why should you settle for boring failures when you can experience failing at something amazing, like coming in a close second in a major election or getting only one of your inventions manufactured or being the twenty-thousandth person to cross the finish line at the Boston Marathon?

The Bottom Line

Confidence comes from taking risks, owning the wins, and learning from the losses. Some people with impostor syndrome embrace uncertainty and have a strong desire to prove themselves. Overall, though, women take fewer risks than men. The reasons are complex but are likely a combination of nurture, nature, and how each perceives the benefits of a given risk.

Women routinely take financial and emotional risks that go unacknowledged by society and themselves. Whether you thrive on the thrill of the risk or you take a more measured approach, you can always build up your risk-taking muscles even more. You don't have to be a "BS artist" to fake it till you make it. But you can enjoy the creativity and potential benefits that come from being a "chutzpah artist."

What You Can Do

- Remember that not taking risks may be the riskiest move of all.
- Recognize those risks you do take that you take for granted.
- Take one step a day to build your risk-taking muscles.
- Practice applying lessons from the "chutzpah artists" you met here to bring a little more confident boldness into your life.

What's Ahead

What you think is your greatest fear may be something else entirely. As you prepare to embark on your new life as someone who feels as competent and successful as you should, there are a few essential insights you need to take with you.

[1 2]

Playing Big

It's not psychologically good for you
to make yourself a little person.
—Liz Smith

From now on everything is going to be different. When you started this journey you thought you were the only one who secretly believed you were fooling others. Now you know that these feelings of ineptness and fraudulence can strike any thoughtful, reflective person with a pulse. You used to assume that your self-doubt was all self-generated, which meant all your energy went into figuring out how to "fix" yourself. Now that you understand that your impostor feelings have a larger social context, you can do far more contextualizing and far less personalizing. This alone is tremendously freeing.

You even have an entirely new competence rule book, one that acknowledges that you can be competent and human at the same time. Now when you nail an assignment, it no longer occurs to you to credit your success to anything other than yourself. If there was a bit of chance involved or if someone put in a good word for you, you think, "So what?" In the end, you know it was you who made your good fortune or connections count. By now you even *sound* different. Instead of pushing compliments away like you used to, today you just smile and say, "Thanks."

And it's going to get even better. From now on, instead of dreading challenges because you're afraid you'll be unmasked, you actually look forward to them and seek them out. You know you don't always have to feel confident to act confident. Even if some of the self-doubts creep back in now and then, you're not worried. This time you know exactly what to do to tame those impostor voices. If you think I'm exaggerating, think again.

Remember Joyce Roché, the former cosmetics-company executive and president and CEO of Girls Inc., whom you met in chapter 1? All you knew about Roché then was that she recalled thinking it was only "a matter of time before you stumble and 'they' discover the truth. You're not supposed to be here. We knew you couldn't do it. We should have never taken a chance on you." But not anymore.

Her transformation from worrying about being unmasked to owning her success and competence offers hope to anyone who worries that she's a hopeless case. Some years later Roché was asked to contribute to a book called *What I Know Now*. In a letter to her younger self she offers some pointed advice that could just as easily be directed at you: "Stop. It. Now. You're not an impostor. You're the genuine article. You have brainpower. You have the ability. You don't have to work so hard and worry so much. You're going to do just fine. You deserve a place at the table. So relax and enjoy your success."

You know she's right. Behind your own mask is a woman who knows she is bright, resourceful, creative, able, and yes, even gifted. And she desperately wants that brilliance to be recognized. Not necessarily by the world (although deep down you probably think that would be pretty cool). Mostly, though, the person you want to see and embrace your brilliance is you. This is all incredibly good news. However, before I send you confidently off into the world, there are a few more things you need to know—and do.

The Flip Side of Your Impostor Story

Linus, the young and gifted character in *Peanuts,* once said, "I am burdened by a great potential." And so are you. You've spent years explaining away your success . . . convinced that you're really not as successful or as competent as everyone else knows you are . . . waiting for the other shoe to drop. But there is another truth and that is:

YOUR FEAR OF BEING INADEQUATE
PALES COMPARED WITH YOUR
FEAR OF BEING EXTRAORDINARY

Consciously you're afraid that people will find out you're inept. But deep down you know you're "smart"—or at least smart enough. As Marianne Williamson famously observed, "Our deepest fear is not that we are inadequate. Our deepest fear is that we are powerful beyond measure. It is our light, not our darkness, that most frightens us."[1]

Buried under all the debris of fear and self-doubt is the certain knowledge that you are infinitely capable. You'll probably even smile when I tell you that leadership expert Manfred F. R. Kets de Vries considers the impostor syndrome to be "the flip side of giftedness." If you don't believe me, then consider the findings by Wake Forest University psychologists that some people who *say* they feel like frauds are secretly more confident than they let on. The conclusion was that such people are in effect "phony phonies." I respectfully disagree. I believe what these researchers really revealed is the other side of impostorism. The side of you that, however small and inconsistent, secretly knows you *are* accomplished and competent and that you really *can* do it.

I wanted to tell you all this from the very beginning. But I knew you wouldn't have believed me. Back then your impostor feelings were far too heavy for you to hear the whole story. That weight has lifted and you're ready now. So repeat after me: *"I am powerful beyond measure."* As cliché as it may sound, you really can do anything you put your mind to. Think about it.

Why Sonia Sotomayor, Suze Orman, or Sue Grafton and not you?
Why Madeleine Albright, Maya Lin, or Martha Graham and not you?
Why Anita Roddick, Kathryn Bigelow, or Marian Wright Edelman and not you?
Why Sally Ride, Dian Fossey, or Grace Hopper and not you?
Why Margaret Mead, Michelle Wie, or Toni Morrison and not you?
Why Meg Whitman, Martha Stewart, or Mary Kay Ash and not you?
Why Louise Hay, Tina Fey, or Jane Goodall and not you?
Why Christiane Amanpour, Salma Hayek, or Amy Tan and not you?

For that matter, why Rick Steves, Stephen King, Gary Vaynerchuk, Bill Gates, Warren Buffett, Richard Branson, Barack Obama, or any man who has achieved his goals and not you? I could go on, of course, but the point is, not one of these amazing women or men are necessarily smarter, better, luckier, or more amazing than you are. True, they've acquired certain knowledge, skills, and experience. But the operative word here is *acquired*. An improbable television phenomenon like Julia Child did not come out of the womb being "Julia Child, cooking legend." She *became* Julia Child—and at forty-nine years old at that. Playwright Wendy Wasserstein's turning point came in her early thirties when a friend told her that "the way to be taken seriously is to take *yourself* seriously."[2]

Oprah Winfrey had none of the advantages of economic class or a stable family life. She spent the first six years of her life being raised by her grandmother in Mississippi before being shuttled north to live with her mother. At thirteen the scars of abuse and molestation drove her to run away from home and subsequently be sent to a juvenile detention facility, only to be denied admission because all the beds were filled. Nothing in Oprah's background would have portended success, never mind megastardom. Yet Oprah was remarkably undaunted. Even after being fired from her television reporter's job and told, "You're not fit for TV,"[3] she remained undaunted and was later said to remark, "I always knew I was destined for greatness." And so are you.

You can be powerful beyond measure without becoming a household name. In fact, it takes just as much courage to walk away from what everyone else considers a "dream job" to follow your own road. It takes not one more ounce of courage or energy to dream big than it does to settle. And you've got a lot more to gain by shooting high than by shooting low.

Who Do You Think You Are to Not Go for It?

Unfortunately, when you dare to step into your genius, resistance is intent on keeping you small. Even if you are fearless, you may feel utterly undeserving (we'll talk more about this in a moment). The closer you get to believing that you actually can do it, the more likely you are to receive an unwanted visit from that niggling inner voice. The one that demands to know, *Who do you think you are?*

In reality the question you should be asking yourself is *Who do I think I am* not *to go for it?* Whether you know it or not, your actions, and conversely your failure to act, have implications that extend far beyond you. It's a lesson I learned while trying to complete the dissertation that set the stage for this book. Each of my subjects had been interviewed and all the recordings had been transcribed. I'd even settled on a title: "A Model of Internal Barriers to Women's Occupational Achievement."

Then the resistance kicked in. I was overwhelmed by the prospect of trying to make sense out of nearly a thousand pages of data. I started second-guessing my topic. I developed a severe case of writer's block. In short, I felt like a fraud. Besides, who did this daughter from a long line of housekeepers and custodians think she was to be "Dr." Valerie Young?

This was in the early eighties, a time when women were inching their way into middle management. My friend Rita Hardiman was leading diversity seminars for managers and executives at some of the largest corporations in the country. Every day she observed amazingly competent women struggling to feel as confident as their oversized shoulder pads implied. Rita had completed her own dissertation only months earlier, so she knew what I was up against. Fearing I might never finish, she sat down and wrote me a letter. There was a lot to it, of course, but the part that stopped me in my tracks was when she said, "Valerie, you have to finish this dissertation. The things you've learned through your research can benefit a lot of women. And if you don't finish, we all lose."

Rita's words forever changed how I viewed the consequences of playing small. My gut response was, "Oh my goodness, how selfish am I? People are waiting for me! I have to hurry!" It was as if someone had flipped a switch inside me. This recognition that my procrastination had consequences for people other than myself became a powerful motivating force.

I've since learned that advocating on someone else's behalf or otherwise serving others is a highly effective way to get women to take action. In an earlier chapter you learned that women who negotiate for more money are perceived to be less nice and more demanding than women who don't ask. I waited until now to tell you the good news. What this study also revealed is that when male and female executives negotiated compensation for themselves, they achieved similar results. But when they bargained *on behalf of someone else,* the women outperformed the men.

The researchers speculate that when acting as an advocate for someone else, women felt more freedom to negotiate assertively, with less fear of being judged unfeminine. Plus, just as men tend to shine in competitive environments, women become energized by cooperative ones, and how better to cooperate than to represent another person's interests?[4]

You already know that you tend to be other-oriented; we talked about it at length in chapter 8. So what if instead of worrying about being unfeminine, you rode the horse in the direction the horse is going? In this case that means that if you want to improve your own outcome, see if you can find a way to link your results to those of others—whether an individual, a group, a community, a country, or humanity as a whole.

This strategy can also improve your chances of achieving a long-held dream. Over the years, I've had countless opportunities to use Rita's advice to help women who find it difficult to let their light shine. One of these was a gifted but unpublished writer named Kim. She had spent years lovingly caring for an ailing parent. After her father passed she began to craft a play about her experience. Kim got only so far before she was stopped by the fear that her play might actually become a hit. Then, she said, "I'd have to play big."

I invited her to imagine a sold-out theater full of people . . . to feel the excitement in the crowd, to know that among them were many women who had been through similar experiences with their own parents, women who were especially eager for their own joy and pain to be honored by the words she'd scripted . . . to watch as the lights dimmed and the curtain rose to reveal an empty stage . . . and then to hear herself, the almost-playwright, step out from the wings and announce to her almost-admirers, *I'm sorry, there will be no play tonight. I was too afraid of being great to write it.*

Can playing big be scary? You bet. It's even harder if you've spent your life putting others' needs before your own. Even when you do manage to convince yourself that you are worthy, to suddenly move your own dream to the front burner can feel selfish. All the more reason you need to see that *everyone loses when you play small.* As Audre Lorde said, "When I care to be powerful—to use my strengths in the service of my vision, then it becomes less and less important whether I am afraid."

Instead of the proverbial question "What would you do if money were no object?" try asking, "What sort of difference could I make if fear were not a factor?" There are people out there right this very minute who want and deserve to benefit from your full range of knowledge, abilities, and skills. Widen the lens even further and you'll see that in a world where poverty and illiteracy disproportionately affect women and children, the world needs all hands on deck. Yours included.

You don't need to run out and end world hunger, secure world peace, or save an endangered species. But you can help raise or mentor the next generation of strong girls and sensitive boys. You can raise your hand in a meeting. You can raise your hand for a project, a promotion, a raise. You can throw your hat into the ring or throw caution to the wind. And if someone is making you feel less capable than you really are, you can raise heck—and plenty of it.

Whatever you do, you owe it to yourself—and to all of us—to start acting as powerful as you really are. If you're ready to use all of the new-found confidence you've acquired here, if you're ready to liberate yourself from the fear of your own greatness, then let's get on with it.

Right the Rules

One thing that keeps people stuck in the impostor syndrome is the belief that they are not entitled to feel, think, or act in certain ways. Below is a list of twenty rights that we're all perfectly entitled to but sometimes act as if we are not. Check off any and all rights that, up until now, you've had trouble always granting yourself. As you read through the list, try to avoid intellectualizing. Instead focus on how you typically respond when your impostor feelings get triggered.

List of Rights[5]

1. The right to say no without feeling guilty
2. The right to feel and express healthy competitiveness and achievement drive
3. The right to make mistakes or to be wrong
4. The right to express pride at my accomplishments
5. The right to occasionally have an off day or not perform up to par
6. The right to fail and to learn from the experience
7. The right to be treated fairly without discrimination due to my sex, race, age, class, sexual orientation, religion, culture, or disability
8. The right to achieve at a level I am comfortable with
9. The right to say, "I don't understand"
10. The right to have things explained to me—even when the person is busy

11. The right to be treated as a competent adult
12. The right to work in nontraditional realms without penalty
13. The right not to be the spokesperson for my entire gender, race, cultural group, et cetera
14. The right to work and raise children at the same time
15. The right to achieve above—or below—family expectations
16. The right to not know all of the answers
17. The right to be treated with dignity and not be patronized
18. The right to have my input considered as valuable as the next person's
19. The right to ask for additional compensation for additional work
20. The right to be in the midst of a learning curve

Next, identify the situation that is most likely to trigger impostor feelings in you. For example, is it whenever you are in a situation where you . . .

- have to defend your work or your ideas?
- are being tested, evaluated, or judged in some way?
- take on a new and unfamiliar assignment?
- are in a classroom or meeting?
- have to present in front of a group?
- show your work to others?
- interact with a person or group of people who are more successful or better educated than you?
- are presented with an opportunity to "play big"?
- other . . .

Now put a star next to the right that is at the core of the impostor scenario you just identified above. In other words, which right are you most denying yourself in that situation? As important, what would you do differently if you really believed you were entitled to this right? If you're not sure, don't worry because you're about to find out.

Creating Your "After" Picture: Who Do You Want to Be?

In chapter 4 you gained insight into unconscious ways you've attempted to evade detection as an impostor. This is also where you identified the negative internal lie you've been telling yourself about yourself known as your "crusher." That was essentially your "before" picture.

Now that you know so much more about the perfectly good reasons you might feel like a fraud, about how society contributes to women seeing themselves as less competent than they really are, about risk taking and the importance of not waiting until you feel confident to demonstrate a bit of chutzpah, you have everything you need to decide who you want to be from this day on.

The "after" picture you create here will be in direct contrast to the "before" snapshot you took in chapter 4. You learned then that the old way of being has become second nature. That's why you need to conjure up a new, self-affirming picture, one that you can have cued up and ready to run the moment your old impostor feelings kick in.

As you prepare to create this new you, remember that acting confident when you feel quite the opposite requires a bit of, well, acting. After all, you're asking yourself to think thoughts you've never thought, feel unfamiliar feelings, and behave in ways that feel quite foreign. Up until now you've typecast yourself as someone who is less competent and capable than you really are. When actors attempt to escape typecasting, they choose roles that are opposite ones they're known for. For you to break out of behavior that is so habitual will require you to dig deep and act against type too.

First you want to get clear about how you would typically respond in this situation. To do this we'll draw again on the work of Gerald Weinstein in *Education of the Self.* To better understand your impostor pattern, complete the following sentences:

- Whenever I'm in a situation where _____
- I usually experience feelings of _____
- The negative voices in my head start saying _____
- And what I typically do is _____

Now I want you to think how you would like this new, confident non-impostor to behave in the same situation by answering these questions:

- What self-affirming things would I *rather feel*?
- What would I like the new *positive voices* in my head to say?
- What would I *rather do* in this situation?

How about feeling powerful, clearheaded, confident, excited, secure, proud, optimistic, eager, curious, capable, or entitled? What about telling yourself things like: "I know I can do this." "I know this stuff." "I love a good challenge." "I'll get better as I get more experience." "It's good enough." "Win or lose, I'll still learn something."

As for your new behaviors, what if you could relax and enjoy the moment? Ask lots of questions so you learn more? Trust that the words will come? Be less concerned with what others think? Wing it a little? Take time to acknowledge and celebrate when you accomplish something?

Before this new way of being can become as automatic and natural as your old self, you need to set a positive foundation that packs enough emotional power to override the negative belief that lies at the heart of your old pattern. This new foundation comes in the form of a one-line declaration that is in direct opposition to your crusher. Unlike that old negative belief, this new "directional statement," as it's called, sets the course for the new positive direction in which you are moving. What about:

"I measure up to myself and no one else. I deserve the success I have achieved and feel proud of my accomplishments."
"I am a creative, intelligent woman with a lot to offer."
"All of my ideas—good, bad, and indifferent—deserve to be heard."
"I have a right to be wrong or have an off day and still be a valuable member of my organization."
"I have the capacity to grow and learn."
"I'm a bright and competent person."
"I am enough."

As you create your own directional statement, there are a few things to keep in mind. First, ideally it will be brief and punchy. That way you'll remember it more easily. Also—and this is important—make sure you phrase it as a positive. So instead of writing, *I'm not as dumb as I think I am,* write, *I am intelligent and capable.* Also, eliminate any hidden qualifiers like *I'm competent—as long as people don't look too closely* or *I measure up to myself—but so what?*

Finally, it's important not to set yourself up to fail with a demand for perfection or grandiose visions. So no unattainable statements like *I am capable of doing everything brilliantly and with ease* or *I am the greatest attorney who ever lived.* Not only are such expectations unrealistic and unnecessary for success, but in the long run imposing these kind of demands on yourself will only rekindle dormant impostor feelings.

With these guidelines in mind, write your new non-impostor directional statement here.

_____

_____

_____

Before moving on, it's important to do a quick test to make sure your new self-confident persona is strong enough to oppose your crusher. You'll know you're on target if:

1. It feels like a lie.
2. It's something you can hardly bring yourself to say out loud.
3. Just the thought of saying it out loud causes a psychological reaction such as blushing, sweaty palms, or tight chest.

If it doesn't fit at least one of these three criteria, go back and work on it until it does. Then trust that with practice you will overcome these reactions and gradually begin to feel the rightness and truth of your statement.

Unlearning the impostor syndrome takes time. To get the ball moving quickly, start not on the feelings front but rather with your thoughts and behaviors. Believe it or not, you can choose to respond differently. Instead of thinking *Who would want to hire me?* you can choose to think, *I have a lot to offer my clients* or, better yet, *They should be so lucky as to have me on the team!* Then you can *act* differently by picking up the phone and delivering your well-rehearsed script stating exactly why you're worth every penny of your fee.

Would you necessarily feel confident and worthy? Probably not. That's because feelings are the hardest things to change, which means that your impostor *feelings* are often the last to go. But as you learned in the last two chapters, the solution is not to wait until you no longer feel afraid, insecure, anxious, inadequate, or undeserving. The solution is to change your thoughts and behaviors first, and let your feelings catch up later.

Final Thoughts

Benjamin Disraeli said, "Fear makes us feel our humanity." If you're hoping for infinite confidence, be careful what you wish for. Some of the most accomplished and creative people are also the most in touch with both the humanity and the utility of fear and self-doubt. It doesn't take a genius to understand why Albert Einstein would say, "I know quite certainly that I myself have no special talent; curiosity, obsession, and dogged endurance, combined with self-criticism, have brought me to my ideas." Did you catch when he said, "combined with self-criticism"?

Remember, it's been found that 70 percent of people have experienced feelings of fraudulence. That begs the question, what's up with the other 30 percent? Given how widespread and *normal* the impostor phenomenon is, why is no one studying the people who've never felt this way? The point is, if feelings of self-doubt and phoniness and self-criticism and fear were all bad, it seems unlikely that they would be so familiar to so many emotionally well-adapted people. Or so useful.

There was a time in Renée Zellweger's career when, she says, she would wake up at night and think, "Oh, damn! Here we go again! What were they thinking? They gave me this role; don't they know I'm faking it?" Zellweger told an Australian reporter that she felt "that luck plays a great part in this journey that I've been experiencing." What's different now is that she understands better the business aspects of the industry and what it takes to prepare for a role as best she can. "So in that way," Zellweger said, she does "feel a little bit better. But never quite. And I'm fine with that, because when you're comfortable, maybe you're also complacent. I think there's a danger in that. And it might be kind of boring too."[6]

Understanding and unlearning the kind of self-limiting philosophies and patterns that drive impostor feelings is not a onetime event. Personal awareness and change take time. There will be moments of profound clarity and abject confusion. There will be victories as well as setbacks.

Fortunately, now when that tired old impostor pattern starts up, a new, more confident person, the one you just met here, will be waiting in the wings to tap you on the shoulder and say, "You are good enough right this minute."

The ball is now in your court. There truly can be no change without changes. If you close this book and do nothing to apply what you've learned, then nothing is exactly what you'll get. I don't expect you to remember everything you've learned here. Hey, I don't remember it all, and I wrote it! But I do expect you to remember to be kind to yourself. In the words of the Hindu yogi Kripalvananda, "Each time you judge yourself, you break your own heart."

The Dirty Little Secret About the Impostor Syndrome

The time has come to let you in on a dirty little secret about the impostor syndrome. It's a secret I've known for some time. I purposely waited until now because if I'd told you at the onset, you may have thrown up your hands. So I'm just going to give it to you straight:

THE IMPOSTOR SYNDROME DOES LESSEN– BUT IT *MAY* NEVER GO AWAY 100 PERCENT

Before you panic, notice I said *may* never totally go away. There are certainly those who insist that their impostor days are behind them. Prior to stepping down as CEO of National Public Radio, Vivian Schiller told a reporter that she'd been intimately acquainted with the impostor syndrome. "You feel as if you're getting away with something and one day you'll get caught. . . . I'd get promoted and I would think, don't they know?" As a former a senior vice president at NYTimes.com and first general manager of Discovery Times Channel, Schiller had been promoted a lot. It took a while, but as the then forty-eight-year-old reported,

"I don't have impostor syndrome anymore. . . . It's the first time I've ever felt that way."[1] That's encouraging for sure.

At the same time, I don't want you to feel discouraged if your own impostor feelings don't vanish quickly—or completely. More likely you'll find your old impostor voices go from a stressful roar to a more manageable whisper. Or they may go into deep hibernation for years at a time until one day, when you step out of your comfort zone in a big way and WHAM—like a cold you thought you'd finally beaten, it's back with a vengeance.

Even the psychologist who first identified the impostor phenomenon, Dr. Pauline Clance, struggled with occasional bouts of self-doubt long afterward. Speaking about her own impostor feelings in a magazine interview, she said, "When I was getting book contracts and I was on the *Donahue* show and the *Today* show and in *Time* magazine, I did begin to feel that way. Fortunately, because I had worked with it, I could say, 'Okay, I'm getting 'impostor feelings.'"

A Funny Thing Happened on the Way to Writing This Book

There's another secret you need to know. This one comes in the form of a personal confession. I had the good fortune to be approached by a phenomenal agent, who arranged for me to interview with seven major publishing houses. Unlike the others, which were in person, my first interview was over the phone. I felt really good afterward. But as the day went on I started second-guessing myself. *Why did I say this? I wish I'd remembered to say that. Was I too long-winded . . . or worse, incoherent?*

The irony of pitching a book on overcoming the impostor syndrome while doing a total number on myself was not lost on me. In the past, a high-stakes situation like this could have easily led to countless days, weeks, even months of obsessive self-guessing. Instead my unexpected bout with doubt lasted less than twenty-four hours. I wasn't any "smarter." I just had the perspective and the tools to talk myself down faster.

Then there was the actual book writing itself. A process I estimated to take no more than nine months ended up taking more than twice that. There were many days when I felt utterly overwhelmed and not at all up to the challenge. All and all, I tossed out as many pages as I ended up keeping. Fortunately there were enough days when the dots connected. Days when I remembered that, like anything else, writing is hard work. It's one word, one paragraph, one page at a time, followed by innumerable edits.

I told you earlier how something Ted Koppel said changed my life. It turns out that a chance encounter with another journalist would shift my thinking as well. During a low point when I thought I should be much farther along, I had the incredibly good fortune to sit next to preeminent investigative reporter and author Bob Woodward on a flight from Washington. As we parted, he graciously wished me luck on my book and told me he'd just handed in the first draft of his sixteenth book that very week, adding that this meant he was *halfway done.* To know that Bob Woodward considers a first draft to be only the halfway mark was tremendously reassuring.

I'm a big fan of vision boards. After using one to find my dream house with a view, I created one for this book. On my most challenging days (of which there were plenty) the words and pictures reminded me of why I was working so hard. Did I still get discouraged? You bet. Then a series of events delayed the book by nearly a year. Normally this wouldn't have been a big deal. But turn the page. Do you see whose picture is smack in the middle of that vision board? My new publish date was scheduled to come just months after the end of the final season of Oprah's quarter-of-a-century run. Talk about a near miss.

Was it "realistic" for me to think I could be on Oprah's show? It was a total long shot. Then again—*why not me?* I vastly prefer dwelling in the world of possibility than in the so-called real world. As Will Smith said, "Being realistic is the most commonly traveled road to mediocrity." The secret is, it didn't matter if I didn't get to be on Oprah or that if I had, I would have been nervous as heck. What matters is that I always believed it was possible.

The reason I'm telling you this is because I know you and how your mind works. And I know how easy it would be for you to finish this book only to run into a situation that triggers your own impostor feelings and say, *See, it didn't work. I'm hopeless.* What you want is sustained confidence 24/7/365. But that's simply not how confidence works. As you've learned, mistakes, failure, and setbacks are to be expected, no one is perfect, and there's always more to learn. And that, my bright and capable impostor friend, is a very good thing.

[NOTES]

Introduction

1. Betty Rollin, "Chronic Self-Doubt: Why Does It Afflict So Many Women?" Hers, *New York Times,* August 19, 1982.
2. Gregory C. R. Yates and Margaret Chandler, "Impostor Phenomenon in Tertiary Students," paper presented at the Annual Conference of the Australian Association for Research in Education, University of South Australia, Adelaide, December 1998; Catherine Cozzarelli and Brenda Major, "Exploring the Validity of the Impostor Phenomenon," *Journal of Social and Clinical Psychology* 9, no. 4 (Winter 1990): 401–17; D. Lester and T. Moderski, "The Impostor Phenomenon in Adolescents," *Psychological Reports* 76, no. 4 (1995): 466; and Sharon Fried-Buchalter, "Fear of Success, Fear of Failure, and the Impostor Phenomenon Among Male and Female Marketing Managers," *Sex Roles* 37, nos. 11–12 (1997): 847–59.
3. Loretta McGregor, Damon E. Gee, and K. Elizabeth Posey, "I Feel Like a Fraud and It Depresses Me: The Relation Between the Imposter Phenomenon and Depression," *Social Behavior and Personality: An International Journal* 36, no. 1 (February 2008): 43–48; K. S. Beason, "The Impostor Phenomenon: Incidence

and Prevalence According to Birth Order and Academic Acceleration" (Psy.D. dissertation, Massachusetts School of Professional Psychology, Boston, 1996); and Shamala Kumar and Carolyn M. Jagacinski, "Imposters Have Goals Too: The Impostor Phenomenon and Its Relationship to Achievement Goal Theory," *Personality and Individual Differences* 40 (2006): 147–57.

4. Mary E. Topping and Ellen B. Kimmel, "The Imposter Phenomenon: Feeling Phony," *Academic Psychology Bulletin* 7, no. 2 (Summer 1985): 213–26.

5. Joan Harvey, Ph.D., with Cynthia Katz, *If I'm so Successful, Why Do I Feel Like a Fake?* (New York: St. Martin's Press, 1985).

[1]

Feel Like an Impostor? Join the Club

1. Ellyn Spragins, *What I Know Now: Letters to My Younger Self* (New York: Crown Archetype, 2006), 143.

2. Leslie Goldman, "You're a Big Success (So Why Do You Feel So Small?)" *Chicago Tribune*, March 30, 2005.

3. Gail M. Matthews, "Impostor Phenomenon: Attributions for Success and Failure," paper presented at the American Psychological Association, Toronto, 1984.

4. Joseph R. Ferrari, "Impostor Tendencies and Academic Dishonesty: Do They Cheat Their Way to Success?" *Social Behavior and Personality* 33, no. 1 (2005): 11–18.

5. "Jodie Foster Reluctant Star," interview with Charlie Rose, *60 Minutes*, January 30, 2000.

[2]

Consider the Source

1. Andy Williams, *Moon River and Me: A Memoir,* reprint edition, 2010.

2. Diane Zorn, "Academic Culture Feeds the Imposter Phenomenon," *Academic Leader* 21, no. 8 (2005): www.magnapubs.com/newsletter/story/l46.

3. Mary E. Topping and Ellen B. Kimmel, "The Imposter Phenomenon: Feeling Phony," *Academic Psychology Bulletin* 7 (1985): 213–26, http://psycnet.apa.org/psycinfo/1986=20664-001.

4. Ellyn Spragins, *What I Know Now: Letters to My Younger Self* (New York: Crown Archetype, 2006).

5. Jonathan Safran Foer interview, *Entertainment Today,* July 5–11, 2002.

6. Kate Winslet interview, *Interview,* November 2000.

7. Don Cheadle interview, *Los Angeles Times,* November 14, 2004.

8. Chris Lee, "A Hard Look at Himself; Colleagues and Reviewers Lavish Praise on Don Cheadle for Distinctive, Eye-Catching Performances but He's His Toughest Critic," *Los Angeles Times,* November 14, 2004.

9. Michael Uslan, quoted in "How to Amp Up Your Charisma," Olivia Fox Cabane, forbes.com, October 22, 2009.

10. A. J. Jacobs, *The Guinea Pig Diaries* (New York: Simon & Schuster, 2009), 67.

11. Meryl Streep, interview by Ken Burns, *USA Weekend,* December 1, 2002. Streep was asked the question, "Will you always act?"

12. Jenny Legassie, Elaine M. Zibrowski, and Mark A. Goldszmidt, "Measuring Resident Well-Being: Impostorism and Burnout Syndrome in Residency," *Journal of General Internal Medicine* 23, no. 7 (July 2008): 1090–94.

13. Carina Sonnak and Tony Towell, "The Impostor Phenomenon in British University Students: Relationships Between Self-Esteem, Mental Health, Parental Rearing Style and Socioeconomic Status," *Personality and Individual Differences* 31, no. 6 (October 15, 2001): 863–74.

14. Neil A. Lewis, "On a Supreme Court Prospect's Résumé: Baseball Savior," *New York Times*, May 14, 2009.

15. Cary M. Watson, Teri Quatman, and Erik Edler, "Career Aspirations of Adolescent Girls: Effects of Achievement Level, Grade, and Single-Sex School Environment," *Sex Roles* 46 nos. 9–10 (2002): 323–35, DOI: 10.1023/A:1020228613796.

16. Sarah Anne Lin, "The Imposter Phenomenon Among High-Achieving Women of Color: Are Worldview, Collective Self-esteem and Multigroup Ethnic Identity Protective?" (Ph.D. dissertation, Fordham University, 2008).

[3]

It's Not All in Your Head

1. Janet K. Swim and Lawrence J. Sana, "He's Skilled, She's Lucky: A Meta-Analysis of Observers' Attributions for Women's and Men's Successes and Failures," *Personality and Social Psychology Bulletin* 22 (1996): 507.

2. "Equality Not Taken for Granted," *Nature* 390 (November 13, 1997): 204.

3. Christine Wenneras and Agnes Wold, "Nepotism and Sexism in Peer-Review," *Nature* 387 (May 22, 1997): 341–43.

4. Claudia Goldin and Cecilia Rouse, "Orchestrating Impartiality: The Impact of 'Blind' Auditions on Female Musicians," *American Economic Review* 90, no. 4 (September 2000): 715–41.

5. Geoff Potvin et al., "Unraveling Bias from Student Evaluations of Their High School Science Teacher," *Science Education* 93 (2009): 827–45, http://onlinelibrary.wiley.com/doi/10.1002/sce.20332/abstract.

6. Rhea Steinpreis, Katie A. Anders, and Dawn Ritzke, "The Impact of Gender on the Review of Curriculum Vitae of Job Applicants and Tenure Candidates: A National Empirical Study," *Sex Roles* 41 (1999): 509–28.

7. Victoria L. Brescoll and Eric Luis Uhlmann, "Can an Angry Woman Get Ahead?

Gender, Status Conferral, and Workplace Emotion Expression," *Psychological Science* 19 (March 2008): 268–75.

8. www.copyblogger.com/James_chartrand_underpants.

9. Eleanor E. Maccoby and Carol Jacklin, *The Psychology of Sex Difference* (Stanford, Calif.: Stanford University Press, 1974).

10. Jacqueline J. Madhok, "The Effect of Gender Composition on Group Interaction," *Locating Power: Proceedings of the Second Berkeley Women and Language Conference,* ed. Kira Hall, Mary Bucholtz, and Birch Moonwomon, vol. 2 (Berkeley, Calif: Berkeley Women and Language Group, University of California, 1992): 371–86.

11. Caroline Simord et al., "Climbing the Technical Ladder: Obstacles and Solutions of Mid-Level Women in Technology" survey of 1,795 technical men and women at seven high-technology companies in the Silicon Valley region (Michelle R. Clayton Institute for Gender Research, Stanford University/Anita Borg Institute for Women and Technology, 2008).

12. Linda J. Sax and Alexander W. Astin, *The Gender Gap in College: Maximizing the Development Potential of Women and Men* (San Francisco: Jossey-Bass, 2008).

13. Joan Biskupic, "Ginsburg: The Court Needs Another Woman: Panel's Lack of Diversity Wears on Female Justice," *USA Today*, May 6, 2009: 1.

14. Dave Barry, "Why Men Can't Help It," *Miami Herald*, November 23, 2003.

15. Rita Hardiman and Bailey Jackson, "Conceptual Foundations for Social Justice Education," in *Teaching for Diversity and Social Justice*, ed. Maurianne Adams, Lee Anne Bell, and Pat Griffin, 2d ed. (New York: Routledge, 2007).

16. K. M. Hayes and S. F. Davis, "Interpersonal Flexibility, Type A individuals, and the Impostor Phenomenon," *Bulletin of the Psychonomic Society* 31 (1993): 323–25.

17. Deborah Tannen, "Power of Talk: Who Gets Heard and Why," *Harvard Business Review*, September 1, 1995.

18. Claude M. Steele and Joshua Aronson, "Stereotype Threat and the Intellectual Test Performance of African Americans," *Journal of Personality and Social Psychology* 69, no. 5 (1995): 797–811.

19. Jennifer Steele and Nalini Ambady, "'Math Is Hard!' The Effect of Gender Priming on Women's Attitudes," *Journal of Experimental Social Psychology* 42, no. 4 (2006): 428–36; and Ilan Dar-Nimrod and Steven J. Heine, "Exposure to Scientific Theories Affects Women's Math Performance," *Science* 314, no. 5798 (October 20, 2006): 435.

20. Mary C. Murphy, Claude M. Steele, and Janes J. Gross, "Signaling Threat: How Situational Cues Affect Women in Math, Science, and Engineering Settings," *Psychological Science* 18, no. 10 (2007): 878–85.

21. P. G. Davies, S. J. Spencer, and C. M. Steele, "Clearing the Air: Identity Safety Moderates the Effects of Stereotype Threat on Women's Leadership Aspirations," *Journal of Personality and Social Psychology* 88, no. 2 (2005): 276–87.

22. Sabine C. Koch, Stephanie M. Müller, and Monika Sieverding, "Women and Computers: Effects of Stereotype Threat on Attribution of Failure," *Computers & Education* 51, no. 4 (December 2008): 1795.

23. P. G. Davies et al., "Consuming Images: How Television Commercials That Elicit Stereotype Threat Can Restrain Women Academically and Professionally," *Personality and Social Psychology Bulletin* 28, no. 12 (2002): 1615–28.

24. Claude M. Steele and Joshua Aronson, "Stereotype Threat and the Intellectual Test Performance of African-Americans," *Journal of Personality and Social Psychology* 69, no. 5 (November 1995): 797–811.

25. Jean-Claude Croizet and Theresa Claire, "Extending the Concept of Stereotype to Social Class: The Intellectual Underperformance of Students from Low Socioeconomic Backgrounds," *Personality and Social Psychology Bulletin* 24, no. 6 (June 1995): 588–94.

26. Anne M. Koenig and Alice H. Eagly, "Stereotype Threat in Men on a Test of Social Sensitivity," *Sex Roles* 52, nos. 7–8 (2008): 489–96.

27. Jeff Stone et al., "Stereotype Threat Effects on Black and White Athletic Performance," *Journal of Personality and Social Psychology* 77, no. 6 (1999): 1213–27.

28. Margaret Shih, Todd L. Pittinsky, and Nalini Ambady, "Stereotype Susceptibility: Identity Salience and Shifts in Quantitative Performance," *Psychological Science* 10

(1999): 80–83; and Margaret Shih, Todd L. Pittinsky, and Amy Trahan, "Domain-Specific Effects of Stereotypes on Performance," *Self and Identity* 5: 1–14.

29. "The Supergirl Dilemma: Girls Grapple with the Mounting Pressure of Expectations," nationwide survey of school-age children conducted for Girls Inc. by Harris Interactive, 2006.

30. Judith Warner, "Women in Charge, Women Who Charge," *New York Times* op-ed, June 5, 2008.

31. Adrienne Rich, *Of Women Born*, reissue (New York: W. W. Norton, 1995).

[4]

Hiding Out

1. Pauline Rose Clance and Suzanne Imes, "The Imposter Phenomenon in High Achieving Women: Dynamics and Therapeutic Intervention," *Psychotherapy Theory, Research and Practice* 15, no. 3 (Fall 1978): 1-8; Clance et al., "Impostor Phenomenon in an Interpersonal/Social Context: Origins and Treatment," *Women & Therapy* 16, no. 4 (1995): 79–96.

2. Ellyn Spragins, *What I Know Now: Letters to My Younger Self* (New York: Crown Archetype, 2006).

3. Donovan Webster, "The Eliot Spitzer Question: Are You an Impostor? Why Do Some Successful Men Self-destruct When They Reach the Top? Are They Phony, Hypomanic, or Just Plain Scared?" *Best Life*, August 2008.

4 Gerald Weinstein, *Education of the Self: A Trainers Manual* (Amherst, Mass.: Mandala Press, 1976).

5. Julie K. Norem, *The Positive Power of Negative Thinking: Using Pessimism to Harness Your Anxiety and Perform at Your Peak* (New York: Basic Books, 2003); and Susan Pinker, "Feeling Like a Fraud," *Globe and Mail*, June 2, 2004: C1.

[5]

What Do Luck, Timing, Connections, and Personality Really *Have to Do with Success?*

1. Marlo Thomas and Friends, *The Right Words at the Right Time* (New York: Atria Books, 2002), 5.
2. Michael E. Raynor, Mumtaz Ahmed, and Andrew D. Henderson, "A Random Search for Excellence: Why 'Great Company' Research Delivers Fables and Not Facts," Deloitte Development 2009.
3. Robin Roberts, *From the Heart: Eight Rules to Live By*, reprint ed. (New York: Hyperion, 2008), xiii.
4. Shannon McCaffrey on Ivanka Trump's presentation at the Glazer-Kennedy Marketing Super Conference, April 2009, *Shannon's Marketing Implementer Newsletter*, June 2009.
5. Daniel Goleman, *Emotional Intelligence* (New York: Bantam Dell: 2006).

[6]

The Competence Rule Book for Mere Mortals

1. Credit for this saying goes to motivational speaker Mike Litman.
2. James Bach, "Good Enough Quality: Beyond the Buzzword," *Computer* 30, no. 8 (August 1997): 96–98.
3. K. A. Ericsson, et al., eds. *Cambridge Handbook of Expertise and Expert Performance* (Cambridge, U.K.: Cambridge University Press, 2006): 658–706.
4. J. McGrath Cahoon, Vivek Wadhwa, and Lesa Mitchell, "Are Women Entrepreneurs Different Than Men?" A study by the Ewing Marion Kauffman Foundation 2010.
5. J. Evans, "Imposter Syndrome? Women, Technology and Confidence," *Globe and Mail*, June 6, 2001.

6. *The Supergirl Dilemma: Girls Grapple with the Mounting Pressure of Expectations*, Girls Inc./Harris Interactive: 2006.

7. "Tina Fey: From Spoofer to Movie Stardom," *Independent*, March 19, 2010.

[7]

Responding to Failure, Mistakes, and Criticism

1. Sharon Fried-Buchalter, "Fear of Success, Fear of Failure, and the Imposter Phenomenon: A Factor Analytic Approach to Convergent and Discriminant Validity," *Journal of Personality Assessment* 58, no. 2 (1992): 368–79.

2. C. S. Dweck and T. E. Goetz, "Attributions and Learned Helplessness," in *New Directions in Attribution Research*, ed. J. Harvey, W. Ickes, and R. Kidd, vol. 2 (Hillsdale, N.J.: Erlbaum, 1978).

3. Deborah Phillips, "The Illusion of Incompetence Among Academically Competent Children," *Child Development* 58 (1984): 1308–20.

4. Betty Shanahan, "Authentic Women and Effective Engineers . . . Create the Future," presentation, Michigan Technical University, November 19, 2008.

5. S. Van Goozen et al., "Anger Proneness in Women: Development and Validation of the Anger Situation Questionnaire," *Aggressive Behavior* 20 (1994): 79–100.

6. Carol S. Dweck, *Mindset: The New Psychology of Success* (New York: Ballantine Books, 2007).

7. Quoted in Marlo Thomas and Friends, *The Right Words at the Right Time* (New York: Atria Books, 2002), 48.

8. Ibid.

9. Karen Wright, "How to Take Feedback," *Psychology Today* (March/April 2011).

[8]

Success and the Female Drive to Care and Connect

1. "The Bottom Line: Connecting Corporate Performance and Gender Diversity,"
    Catalyst study, January 2004, http://catalyst.org/publication/82/the-bottom-line-
    connecting-corporate-performance-and-gender-diversity.

2. Anna Fels, *Necessary Dreams: Ambition in Women's Changing Lives* (New York:
    Pantheon, 2004).

3. Suzie Mackenzie, "Talented, Clever, Sexy . . . and Guilty," *Guardian Unlimited*,
    March 22, 1999, www.guardian.co.uk.

4. "Spellbound," *Dateline*, December 22, 2000.

5. Mariah Burton Nelson, "Sisters Show How to Compete—and Care," *Newsday*,
    September 11, 2001.

6. Lee Anne Bell, "Something's Wrong Here and It's Not Me: Challenging the
    Dilemmas That Block Girl's Success," *Journal for the Education of the Gifted* 12, no.
    2 (1989): 118–30.

7. Georgia Sassen, "Success Anxiety in Women: A Constructivist Interpretation of
    Its Sources and Its Significance," *Harvard Business Review* (1980).

8. Carol Stocker, "When Even the Most Successful People Have a Gnawing Feeling
    They're Fakes," *Boston Globe*, March 22, 1986.

9. Sheryl Sandberg, "Why We Have Too Few Women Leaders," speaking at TED
    Conference, December 21, 2010.

10. M. C. Murphy, C. M. Steele, and J. J. Gross, "Signaling Threat: How Situational
    Cues Affect Women in Math, Science, and Engineering Settings," *Psychological
    Science* 18 (2007): 879–85.

11. Clay Shirky, "A Rant About Women," January 15, 2010, www.shirky.com/
    weblog/2010/01/a-rant-about-women.

12. Richard L. Luftig and Marci L. Nichols, "An Assessment of the Social Status and
    Perceived Personality and School Traits of Gifted Students by Non-Gifted Peers,"
    Roeper Review 13, no. 3 (1991): 148–53.

13. Kimberly Daubman and Harold Sigall, "Gender Differences in Perceptions of How Others Are Affected by Self-disclosure About Achievement," *Sex Roles* 37, nos. 1–2 (1997): 73–89.

14. Hannah Riley Bowles, Linda Babcock, and Lei Lai, "Social Incentives for Gender Differences in the Propensity to Initiate Negotiations: Sometimes It Does Hurt to Ask," *Organizational Behavior and Human Decision Processes* 103, no. 1 (May 2007): 84–103.

15. Girl Scouts of USA study, "Change It Up! What Girls Say About Redefining Leadership, 2008.

16. Pat Heim and Susan Murphy, *In the Company of Women; Indirect Aggression Among Women; Why We Hurt Each Other & How to Stop* (New York: Tarcher, 2003), 53.

[9]

Is It "Fear" of Success or Something Else?

1. Sharon Hadary, former founding executive director of the Center for Women's Business Research, "Why Are Women-Owned Companies Smaller Than Men-Owned Companies?" *Wall Street Journal* post, May 17, 2010.

2. Ann J. Brown, William Swinyard, and Jennifer Ogle, "Women in Academic Medicine: A Report of Focus Groups and Questionnaires, with Conjoint Analysis," *Journal of Women's Health* 10 (2003): 999–1008.

3. J. McGath Cohoon, Vivek Wadhwa, and Lesa Mitchell, "Are Successful Women Entrepreneurs Different from Men?" Ewing Marion Kauffman Foundation, May 2010.

4. Lorraine S. Dyke and Steven A. Murphy, "How We Define Success: A Qualitative Study of What Matters Most to Women and Men," *Sex Roles: A Journal of Research* 55, nos. 5–6 (2006): 357–71.

5. Akira Miyake et al., "Reducing the Gender Achievement Gap in College Science:

A Classroom Study of Values Affirmation," *Science* 330, no. 1006 (November 26, 2010): 1234–37.

6. Peggy McIntosh, "Feeling Like a Fraud: Part I," Paper No. 37 (1989); "Feeling Like a Fraud: Part II," Paper No. 18 (2002), Work in Progress Series, Stone Center for Developmental Services and Studies, Wellesley, Mass.

7. Response to a question following a 2006 appearance at the Women's High-Tech Coalition, a Silicon Valley group.

8. "Leaders in a Global Economy: A Study of Executive Women and Men," joint study by Catalyst, the Families and Work Institute, and the Center for Work and Family at Boston College, January 2003.

9. Lin Chiat Chang and Robert M. Arkin, "Materialism as an Attempt to Cope with Uncertainty," *Psychology & Marketing* 19, no. 5 (2002): 389–406.

10. Kathleen D. Vohs, Nicole L. Mead, and Miranda R. Goode, "The Psychological Consequences of Money," *Science* 314, no. 5802 (November 17, 2006): 1154–56.

11. Elizabeth W. Dunn, Lara B. Aknin, and Michael I. Norton, "Spending Money on Others Promotes Happiness," *Science* 319, no. 5870 (March 24 2008): 1687–88.

12. Rosie O'Donnell interview conducted by Troy Roberts, CBS *Sunday Morning*, July 7, 2009.

13. Mary Godwyn and Donna Stoddard, *Minority Women Entrepreneurs: How Outsider Status Can Lead to Better Business Practices* (Greenleaf, Stanford University Press, 2011).

14. Gary S. Cross, *Time and Money: The Making of Consumer Culture* (New York: Routledge, 1993).

15. Daniel McGinn, "The Trouble with Lifestyle Entrepreneurs," *Inc.*, July 2005.

16. "Chris Rock Is Ready to Rock Broadway," interview by Harry Smith on *CBS Sunday Morning*, April 3, 2011.

[1 0]

Why "Fake It Till You Make It" Is Harder for Women— and Why You Must

1. William Fleeson, "Towards a Structure- and Process-Integrated View of Personality: Traits as Density Distributions of States," *Journal of Personality and Social Psychology* 80, no. 6 (2001): 1011–27.

2. Erica Heath, "Incompetents Who Sing Strengths Go Far," *Rocky Mountain News*, March 25, 2006.

3. Steve Schwartz, "No One Knows What the F*ck They're Doing (or 'The Three Types of Knowledge')," http://jangosteve.com/post/380926251/no-one-knows-what-theyre-doing, February 9, 2010.

4. Traci A. Giuliano et al., "An Empirical Investigation of Male Answer Syndrome," paper presented at the 44th Annual Convention of the Southwestern Psychological Association, New Orleans, La., April 1998.

5. Rebecca Solnit, "Men Who Explain Things," *Los Angeles Times*, April 13, 2008.

6. *Newsweek on Campus*, November 1985, 10.

7. Harry G. Frankfurt, *On Bullshit* (Princeton, N.J.: Princeton University Press, 2005).

8. Deborah Tannen, *Talking from 9 to 5: Women and Men at Work*, (New York: Harper Paperbacks, 1995).

9. Jeanne Wolf, "You've Got to Be a Fighting Rooster," *Parade*, June 15, 2008, 4–5.

10. Steve Schwartz, "No One Knows What the F*ck They're Doing (or 'The 3 Types of Knowledge').

11. Robert Siegel, "Daniel Schorr: 90 Years in a Newsworthy Life," *Morning Edition*, National Public Radio, August 31, 2006.

12. In the 1988 vice presidential debate between Lloyd Bentsen and Dan Quayle, Bentsen was responsible for one of the most memorable moments of the campaign. When Quayle compared his length of time in the Senate to that of the late president John F. Kennedy, Bentsen, famously replied, "Senator, I served with

Jack Kennedy, I knew Jack Kennedy, Jack Kennedy was a friend of mine. Senator, you're no Jack Kennedy."

13. Video interview with Harry G. Frankfurt, http://press.princeton.edu/titles/7929 .html.

[11]
Rethinking Risk Taking and Cultivating Chutzpah

1. Jacqueline Reilly and Gerry Mulhern, "Gender Differences in Self-Estimated IQ: The Need for Care in Interpreting Group Data," *Personality and Individual Differences* 18, no. 2 (1995): 368–73.

2. Christine R. Harris, Michael Jenkins, and Dale Glaser, "Gender Differences in Risk Assessment: Why Do Women Take Fewer Risks Than Men?" *Judgment and Decision Making* 1, no. 1 (2006): 48–63.

3. M. H. Matthews, "Gender, Home Range, and Environmental Cognition" *Transactions of the Institute of British Geographers* 12, no. 1 (1987): 43–50; and *Making Sense of Place: Children's Understanding of Large Scale Environments* (Hertfordshire, U.K.: Harvester Wheatsheaf, 1992).

4. Ruth Sunderland, "Women Hedgies Leave Guys in the Shade," *Sydney Morning Herald*, October 21, 2009.

5. Elke U. Weber, Ann-Renee Blais, and Nancy E. Betz, "A Domain Specific Risk-Attitude Scale: Measuring Risk Perceptions and Risk Behaviors," *Journal of Behavioral Decision Making* 15 (2002): 263–90.

6. Shamala Kumar and Carolyn M. Jagacinski, "Impostors Have Goals Too: The imposter Phenomenon and Its Relationship to Achievement Goal Theory," *Personality and Individual Differences* 40, no. 1 (2006): 147–57.

7. Mark McGwire, interview by Ken Burns, *USA Today*, April 23, 1999, 6W.

8. Richard Corliss, "I Dream for a Living: Steven Spielberg, the Prince of Hollywood, Is Still a Little Boy at Heart," *Time*, July 15, 1985.

9.   Stephen Shadegg, *Clare Boothe Luce: A Biography* (New York: Simon & Schuster, 1970).

10. James R. Haggerty, *Wall Street Journal,* February 19, 1999.

11. Claudia Jessup, *Supergirls: The Autobiography of an Outrageous Business* (New York: Harper & Row, 1972). Thanks to my friend Barbara Winter for turning me on to these women's stories.

12. Denzel Washington, interview by George Stephanopoulos, *Good Morning America,* April 10, 2010.

13. Elizabeth Alexander, interview by Erin Moriarty, *48 Hours,* January 2009.

14. Presentation-skills tips come from the training company Communispond.

15. Helen Gurley Brown, *I'm Wild Again: Snippets from My Life and a Few Brazen Thoughts* (New York: St. Martin's Press, 2000), 67.

16. Garrison Keillor, commencement address, Macalester College, St. Paul, Minn., 2002.

[1 2]

Playing Big

1. Marianne Williamson, *A Return to Love* (New York, HarperCollins, 1992).

2. Marlo Thomas and Friends, *The Right Word at the Right Time* (New York: Atria Books, 2002), 364.

3. Steve Young, *Great Failures of the Extremely Successful: Mistakes, Adversity, Failure, and Other Stepping Stones to Success* (Los Angeles: Tallfellow Press, 2002), preface.

4. Hannah Riley Bowles, Linda Babcock, and Kathleen L. McGinn, "Constraints and Triggers: Situational Mechanics of Gender in Negotiation," *Journal of Personality and Social Psychology* 89, no. 6 (December 2005): 951–65.

5. Back in the early eighties a lot of my fellow students in the School of Education at the University of Massachusetts created some groundbreaking educational materials. In our naïve desire to share and learn, many of us put our work out there for all to

use. Not only did it never occur to us to copyright it, but more often than not, we never even put our names on the document! This list of rights was one of those wonderful documents that circulated among the students in my department at the time, most likely from the Education of the Self program. I've modified it over the years, but the true credit lies with its very wise, generous, and unrecognized creator.

6. Melinda Houston, "Diary of a Bluffer," The Age.com.au, November 7, 2004. http://www.theage.com.au/articles/2004/11/06/1099547433417.html?from=storyhs.

Appendix

1. "The Most Powerful Woman in Media? Vivian Schiller, CEO of NPR, Talks to Lynn Sherr," *More*, September 29, 2009.

[ACKNOWLEDGMENTS]

I would have undoubtedly continued to speak on the impostor syndrome for many years to come. However, this book itself would not have happened were it not for a few key people. The first is my agent, Elisabeth Weed. During the course of two days I received publishing inquiries from four literary agents all in response to a feature in the *Chronicle of Higher Education* about a recent presentation at Columbia University. I was flattered but felt obligated to let them know that a previous literary agency had tried and failed to find a publisher for me. At that everyone politely backed away—except for Elisabeth, who said, "That was them. This is me. I can sell this book." And sell she did—brilliantly. Since then I've come to rely on Elisabeth as a savvy sounding board and advocate.

My journey with Crown Publishing began with two brilliant and enthusiastic champions of this book, Tina Constable and Heather Jackson. Heather was my first editor. We worked together for a year until, after two extraordinarily successful decades in publishing, she decided to leave to blaze her own trail. Gratefully it was Heather's early edits that helped me to both shape the book and to find my own voice.

My new editor, Suzanne O'Neill, jumped in to pick up where Heather and I left off. I can only imagine the challenge of entering the editorial process so late in the game. Her many editorial suggestions were invaluable in smoothing out the rough spots and helping me to be more succinct. No easy task. Suzanne also deserves all the credit for coming up with the title of this book.

The instant I met my marketing team at Crown—Rachel Rokicki, Jennifer Robbins, Courtney Snyder, Meredith McGinnis, and Katie

Conneally—I knew I was in good hands. Also on a marketing note, thanks to the generosity of social media guru Gary Vaynerchuk and his brother A.J., I had the opportunity to learn firsthand from marketing staffer Sam Taggart about the behind-the-scenes mechanics of Gary's bestselling book launches. Sam's insights were invaluable.

I will be eternally grateful to two friends who, despite busy schedules of their own, diligently read and edited every page of the early versions of the manuscript. When my words were muddled or rambling, I could always count on Diana Weynand, a well-regarded author in her own right, to tell it like it was in her gentle old-soul way. As a fellow entrepreneur, Diana also helped to keep me (relatively) sane throughout the process of running a business while simultaneously writing a book. My multi-talented friend Cathy McNally brought her own keen writing and editing skills, from which I benefited greatly. Famous for her quick wit, Cathy also brought much needed levity to both this endeavor and my life.

As I was getting down to the wire, my friend Linda Marchesani was invaluable in helping me think through how to edit a particularly pesky chapter, during her vacation, no less. Others whose comments and suggestions helped tremendously are Kerry Beck, Susan Merzbach, Rita Hardiman, Lee Bell, Rene Carew, and Matt Ouellett. Also a heartfelt thank-you to Gerry Weinstein, who over the years has generously allowed me to adapt from his groundbreaking work on humanistic education and self-awareness training both in my workshops and in this book.

Everyone needs a cheering section and mine ran several bleachers high and a mile deep: My father, Edward Young, and the second love of his life, Leslie Fitzgerald; my aunt Marion Lapham and adopted uncle Art Warren; and my four siblings, Susan, Debbie, Peter, and Mark, and their spouses.

I feel blessed to be surrounded by family and friends who for three years waited patiently for the day I would no longer reply to their calls and invitations with "Sorry I can't talk/go/stay, I'm working on the book." Among these are my dear friends Susan DeSisto, Ange DiBenedetto, Lynn Werthamer, and Keitheley Wilkinson. Thanks too for virtual support from Barbara Winter, Steve Coxsey, and Dyan DiNapoli, as well as to Suzanne Evans and all the members of my business mastermind group—you know who you are.

My work ethic I credit entirely to my mother, Barbara Young. While I was in graduate school doing the research on what would ultimately form the basis of this book, my mother was working tirelessly as a second-shift custodian at the same university. Were she alive today, I know my mother would beam with pride at her "author daughter."

To all 23,000 subscribers of my *Changing Course* newsletter and to everyone in the Profiting from Your Passions® career-coach community, a heartfelt thanks for understanding when an issue was late or I was otherwise not always 100 percent present. Special thanks goes to my virtual assistant (and so much more) Lisa Tarrant, who did a great job of holding down the fort at both ChangingCourse.com and ImpostorSyndrome.com while I was preoccupied with the book.

Moving back through time . . . I owe much to those who were at the very inception of my own journey with the impostor syndrome. This includes the original fifteen women I interviewed for my doctoral research on internal barriers to women's occupational achievement, whose insights and observations informed my thinking about all my work that would follow. My friend Lee Anne Bell with whom I designed and cofacilitated the first impostor-syndrome workshops some three decades ago. And to the founding faculty in the Social Justice in Education program at the University of Massachusetts for helping to widen my lens.

Most important, I will forever be indebted to the tens of thousands of women and men who have attended my workshops over the years and without whom this book would not have been possible. Many pulled me aside to share their own impostor story privately. Others bravely spoke up during the workshop itself, voluntarily sharing their stories often in front of several hundred strangers. Thanks as well to the countless people who have emailed me over the years to share their own sometimes painful impostor experiences. In one way or another all of their voices are reflected here.

Finally, I must thank the codiscoverers of the impostor phenomenon, psychologists Pauline Clance and Suzanne Imes, to whom this book is dedicated.

For girls and women the gap between capability and confidence is an individual as well as a collective experience. Now that you've learned how to let your own light shine I invite you also to volunteer for or financially support nonprofit organizations dedicated to empowering girls and women locally and around the world. Here are two of my favorite nonprofits, both of which are making a dramatic difference in our world. You can learn more about these and other national and international organizations at www.ImpostorSyndrome.com.

girls inc.®

Girls Inc. delivers life-changing programs that inspire girls to be strong, smart, and bold. Research-based curricula delivered by trained professionals equip girls to achieve academically; lead healthy and physically active lives; manage money; navigate media messages; and discover an interest in science, technology, engineering, and math. In 2010, the network of local Girls Inc. nonprofit organizations served 150,000 girls ages 6 to 18 at over 1,400 sites in 350 cities across the United States and Canada. For more information visit www.GirlsInc.org.

WOMEN'S
FUNDING
NETWORK

Women's Funding Network (WFN) is the largest philanthropic network in the world dedicated to improving the lives of women and girls. A network of 166 women's funds in twenty-six countries, WFN supports and champions the work of women's funds that believe a better world for women and girls is a better world for all. Learn more at www.womens fundingnetwork.org.

[I N D E X]

[ABOUT THE AUTHOR]

After impostor feelings threatened to derail her own academic and career aspirations Valerie Young made it her mission to understand why it is that so many intelligent, capable women in particular often feel anything but. Since then she's addressed more than 40,000 people at such diverse organizations as IBM, Boeing, Intel, Chrysler, UBS, Bristol Meyers Squibb, EMC, Procter & Gamble, Ernst & Young, American Women in Radio and Television, and the Society of Women Engineers.

Her insight and humor have also made her a popular speaker among students and faculty at more than sixty colleges and universities, including Harvard, Stanford, MIT, Caltech, Johns Hopkins, Cornell, Princeton, Columbia, Smith, Dartmouth, New York University Medical School, the University of Michigan, and the University of Pennsylvania. Her career-related tips have been cited around the world in the *Wall Street Journal, USA Today Weekend, Kiplinger's, More, Psychology Today, Woman's Day, Entrepreneur, Redbook,* the *Chicago Tribune,* the *Boston Globe, Glamour UK,* the *Globe and Mail,* the *Sydney Morning Herald, Grazia* magazine, and elsewhere.

Valerie is also the founder and Dreamer in Residence at ChangingCourse.com and the creator of the Profiting from Your Passions® career-coach training program. Prior to becoming an entrepreneur, Valerie was a manager of marketing and communications at a Fortune 200 company. She earned her doctoral degree in education at the University of Massachusetts in Amherst, where she was also the founding coordinator of the School of Education's Social Justice in Education program. She can be reached at www.ImpostorSyndrome.com.